LAW, CRIME AND LAW ENFORCEMENT

NATIONAL STRATEGY FOR CHILD EXPLOITATION PREVENTION AND INTERDICTION

(EDITED & ABRIDGED)

LAW, CRIME AND LAW ENFORCEMENT

Additional books in this series can be found on Nova's website under the Series tab.

Additional E-books in this series can be found on Nova's website under the E-books tab.

LAW, CRIME AND LAW ENFORCEMENT

NATIONAL STRATEGY FOR CHILD EXPLOITATION PREVENTION AND INTERDICTION

(EDITED & ABRIDGED)

JEREMY R. BARNES
AND
ASHLEY P. DAVIS
EDITORS

Nova Science Publishers, Inc.
New York

For permission to use material from this book please contact us:
Telephone 631-231-7269; Fax 631-231-8175
Web Site: http://www.novapublishers.com

LIBRARY OF CONGRESS CATALOGING-IN-PUBLICATION DATA

National strategy for child exploitation prevention and interdiction : (edited & abridged) /
editors, Jeremy R. Barnes and Ashley P. Davis.
p. cm. -- (Law, crime and law enforcement)
Includes bibliographical references and index.
ISBN 978-1-61122-853-3 (hardcover : alk. paper)
1. Sexually abused children--United States. 2. Teenage sex
offenders--United States. I. Barnes, Jeremy R. II. Davis, Ashley P.
HV6570.2.C53 2011
362.76'5610973--dc22
2010046850

Published by Nova Science Publishers, Inc. † New York

Contents

Preface

The sexual abuse and exploitation of children rob the victims of their childhood, irrevocably interfering with their emotional and psychological development. Ensuring that all children come of age without being disturbed by sexual trauma or exploitation is more than a criminal justice issue, it is a societal issue. Despite efforts to date, the threat of child sexual exploitation remains very real, whether it takes place in the home, on the street, over the Internet or in a foreign land. Because the sexual abuse and exploitation of children strikes at the very foundation of our society, it will take our entire society to combat this affront to the public welfare. This authors of this book examine the nature of the child exploitation problem and the significant efforts being undertaken by federal, state and local agencies to address this epidemic.

Chapter 1- The sexual abuse and exploitation of children rob the victims of their childhood, irrevocably interfering with their emotional and psychological development. Ensuring that all children come of age without being disturbed by sexual trauma or exploitation is more than a criminal justice issue, it is a societal issue. Despite efforts to date, the threat of child sexual exploitation remains very real, whether it takes place in the home, on the street, over the Internet, or in a foreign land.

Chapter 2- In the United States, estimates suggest that as many as 300,000 children may become victims of commercial sexual exploitation each year (Estes and Weiner, 2001). This bulletin describes the findings of a study that the Urban Institute conducted to examine the effects of the passage of the Victims of Trafficking and Violence Protection Act of 2000 (TVPA) on the federal prosecution of commercial sexual exploitation of children (CSEC) cases. It discusses U.S. enforcement of TVPA and succeeding laws enacted to strengthen penalties against CSEC, describes features of successful prosecutions, and examines how the legislation has affected court penalties and service providers. The authors also discuss recommendations for policymakers and practitioners who work with children and youth who have been the victims of commercial sexual exploitation.

Chapter 3- Although those who commit sex offenses against minors are often described as "pedophiles" or "predators" and thought of as adults, it is important to understand that a substantial portion of these offenses are committed by other minors who do not fit the image of such terms.

Interest in youth who commit sexual offenses has grown in recent years, along with specialized treatment and management programs, but relatively little population-based epidemiological information about the characteristics of this group of offenders and their offenses has been available. The National Incident-Based Reporting System (NIBRS) offers perspective on the characteristics of the juvenile sex offender population coming to the attention of law enforcement.

In: National Strategy for Child Exploitation Prevention... ISBN: 978-1-61122-853-3
Editor: Jeremy R. Barnes and Ashley P. Davis

Chapter 1

NATIONAL STRATEGY FOR CHILD EXPLOITATION PREVENTION AND INTERDICTION (EDITED AND ABRIDGED)

United States Department of Justice

"There can be no keener revelation of a society's soul than the way in which it treats its children."[1] "Given the current statistics surrounding child pornography, we are living in a country that is losing its soul."[2]

I. EXECUTIVE SUMMARY

The sexual abuse and exploitation of children rob the victims of their childhood, irrevocably interfering with their emotional and psychological development. Ensuring that all children come of age without being disturbed by sexual trauma or exploitation is more than a criminal justice issue, it is a societal issue. Despite efforts to date, the threat of child sexual exploitation remains very real, whether it takes place in the home, on the street, over the Internet, or in a foreign land.

Because the sexual abuse and exploitation of children strikes at the very foundation of our society, it will take our entire society to combat this affront to the public welfare. Therefore, this National Strategy lays out a comprehensive response to protect the right of children to be free from sexual abuse and to protect society from the cost imposed by this crime.

In the broadest terms, the goal of this National Strategy is to prevent child sexual exploitation from occurring in the first place, in order to protect every child's opportunity and right to have a childhood that is free from sexual abuse, trauma, and exploitation so that they can become the adults they were meant to be. This Strategy will accomplish that goal by efficiently leveraging assets across the federal government in a coordinated manner. All entities with a stake in the fight against child exploitation—from federal agencies and investigators and prosecutors, to social service providers, educators, medical professionals, academics, non-governmental organizations, and members of industry, as well as parents, caregivers, and the threatened children themselves—are called upon to do their part to prevent these crimes, care for the victims, and rehabilitate the offenders.

BACKGROUND

In 2008, Congress passed and President Bush signed the Providing Resources, Officers, and Technology to Eradicate Cyber Threats to Our Children Act of 2008 (the "PROTECT Our Children Act" or the "Act"). This Act requires the Department of Justice (the "Department") to formulate and implement a National Strategy to combat child exploitation. The Act also requires the Department to submit a report on the National Strategy (the "National Strategy" or "Report") to Congress every other year. The Act mandates that the National Strategy contain a significant amount of information, including: (1) an assessment of the magnitude of child exploitation;[3] (2) a review of the Department and other state and federal agencies' efforts to coordinate and combat child exploitation;[4] and (3) a proposed set of goals and priorities for reducing child exploitation.[5] In this inaugural National Strategy report, the Department describes its first-ever threat assessment of the danger that faces the nation's children, its current efforts to combat child exploitation, and posits some goals and plans to fight the threats that are facing our Nation's children.

THE THREAT ASSESSMENT

This chapter attempts to marshal a massive amount of information about the nature of the child exploitation problem and the significant efforts being undertaken by federal, state, and local agencies to address this epidemic. To evaluate the extent and forms of child exploitation, between approximately February 2009 and February 2010, the National Drug Intelligence Center ("NDIC") prepared a threat assessment (the "Threat Assessment" or "Assessment") that is summarized in this chapter. In conducting the Threat Assessment, NDIC interviewed over a hundred prosecutors, investigators, and other experts in the field, conducted interviews to collect information, reviewed thousands of pages of documents from investigations, cases, relevant research, and analyzed data from the National Center for Missing & Exploited Children. In addition to conducting the Threat Assessment, the Department and the Library of Congress have gathered and reviewed an extensive amount of studies and research relevant to the field of child exploitation to help inform the Department and its partners of the most recent information available from academia on this subject.[6]

The Threat Assessment research indicates that the threat to our nation's children of becoming a victim of child exploitation is a very serious one. For example, investigators and prosecutors report dramatic increases in the number, and violent character, of the sexually abusive images of children being trafficked through the Internet. They also report the disturbing trend of younger children depicted in these images, even including toddlers and infants. Further, offenders have become proficient at enticing children to engage in risky behavior, like agreeing to meet for sexual activity, or even to display themselves engaging in sexual activity through images or webcams. In addition, the offenders have been able to master Internet technologies to better mask their identities.

To address the threat to our nation's children, the National Strategy focuses on the following types of child sexual exploitation: (1) child pornography, often called images of child sexual abuse; (2) online enticement of children for sexual purposes; (3) commercial sexual exploitation of children, and (4) child sex tourism.

Child Pornography: The expansion of the Internet has led to an explosion in the market for child pornography, making it easier to create, access, and distribute these images of abuse. While "child pornography" is the term commonly used by lawmakers, prosecutors, investigators, and the public to describe this form of sexual exploitation of children, that term largely fails to describe the true horror that is faced by hundreds of thousands of children every year. The child victims are first sexually assaulted in order to produce the vile, and often violent, images. They are then victimized again when these images of their sexual assault are traded over the Internet in massive numbers by like-minded people across the globe.

The anonymity afforded by the Internet makes the offenders more difficult to locate, and makes them bolder in their actions. Investigations show that offenders often gather in communities over the Internet where trading of these images is just one component of a larger relationship that is premised on a shared sexual interest in children. This has the effect of eroding the shame that typically would accompany this behavior, and desensitizing those involved to the physical and psychological damage caused to the children involved. This self-reinforcing cycle is fueling ever greater demand in the market for these images. In the world of child pornography, this demand drives supply. The individual collector who methodically gathers one image after another has the effect of validating the production of the image, which leads only to more production. Because the Internet has blurred traditional notions of jurisdiction and sovereignty, this urgent crime problem is truly global in scope, and requires a coordinated national and international response.

Online Enticement of Children: Child predators often use the internet to identify, and then coerce, their victims to engage in illegal sex acts. These criminals will lurk in chat rooms or on bulletin board websites that are popular with children and teenagers. They will gain the child's confidence and trust, and will then direct the conversation to sexual topics. Sometimes they send the child sexually explicit images of themselves, or they may request that the child send them pornographic images of themselves. Often, the defendants plan a face-to-face for the purpose of engaging in sex acts.

The Commercial Sexual Exploitation of Children: Children are being recruited and coerced into the world of prostitution in our own cities. Teen runaways - who are often trying to escape abusive homes – may turn to prostitution as a means of survival. They also frequently fall prey to "pimps" who lure them in with an offer of food, clothes, attention, friendship, love, and a seemingly safe place to sleep. Once the pimps gain this control over the children, they often use acts of violence, intimidation, or psychological manipulation to trap the children in a life of prostitution. Pimps will also cause the children to become addicted to drugs or alcohol (or will increase the severity of a pre-existing addiction) in order to ensure complicity. These children are taught to lie about their age and are given fake ID.

They are also trained not to trust law enforcement and to lie to protect their pimps. As a result, these victims are often not recognized as victims, and may be arrested and jailed. The dangers faced by these children– from the pimps, from their associates, and from customers—are severe. These children become hardened by the treacherous street environment in which they must learn to survive. As such, they do not always outwardly present as sympathetic victims. These child victims need specialized services that are not widely available given that they often present with illnesses, drug additions, physical and sexual trauma, lack of viable family and community ties, and total dependence – physical and psychological – on their abusers, the pimps.

Child Sex Tourism: "Child sex tourism" refers to Americans or U.S. resident aliens traveling abroad for the purpose of sexually abusing foreign children (usually in economically disadvantaged countries). Americans, capitalizing on their relative wealth and the lack of effective law enforcement in the destination countries, easily purchase access to young children to engage in illicit sex acts, sometimes for as little as $5. Like child pornography and other Internet-facilitated crimes against children, the Internet has revolutionized the child sex tourism industry. As a result, a new, emboldened crop of offenders are finding the navigation of travel in developing countries much easier than in the past. Additionally, the Internet allows like-minded offenders to gather and exchange information on how and where to find child victims in these foreign locations, making the offenders better informed about where sex tourism is prevalent and where law enforcement is lax. Numerous countries in Southeast Asia are so well-known for child sex tourism that there are entire neighborhoods which are considered brothels, and there are open-air markets where children can be purchased for sex.

In short, the threat of sexual exploitation faced by children today is very real.

Brief Overview of the Nation's Efforts to Combat Child Exploitation

While the threat has increased, so, too, have the resources dedicated to addressing this issue. This chapter provides an overview of the significant efforts of the Department and numerous other federal, state, and local agencies that are working to prevent and interdict child exploitation. The efforts are multi-faceted and many of these groups work cooperatively to address this ever-expanding problem.

The Department has a number of components, offices, and agencies that devote personnel, resources, and time to the issue of preventing, investigating, and prosecuting child exploitation, as well as to providing services to victims and families. These components include, but are not limited to: the Office of the Deputy Attorney General (ODAG), the Federal Bureau of Investigation (FBI), the U.S. Marshals Service, Interpol Washington, the U.S. Attorney's Offices, the Criminal Division's Child Exploitation and Obscenity Section (CEOS), and the Office of Justice Programs (OJP).

The ODAG helps to direct all of the Department's efforts to combat child exploitation. The Department has appointed a National Coordinator for Child Exploitation Prevention and Interdiction, who is an official within the Office of the Deputy Attorney General.

The FBI leads the Department's investigative efforts and as a part of that mandate created the Innocent Images National Initiative which focuses on technology-facilitated child exploitation. Between 1996 and 2007, there was a 2062% increase in child exploitation investigations throughout the FBI. In 2004, the FBI launched the Innocent Images International Task Force, which has brought dozens of investigators from all over the world to train with the FBI and foster international cooperation in the global fight against child exploitation.

The Marshals Service is tasked under the Adam Walsh Act with the primary responsibility for locating and apprehending sex offenders who have failed to register on a sex offender registry. As part of the Adam Walsh Act, the Marshals Service has three principle responsibilities: assisting state, local, tribal and territorial authorities in the location and apprehension of noncompliant and fugitive sex offenders; investigating violations of the Adam Walsh Act for federal prosecution; and assisting in the identification and location of sex offenders relocated as a result of a major disaster. Dozens of Deputy U.S. Marshals lead task forces of federal, state, and local partners to track down and apprehend these offenders. In addition, the Marshals Service has formed a Sex Offender Investigations Branch. In Fiscal Year 2009, this Branch arrested more than 10,000 fugitives, wanted for failing to register and/or actual sex offenses, and conducted thousands of compliance checks.

INTERPOL Washington is the official U.S. representative to the International Criminal Police Organization (INTERPOL). As the national point of contact for INTERPOL in the United States, INTERPOL Washington routinely exchanges criminal investigative data with international counterparts on behalf of the more than 18,000 federal, state, local and tribal law enforcement agencies in the United States. In addition to providing support to NCMEC, ICE and the FBI, INTERPOL Washington tracks sex offenders who travel overseas, and coordinates a number of international alerts relating to child exploitation.

The 94 United States Attorney's Offices prosecute federal child exploitation cases throughout the country and coordinate Project Safe Childhood within their districts, the Department's 2006 national initiative to marshal federal, state, and local resources to prevent and interdict child exploitation. Since 2006, the number of cases and defendants prosecuted by United States Attorney's Offices has increased by 40%, with 2,315 indictments against 2,427 defendants filed in Fiscal Year 2009.

CEOS, situated within the Department's Criminal Division, consists of approximately twenty attorneys and a six-person High Technology Investigative Unit ("HTIU"). CEOS leads the Criminal Division's campaign against the sexual exploitation of children by investigating and prosecuting the most challenging child sexual exploitation cases, and then by drawing from those experiences to shape domestic and international policy, launch nationwide investigations against the worst offenders, and provide guidance and training to other prosecutors and agents, both within and outside the federal government. CEOS is able to leverage a small amount of resources into extraordinary results. For example, in the last three years CEOS has spearheaded 18 national operations that have resulted in the investigation of over 2,000 individuals. Since 2001, the number of cases and investigations handled by CEOS Trial Attorneys has increased by 1,100%.

The OJP oversees the disbursement of millions of dollars in grants to federal, state, and local agencies to aid in the fight against child exploitation. OJP's efforts help provide communication and coordination to dozens of groups, including the Internet Crimes Against Children (ICAC) Task Force Program which is a fundamental component to our Nation's fight against child exploitation. Since 1998, the Department, through the Office of Justice Programs, has funded the ICACs which are a collection of 61 separate tasks forces throughout the country, with at least one in each state, that work to coordinate federal, state, local and tribal investigative and prosecution agencies to coordinate efforts to interdict child exploitation. Since 1998, ICAC task forces have arrested nearly 17,000 offenders.

Moreover, there are numerous other Federal agencies that are partners in the fight against child exploitation. This includes the United States Postal Inspection Service, the Department of Homeland Security through Immigration and Customs Enforcement and the United States Secret Service, the Department of Health and Human Services, the Department of Defense, the Department of State, the Department of Labor, and the Department of Commerce. Non-governmental organizations work alongside federal, state, local, and tribal partners to combat child exploitation as well. These include the National Center for Missing & Exploited Children, Child Help, Darkness to Light, Girls Educational and Mentoring Services, Inc., Enough is Enough, i-Safe, Kristi House, Inc., Nevada Child Seekers, Paul and Lisa Program, Inc., Web Wise Kids, San Diego Police Foundation, Self-Reliance Foundation, Washtenaw Area Council for Children, INOBTR, TechMissionYouth Program, PROTECT, ECPAT-USA, and many others.

One of the chief mandates of the Act was that the Department expand its efforts to coordinate and cooperate with federal, state, local and international organizations and agencies to combat this scourge. While the Department has long coordinated with all levels of government within the United States and with law enforcement internationally to fight child exploitation, additional high-level working meetings have begun between the Department and other federal government agencies, as well as state, local, and international partners. The Department already belongs to several inter-agency working groups related to child exploitation, like the Federal Inter-Agency Task Force on Missing and Exploited Children. Additionally, the Department provides funding for the Amber Alert program, many child advocacy centers, and many state and local agencies through grants and funding administered by the Office of Juvenile Justice and Delinquency Prevention, the Bureau of Justice Assistance, the National Institute of Justice, the Office for Victims of Crime, and others.

THE CONTINUING FIGHT AGAINST CHILD EXPLOITATION

As outlined in this chapter, the Department is diligently working to combat child exploitation. For example, the Department has increased the number of agents and prosecutors dedicated to child exploitation cases. The FBI has increased the digital forensic capacity at Regional Computer Forensics Labs, which will lead to more expeditious reviews of the critical evidence in these cases. The Department has funded, and will continue to fund, the ICAC Task Force Program. CEOS advises and provides training to the nation's prosecutors, and also conducts high-tech and complex investigations. The U.S. Marshals pursue and have successfully captured thousands of individuals who abscond from their responsibility to register as sex offenders and those who offend and become fugitives. However, as the Threat Assessment evidences, more work must be done to combat the expanding number of predators and, more importantly, to prevent them from harming a child in the first instance.

At its core, the goal of this National Strategy is to reduce the incidence of the sexual exploitation of children. This goal is the guiding principle for all the Department's current and future efforts.

The Department's approach for achieving this goal is multifaceted and includes: (1) an overarching statement of broad goals that will be used to direct the National Strategy; (2) more specific goals to address the dangers identified by the Threat Assessment; (3) programmatic goals that can provide some measurable information and results to help guide the Strategy going forward; and (4) individualized goals by relevant Department components that are designed to support both the broad goals of the Strategy and the programmatic goals of the Department.

The following broad goals will direct the effort of the National Strategy going forward.

1. *The Department will continue to partner closely with state, local, tribal, and non-governmental entities, as well as other federal agencies and the private sector to implement the National Strategy in a coordinated fashion.*
2. *The Department will increase its commitment to a leadership role in finding a global solution to the transnational problem of the sexual exploitation of children.*
3. *The Department will continue to partner with Industry to develop objectives to reduce the exchange of child pornography.*
4. *The Department will explore opportunities to increase the education and awareness of federal, state, local and tribal judges of the difficult issues involved in child sexual exploitation.*
5. *The Department will work toward improving the quality, effectiveness, and timeliness of computer forensic investigations and analysis.*
6. *The Department will increase its commitment to effective and sophisticated training for prosecutors and investigators.*
7. *The Department will build on the success of the Project Safe Childhood initiative.*

Beyond these broad goals, this National Strategy seeks to best marshal all of the Department's resources in a more coordinated, integrated, and strategic way.

As outlined in this chapter, the Department, in partnership and cooperation with other federal, state, local, tribal, and international partners is aggressively pursuing those who would steal the innocence from the soul of our children. Thousands of federal, state, and local investigators and prosecutors, without fanfare or even adequate public recognition of the difficulty of their work, fight this battle fiercely every day. Dedicated professionals in non-governmental organizations, child protective services, and child advocacy centers devote massive time and energy to protecting children, again largely without society fully recognizing the importance of their work. This National Strategy outlines how we will, and must, act together as a nation to protect our children and provides a unique opportunity for us to act together as a nation to protect, as Nelson Mandela said, our society's soul by vigorously pursuing those who violate our children.

II. A Grave Threat to a Precious Resource: An Assessment of Current Child Exploitation Threats

In 2008, the enactment of the PROTECT Our Children Act of 2008 (Public Law 110-401, hereafter, "the Act") required that the Department of Justice (the "Department") conduct a threat assessment of the risks posed to children by child exploitation. The National Child Exploitation Threat Assessment 2010 (the "Threat Assessment" or "Assessment") is the first national assessment by the Federal government of the risks posed by child exploitation.[7] To complete the Assessment, the National Drug Intelligence Center ("NDIC") invested more than a year of its time and interviewed more than one hundred child exploitation prosecutors, investigators, and experts in the field, and reviewed thousands of pages of documents from investigations, criminal cases, research studies, and the National Center for Missing & Exploited Children to compile this Assessment. The Department determined that, in order to report to Congress on the threat that child exploitation presents, any assessment should focus on five key areas: (1) child pornography, often called images of child sexual abuse; (2) online enticement of children for sexual purposes; (3) commercial sexual exploitation of children, (4) child sex tourism; and (5) child exploitation in Indian Country. These five areas form the bulk of federal child exploitation investigations by federal, state, local, and tribal investigators. This chapter provides a summary of the findings of the Assessment relating to these five areas.[8]

The results of the Threat Assessment reveal that there has been a dramatic increase in cases of sexual exploitation of children, including the possession, distribution, and manufacture of child pornography; the online enticement of children for sexual acts; commercial sexual exploitation of children; child sex tourism; and child sexual molestation, since the 1990s. For example, in 2006 U.S. Attorneys handled 82.8 percent more child pornography cases than they had in 1994. State and local law enforcement agencies involved in Internet Crimes Against Children Task Forces reported a 230 percent increase in the number of documented complaints of online enticement of children from 2004 to 2008. In the same time period ICAC Task Forces noted a more than thousand percent increase in complaints of child prostitution.

A. Child Pornography— Images of Child Sexual Abuse

Child pornography refers to the possession, trade, advertising, and production of images that depict the sexual abuse of children. The term *child pornography* is used throughout this Assessment because it is the legal and accepted term for *images of child sexual abuse*; however, many experts in the field believe that use of that term contributes to a fundamental misunderstanding of the crime—one that focuses on the possession or trading of a picture and leaves the impression that what is depicted in the photograph is pornography. Child pornography is unrelated to adult pornography; it clearly involves the criminal depiction and memorializing of the sexual assault of children and the criminal sharing, collecting, and marketing of the images.

State and federal investigators and prosecutors universally report seeing dramatic increases in the number of child pornography images traded on the Internet, the number of child pornography offenders, and the number of children victimized by child pornography. They also report an increase in the sadistic and violent conduct depicted in child pornography images and that they are encountering more young victims than before—particularly infants and toddlers. In addition, law enforcement officers and prosecutors interviewed for this Assessment universally report connections between child pornography offenses and sexual contact offenses against children.

The Internet and advances in digital technology have provided fertile ground for offenders to obtain child pornography, share child pornography, produce child pornography, advertise child pornography, and sell child pornography. The Internet also has allowed offenders to form online communities with global membership not only to facilitate the trading and collection of these images, but also to facilitate contact (with each other and children) and to create support networks among offenders. Rather than simply downloading or uploading images of child pornography to and from the Internet, offenders also use current technologies to talk about their sexual interest in children, to trade comments about the abuse depicted in particular images— even as images are shared real-time—to validate each other's behavior, to share experiences, and share images of themselves abusing children as they do so.

This Section provides an overview of the Threat Assessment findings as they relate to child pornography which include the following: (1) research that indicates child pornography poses a danger to both the victims and other children; (2) indicators that suggest a significant increase in the proliferation of child pornography; (3) evidence that child pornographers are becoming more sophisticated in the production and distribution of materials; and (4) information that organized crime syndicates are involved in the child pornography trade. In addition, this Section outlines some of the steps that law enforcement agencies are taking to identify the most dangerous child pornographers.

1. Child Pornography Offenses Present A Real Threat To Children

The children whose abuse is captured in child pornography images suffer not just from the sexual abuse graphically memorialized in the images, but also from a separate victimization, knowing that the images of that abuse are accessible, usually on the Internet, and are traded by other offenders who receive sexual gratification from the children's distress. According to academic researchers, medical professionals, and child pornography victims themselves, knowing that all copies of child pornography images can never be retrieved compounds the victimization. The shame suffered by the children is intensified by the fact that the sexual abuse was captured in images easily available for others to see and revictimizes the children by using those images for sexual gratification. Unlike children who suffer from abuse without the production of images of that abuse, these children struggle to find closure and may be more prone to feelings of helplessness and lack of control, given that the images cannot be retrieved and are available for others to see in perpetuity. They experience anxiety as a result of the perpetual fear of humiliation that they will be recognized from the images. This harm is best described by the mother of a victim.

A Mother's Story of Child Pornography Victimization

[M]y daughter was abused repeatedly to produce images for the purpose of being traded [and] shared over the [I]nternet. Without a market to receive and trade those images, without the encouragement of those who wanted to acquire the images, I truly believe this abuse would not have occurred.

All those who trade these images and thereby create the demand for lurid and violent depictions of children are participants in the exploitation of my daughter. Each traded picture that placed a value on inventiveness, novelty, or cruelty played a role in egging on the abuser to even more vile acts.

The pictures of my daughter were 'made for trade'— her abuser adapted to serve his market— whatever his audience was looking to acquire, that's what happened to her ...

Producer, distributor, and consumer-—everyone who participates in this evil exchange helps create a market, casting a vote for the next abuse. Regardless of whether they directly abused children themselves, reveled in the images of suffering, or persuaded others to abuse children on their behalf (to provide images of the abuse) each participant has a responsibility for the effects...

[A] shadow... comes over her face if a stranger gives her an expected compliment. The pictures are still out there...

Now that she's growing older and realizing the extent of the [I]nternet, she's also beginning to grasp the darker side of the story— how many people see those same pictures as something to enjoy rather than abhor.

We have no way of knowing how many pedophiles used the pictures of her being tortured and degraded as an opportunity for personal gratification ...

I can find no words to express the fury I feel at those who participate in this evil, or my scorn for any attempt to minimize responsibility by feeble claims that the crime was 'victimless.' My daughter is a real person. She was horribly victimized to provide this source of 'entertainment." She is exploited anew each and every time an image of her suffering is copied, traded, or sold. While the crime is clearly conscienceless, it is hardly 'victimless.'

I asked my daughter what she most wanted to ask of the judge. Her request: "Please, don't let them pretend no one's getting hurt."

A.Available Indicators Suggest Child Pornography Is Increasing

i. Indicators relating to the volume of child pornography.

Experts interviewed for this Assessment, most of whom have longtime experience in this area of law enforcement, concluded that the market—in term of numbers of offenders, images, and victims—has been trending significantly upward. Approximately two-thirds of the child exploitation experts interviewed by NDIC for this Assessment reported that child pornography either is growing exponentially or there has been an overwhelming increase in the volume of child pornography images available.[9] For example, Cybertipline reports, sent by electronic service providers and the public to the National Center for Missing & Exploited Children ("NCMEC"), increased by 69% between 2005 and 2009. Additionally, NCMEC's Child Victim Identification Program has seen a 432% increase in child pornography movies and files submitted for identification of the children depicted during that same time period. However, precisely quantifying the volume of the child pornography market is impossible; the number of offenders accessing the images and videos and the quantity of images and videos being traded is unknown.

> Between 2005 and 2009, the National Center for Missing & Exploited Children's Child Victim Identification Program has seen a 432% increase in child pornography movies and files submitted for identification of the children depicted.

Although documenting the precise quantity of child pornography is difficult, it is evident that technological advances have contributed significantly to the overall increase in the child pornography threat. Offenders can easily produce child sex abuse images using digital technologies and distribute the images over the Internet. From 2005 through 2009, U.S. Attorneys prosecuted 8,352 child pornography cases, and in most instances, the offenders used digital technologies and the Internet to produce, view, store, advertise, or distribute child pornography.

Prior to the mid-1990s, Internet access and the availability of digital home recording devices (still, video, and web cameras) were very limited, thereby confining the production and distribution of child pornography material to relatively few individuals. Today, the ease with which a person can move from viewing child pornography to producing and distributing child pornography is illustrated in numerous cases.[10] In addition, advances in computer memory storage, the speed of downloading and uploading, and advances in file sharing technologies make it very easy to quickly transfer or receive large volumes of child sex abuse images. Numerous technologies are used by offenders—including P2P networks, Internet Relay Chat (IRC), newsgroups, bulletin boards, photo sharing sites, and social networking sites, among others. Experts posit, and common sense suggests, that the easy accessibility to this material online draws new offenders to the crime.

As home digital recording and computer technology have improved and child pornography production and sharing have increased, so too have the illicit images and videos typically stored by offenders. Increased home computer storage capacity has enabled many child pornography offenders to store huge collections of images (some containing 1 million) and numerous video files (often 1 hour in length).[11] For example, more than 15,000 stored videos were found on various media and the offender's computer in Philadelphia in 2007. Holding vast libraries of child pornography material enables offenders to share more illicit images and videos of greater variety than was possible in past years.

ii. Research relating to the number of computers or computer users engaging in Peer-to-Peer file sharing of child pornography.

The Act specifically directs the Department to evaluate data relating to the overall magnitude of child pornography trafficking including the number of computers with which offenders view child pornography or engage in peer-to-peer file sharing.[12] At this time, there is no method for identifying every individual that views or facilitates the production or sharing of child pornography. Similarly, at this time, it is not possible to provide a definitive number of computers or computer users engaged in peer-to-peer file sharing of child pornography because there is no surveillance mechanism to accomplish this task. However, law enforcement agencies are taking steps to address this issue by employing a variety of investigative techniques that can identify the number of unique Internet Protocol (IP) addresses linked to computers sharing known files containing child pornographic material on particular networks. In addition, the law enforcement agencies have begun to identify and catalog child pornography images. By identifying IP addresses and cataloging unique images, the law enforcement agencies can help gauge the volume of child pornography that is being distributed online.

Two programs currently used by law enforcement agencies to identify IP addresses and catalog images include: Operation Fairplay, supported by the Wyoming Division of Criminal Investigations and the Palm Beach County (FL) State's Attorney Office and Operation RoundUp, developed by the University of Massachusetts under a grant from the National Institute of Justice. Since Operation Fairplay's inception in 2006 and Operation Roundup's inception in late 2009, the two programs have identified over 20 million different IP addresses offering child pornography files (pictures, videos) on a Peer-to-Peer file-sharing network. Further, the programs have identified thousand of unique images. For example, Operation Fairplay has a "watch list" of 170,000 child pornography files.[13] Operation RoundUp currently has a watch list of 120,000 child pornography files. In both of these tools, the files on the "watch list" are those the developers (law enforcement officers) deem to represent some of the "worst" (movies and photographs of the most violent assaults, with the youngest victims) of the child pornography images they have seen.[14]

These two applications (Fairplay, RoundUp) are currently the only sources of data in the United States known to the Department on the volume of child pornography traded over peer to peer networks. They do not, however, represent the total volume of child pornography traded over the Internet for these reasons:

- The number and names of child pornography files change every minute. It is therefore impossible to determine an accurate, absolute count of all child pornography files on the Internet. Both Fairplay and RoundUp limit their hits to a discrete number of known files (for technological and investigative efficiency reasons).
- Some computers and computer users are exchanging files currently unknown to law enforcement or not on the watch list for Fairplay and RoundUp; those files, computers, and computer users cannot be counted.
- The tools we have to monitor the trading of child pornography on the Internet work on some of the most widely used computer file sharing clients.[15] There is file trading traffic, some of it presumably child pornography, on other peer-to-peer file sharing applications that are not accounted for by these tools.
- Beyond peer-to-peer file sharing tools, child pornography is traded over the internet via e-mail applications, chat rooms, IRC, web site downloads and other applications. These forms of child pornography trading are not included in the counts from Operation Fairplay and RoundUp.
- Not all unique IPs identified by Operations Fairplay and RoundUp represent an individual who is *intentionally* trading in child pornography. There have been cases identified through these operations of users who unintentionally downloaded a single file of child pornography over the Peer-to-Peer file sharing network (e.g., while searching for adult pornography). While these unintentional down loaders are

contributing to the global problem of the online availability of child pornography, they are not themselves consumers of child pornography. Further, IP addresses are not static, so a consumer of child pornography may be counted numerous times by these operations as his IP address changes over time.

Over 100 search warrants have been completed from leads generated by Operation RoundUp since its initiation last year.

The Table below shows the number of unique IP addresses logged by Operations Fairplay and RoundUp.

The Table below shows the percentage of unique IP addresses and new GUIDs[16] in the United States identified by Operation RoundUp over a 3 week period in September-October, 2009.

The Figure below shows the number of files available for peer-to-peer sharing by unique IPs identified by Operation RoundUp between October 5, 2008 and October 4, 2009. Over 630,000 of the unique IP addresses identified had only one identified child pornography file. The greatest number of identified child pornography files available from a single unique IP address was 2,365.

Unique IP Addresses Users Engaging in Peer-to-Peer File Sharing of Child Pornography

	Operation Fairplay Fiscal Year 2008	**Operation Fairplay January -June 2009**	**Operation RoundUp October 5, 2008- October 4, 2009**
Domestic	1,717,522	1,424,734	9,793,430
International	2,891,159	2,325,035	11,877,014
Total	4,608,681	3,749,769	21,670,444

Source: Wyoming Division of Criminal Investigations, Palm Beach County State's Attorney Office and Massachusetts State Police

Unique IP Addresses Users and GUIDs Engaging in Peer-to-Peer File Sharing of Child Pornography September-October, 2009 [Operation RoundUp]

Date	**Total Records**	**US Records**	**% US**	**US Unique IP**	**New US IP**	**US GUID**	**New US Guid**	**New Guid/IP**
9/19/09	18,965,165	8,781,521	46.30%	1,033,134		114,175		
9/27/09	20,144,735	9,226,370	45.80%	1,052,217	19,083	121,232	7,057	36.98%
9/30/09	20,862,015	9,493,631	45.51%	1,060,522	8,305	123,916	2,684	32.32%
10/3/09	21,425,113	9,698,666	45.27%	1,067,617	7,095	127,394	3,478	49.02%
10/4/09	21,670,444	9,793,430	45.19%	1,073,065	5,448	128,335	941	17.27%

Source: Massachusetts State Police

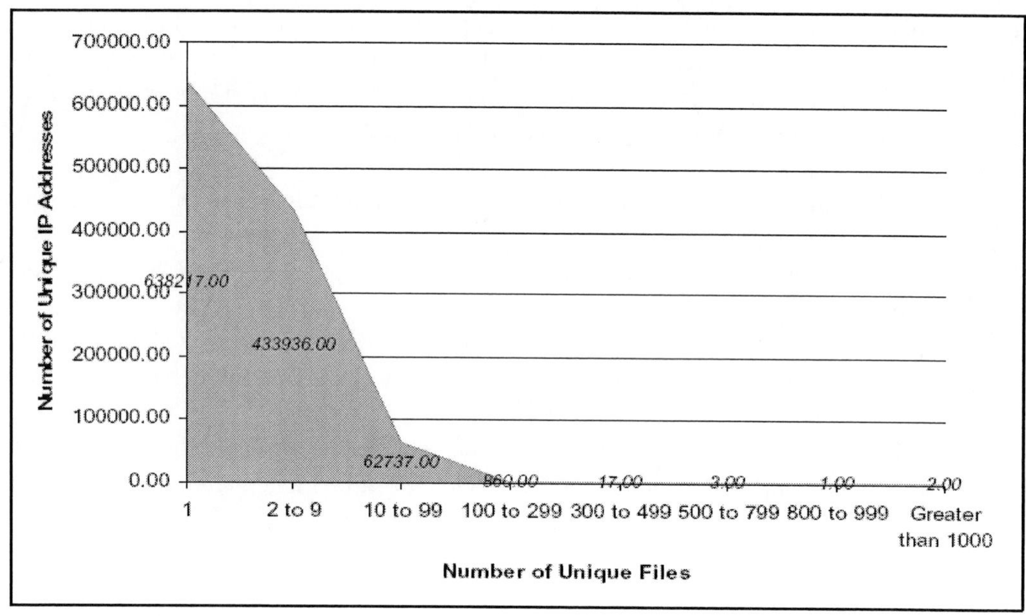

Source: Massachusetts State Police

Number of Identified Child Pornography Files Available from Unique IP Addresses [Operation RoundUp]

As this chapter noted above, it is not possible to provide an exact number of people trading child pornography across the world. UNICEF and the United Nations have provided some estimates, however, their inclusion here does not indicate that the Department endorses these figures. UNICEF estimates that there are more than four million websites featuring sexually exploited minors. Further, the number of child pornography websites is growing: 480,000 sites were identified in 2004 compared to 261,653 in 2001. More than 200 new images are circulated daily, and UNICEF estimates that the production and distribution of child pornographic images generates in between 3 and 20 billion dollars a year.[17]

The United Nations released a report in July 2009 asserting that there are approximately 750,000 sexual predators using the Internet to try to make contact with children for the purpose of sexually exploiting them.[18]

The National Center for Missing & Exploited Children maintains the CyberTipline, an online reporting system for (internet service providers) ISPs and the public to report online child pornography. The Table below shows the number and type of CyberTipline reports in 2008 and 2009.

For FY 2008, ICAC Task Forces reported 34,829 documented complaints,[19] which include child pornography (manufacture, distribution, or possession), traveler, enticement, obscenity directed to minors, and child prostitution, resulting in 12,248 investigations. For the first six months of 2009, Task Forces reported 18,331 documented complaints, resulting in 5,936 investigations. The Table below shows the number and types of documented complaints to ICAC Task Forces.

CyperTipline Reports by Incident Type

Type of Incident	*FY 2008*	*Jan-June 2009*
Child Pornography (possession, manufacture, and distribution)	86,705	44,924
Child Prostitution	1,206	592
Child Sex Tourism	433	121
Child Sexual Molestation (not by family member)	1,998	848
Misleading Domain Name	2,716	334
Online Enticement of Children for Sexual Acts	10,151	3,492
Misleading Words or Digital Images on the	0	1,601
Unsolicited Obscene Material Sent to a Child	1,417	517
Total	104,626	52,429

Source: National Center for Missing & Exploited Children

Documented Complaints to ICAC Task Forces (N=59)

ICAC Complaints		**Type**	**FY 2008 Number of Complaints**	**Jan. – June 2009 Number of Complaints**
Traveler		Proactive Reactive	1,197 411	476 265
Enticement		Proactive Reactive	3,257 3,448	1,240 2,370
Obscenity Directed to Minors		Proactive Reactive	1,240 1,382	479 1,073
Child Prostitution		Proactive Reactive	85 260	76 162
Child Pornography	Manufacture	Proactive Reactive	224 799	193 585
	Distribution	Proactive Reactive	9,935 3,007	2,375 2,367
	Possession	Proactive Reactive	3,263 6,321	2,688 3,982
TOTAL COMPLAINTS			**34,829**	**18,331**

Source: Reports from ICAC Task Forces

B. The Thriving Market For Child Pornography Promotes The Fresh Abuse Of Children

Most indicators reviewed by NDIC for this Assessment point to a steady and significant increase in the volume of child pornography traded over the Internet, and they similarly suggest the existence of a large and global market. This growing and thriving market for child pornographic images is responsible for fresh child sexual abuse—because the high demand for child pornography drives some individuals to sexually abuse children and some to "commission" the abuse for profit or status.

In one case, a predator victimized more than 150 children for profit by before he was arrested by U.S. Postal Inspectors.[20] In another case, the defendant was a "photographer" who traveled throughout several European countries to arrange, witness, and film the sexual abuse of approximately 20 underage girls. The "photographer" then sold the abusive images worldwide through his commercial web site. The initial exposure was estimated to have reached more than 3,000 active traders in approximately 28 countries. He also offered his customers the opportunity to make special requests for videos, purchase the child-sized lingerie used in some of the videos, and, in one case, the opportunity to travel to Europe to photograph the underage girls with him.[21]

Another investigation revealed that offenders would congregate with like-minded people on the Internet and sometimes encourage each other to act out their fantasies and share proof. In Operation Hamlet, offenders abused their own children and made them available to other members of the group for the same purpose.[22] Another case revealed that some child pornography offenders are driven to abuse children because providing new images to their online communities gives them "status."[23] Some communities have restricted memberships, allowing entry only to those who contribute an image not already possessed by the group. In some instances, fathers have abused their own children, not out of any apparent sexual attraction to their children, but because they wanted to reap the benefits of producing and introducing a new child pornographic image into the market and their children were easily accessible targets.[24]

In one highly publicized investigation, Federal Bureau of Investigation (FBI) agents interviewed a man who admitted molesting his daughter and videotaping the sometimes violent assaults. The child, who was 9-years-old when interviewed, said her father began assaulting her when she was 5-years-old. She said he would assault her and immediately publish the assaults on the Internet. The man told agents that he began molesting his daughter because he needed "fresh" images to provide others on the Internet before they would trade their own newest or least-circulated images with him. He described his desire for images he had not seen and said that, to get them, he was required to provide images others had not seen in trade.

Some researchers suggest that viewing child pornography desensitizes the viewer and may reduce inhibitions, increasing the risk that the child pornography offender might engage in a contact offense against a minor.

The facts in *U.S. v. Curry*[25] illustrate a situation in which viewing child pornography can cause an offender to desire to commit contact offenses and, in fact, prepare to commit contact offenses.

C. Child Pornography Offenses Often Are Linked To Contact Offenses

A number of studies indicate a strong correlation between child pornography offenses and contact sex offenses against children. The National Juvenile Online Victimization (NJOV) study revealed contact offenses in one of every six cases that began as a child pornography investigation with no prior knowledge by law enforcement of possible contact offenses by the target.[26] While no study can quantify the risk that any given child pornography offender poses for future contact offenses against children, the significant correlation between child Pornography offenses and contact offenses signals that the risk is present.

In 2009, The Department's Child Exploitation and Obscenity Section (CEOS) helped organize an international symposium through the Group of Eight (G8) titled "Global Symposium for Examining the Relationship Between Online and Offline Offenses and Preventing the Sexual Exploitation of Children". The symposium was held April 5-8, 2009, at the University of North Carolina in Chapel Hill, North Carolina and brought together researchers and other experts from around the world who have worked with child pornography offenders and victims. The symposium was designed for these experts to share their research and individual findings, and develop consensus on the risks to children and society posed by child pornography offenders and also to identify gaps in research and knowledge. Among the most notable points of consensus developed include a finding that there is sufficient evidence of a relationship between possession of child pornography and the commission of contact offenses against children to make it a cause of acute concern, and that the greater availability of child sexual exploitation materials has stimulated the demand and production of even more extreme, sadistic, and violent images of children and infants. The findings and gaps in research were incorporated into a report written by CEOS, entitled *"Report to LEPSG on the 'Global Symposium for Examining the Relationship Between Online and Offline Offenses and Preventing the Sexual Exploitation of Children'"*. On May 30, 2009, the G8 Ministers of Justice and Home Affairs issued a declaration titled *"The Risk to Children Posed by Child Pornography Offenders"* which specifically recognizes the findings made by the experts at the symposium as noted in the report written by CEOS.

In the words of one prosecutor:

"Imagine an offender who spends several hours every night on the Internet 'enjoying' and fantasizing to images of children being sexually abused, and congregating with like-minded people in these trading communities, where they validate and normalize each other's behavior and desires. Assume that he does this several times a week, for several months, maybe even years —which is not at all unusual. Common sense tells you that his 5-year-old daughter, sleeping in the bedroom next door, is at great risk— particularly if the images he collects involves girls in that age bracket. Can we say for certain that he will act out his fantasies on the little girl? No, we can't. But there's real cause to fear for her safety."

Source: U.S. Department of Justice, Child Exploitation and Obscenity Section.

Law enforcement officers and prosecutors interviewed for this Assessment overwhelmingly report discovering contact offenders through the course of child pornography investigations. FBI investigations conducted as part of an Innocent Images Operations Unit (IIOU) Initiative[27] have determined that mass distributors of child pornography using publicly available file sharing software that allows individuals to establish private "friend" groups were found to have committed contact offenses against minors at a very high rate. In fact, FBI analysis of statistics generated through the IIOU Initiative indicated that the software is used for the mass distribution of child pornography by producers and repeat child sex offenders at a higher observed rate than any other online application. As of January 22, 2010, 102 investigations were initiated from 170 IIOU disseminated leads. The 102 cases resulted in 50 new victims of sexual abuse being identified and saved, with another 16 previously victimized minors identified. In total, 66 victims of contact sexual abuse were discovered from these 102 investigations. As of January 22, 2010, eleven (11) of the subjects investigated were found to have been convicted sex offenders, with eight (8) additional subjects previously charged, but not convicted for various reasons, with sex offenses against a child.

Each of these investigations was predicated on the distribution of child pornography with the discovery of contact offenses made at a later stage in the investigation. An analysis of 1,663 federally prosecuted child pornography cases indicates contact offenses were discovered in approximately one-third of cases.[28] Our review of child pornography case summaries from 2005 to 2009 confirms that reporting.[29] United States Postal Inspection Service (USPIS) data also support the correlation between child pornography offenders and contact offenders.[30] Several national child pornography operations uncovered a number of contact sex offenders.[31]

Law enforcement experts in the area of child pornography report that interactive online communities for child pornography offenders, which typically include members from around the world, create a greater risk than ever before. Some online communities are limited to the exchange of images, but others allow the exchange of information, chat, and even surveys for the members—creating real communities. Offenders effectively validate and normalize each other's behavior.[32]

Law enforcement experts perceive "trading" communities as risky enough; however, when a community allows and promotes communications between offenders regarding their sexual interests in children and their desires and experiences abusing children, that behavior also becomes normalized, increasing the risk that it drives some to act on those desires. Academic research also supports the conclusion that repeated viewing of the images, exposure to the community of other offenders, and the resulting normalization of the aberrant behavior, along with the community's encouragement of sexual abuse of children, increases the risk that offenders will sexually abuse children.[33]

D. The Children Most Vulnerable And At Risk Are Those The Offenders Can Easily Access And Manipulate

No matter what the motivation to produce child pornographic images—self-gratification, status in and entrée to exclusive online groups, or profit—most often, the offenders turn to children who are most easily available to them. It is no surprise then, that most sexual abuse of children can be attributed to those who have a relationship of trust and authority relative to the child in addition to ready access to the child. National Center for Missing & Exploited

Children (NCMEC) data indicates that the vast majority of identified child pornography victims (69% of their data set) were abused/exploited by people familiar to the children. In the NCMEC data set these people included parents, other relatives, neighbors, family, friends, babysitters, coaches, and guardians' partners; only a small fraction of victims (4% of the NCMEC data set) were victimized by individuals with whom the child had no relationship.[34] The abuse typically happens in the privacy of a home—away from prying eyes—and the victim is easily manipulated and shamed or scared into submission and silence.

While some of these images clearly depict children in great distress, others depict the children as appearing compliant. The abuse is rarely a one-time event, but rather an ongoing victimization that can last and progress for many years. The offender usually takes great care to groom the child so the sexual behavior becomes normalized. Additionally, because the abuser is typically a person the child trusts, it is easier to convince the child to agree to sexual acts. Thus, a 12-yearold child in a sexually abusive image may appear compliant, but that same child, when first abused at age 6, could have presented a completely different image to the viewer. It is important to note that depictions showing a so-called "compliant child" also provide collectors of child pornography support for their delusion that the child is not suffering abuse, a conclusion that lets them rationalize their collection of images and brings them potentially closer to contact abuse themselves.

Grooming usually involves normalizing sexualized behavior in the offender-child relationship by introducing increasingly intimate physical contact by the offender toward the victim, very gradually sexualizing the contact, and sometimes using child pornography to break down the child's barriers. This gradual process and the relationship of trust and authority that the offender usually holds over the child, along with the child's immaturity and subservience, serves to break down the child's resistance. These children have a difficult time understanding what is happening to them and why and have very little control over their circumstances.

Once child sexual abuse has occurred, offenders often are very successful at ensuring that the children stay silent about the abuse. Children rarely report the victimization. They may remain silent out of a sense of loyalty or obligation to the abuser, shame, guilt, or fear. The child may fear that they will appear complicit in the abuse, or they may be humiliated by the thought of others' viewing the images. Often, the child will have a significant emotional relationship with the offender prior to the abuse, making it difficult for the child to report the abuse. Also, children often are aware of the consequences to the family of disclosure and are loath to cause turmoil in their families.

E. Law Enforcement Officers Are Seeing More Prepubescent Children And Infants In Child Pornography Images And More Images Depicting Violent, Sadistic Acts

Among NDIC interviewees, 82 percent of respondents reported victims (all of whom were minors) in all age brackets, 51 percent reported that most investigations involved prepubescent children, and 67 percent reported that victims are getting younger. Also according to the NDIC interviewees, 63 percent of respondents reported increased violence toward child pornography victims, 42 percent more bondage, 38 percent more sadism and masochism, and 15 percent more bestiality. Although 21 percent reported no change in violence, no respondents reported decreased violence. One agency representative interviewed by NDIC reported occasionally discovering child pornography images that appear to represent autopsies.[35]

U.S. Sentencing Commission data between 2002 and 2008 shows a 65 percent increase during that period regarding enhancements for sadistic, masochistic, or violent images[36] The NJOV study found that 21 percent of child pornography offenders had images that depicted violence "such as bondage, rape or torture," adding that most of these images involved children who were "gagged, bound, blindfolded, or otherwise enduring sadistic sex."[37]

2. Child Pornographers Are Increasing Their Efforts To Avoid Being Identified

Technology has increased the production and distribution of child pornography and is being utilized extensively by pornographers to help avoid being caught. For example, offenders often connect to the Internet using free Wi-Fi, a wireless system at public access points or connect to unsecured wireless routers installed in private residences rather than accessing Internet sites from their personal Internet accounts. Offenders also use anonymizers, software applications that enable them to access the Internet while hiding the source computer's identifying information. In many instances, offenders hide their actual Internet Protocol (IP) addresses[38] by using use proxy servers.[39] Even when offenders do not employ these measures, often identifying information through IP addresses is not retained for long periods by Internet Service Providers, which unintentionally provides anonymity to offenders.[40] Offenders also diminish the ability of law enforcement officials to investigate child pornography storing images in encrypted files and by erasing images using evidence eliminating software. Offenders also increasingly access streaming web cam video to view victims in real time without actually producing or storing images or videos that could later be discovered by law enforcement.[41] Predators also rely on "throw-away" free e-mail accounts, "secure" e-mail accounts such as hush mail, and counter-surveillance methods.

ILLICIT USE OF A LEGITIMATE IP ADDRESS TO DISTRIBUTE CHILD PORNOGRAPHY

In 2004, Las Vegas, Nevada, Internet Crimes Against Children (ICAC) Task Force officers identified an IP address that was used to distribute child pornography. The IP address was associated with a business in Australia. Law enforcement further investigated and discovered that a Russian criminal organization had, in fact, stolen the IP address and used a server in Fairfax, Virginia, to operate the site. The stolen IP address and remote server were used to conceal the identity and location of the actual site operators so they could continue to sell child pornography and evade law enforcement.

Source: Las Vegas, Nevada, Internet Crimes Against Children Task Force.

Predators are also engaging in specific counter-surveillance activities such as researching cases in the news and topics presented by law enforcement at law enforcement only conferences. To further shield their identities, offenders occasionally will deviate from the common use of traditional credit cards and rely on digital currencies and prepaid credit cards to conceal transactions. The use of counter forensic tools such as proxies and onion routers[42] by online predators to remain anonymous when accessing the Internet also has increased. When effective methods of countering law enforcement efforts are developed, the information typically is shared among predators—including the suspected law enforcement officers screen name— often enabling even inexperienced offenders to operate undetected.

IDENTIFICATION OF A CHILD PORNOGRAPHY VICTIM

In January 2006, the FBI and NCMEC began conducting exhaustive analysis in an attempt to identify the child victim in a widely circulated child pornography series on the Internet. Images in this series began to surface in 2005 and documented an increasing level of sexual molestation to the minor victim as she aged over at least 4 years. A prominent clue that produced the strongest lead for law enforcement authorities was found in the background of one of the images. It was a decorative plate bearing a birth date and a girl's name hung on a wall. This information was used to obtain a court order directing the Social Security Administration in coordination with the Internal Revenue Service to provide information on all filers in the tax year 2006 who claimed a dependent child matching the girl's name from the wall or any variation of it.

The information received resulted in the dissemination of action leads to 29 field offices that directed them to compare the dependent children residing in their territory to sanitized images depicting the girl. On March 18, 2009, the FBI sent an immediate lead to one of the field divisions to follow up on two children residing within their territory who had pedigree information consistent with the girl in the images. On March 25, 2009, the FBI received confirmation from the field division that a child residing in its area was the child depicted in the series. On March 30, 2009, the victim was interviewed, and she identified the subject and disclosed the activity that had taken place. The field division also obtained items of evidentiary value that were visible in the explicit images. From the investigation, an immediate lead regarding the subject was disseminated to another field division. In turn, this second field division conducted surveillance on the subject's home. During surveillance, the subject was observed exiting his residence. Agents were able to obtain written consent to search his home, car, and shed. Jewelry visible in the explicit images was seized from the shed during the consent search. The subject was arrested, confessed, and provided a signed sworn statement to FBI agents.

Further, producers of child pornography are increasingly taking precautions to hide their identities and the identities of their victims in images and videos. Before production, many offenders hide or cover their faces and the faces of the victims. They also remove items within a setting that would allow law enforcement to identify the location. After production, offenders edit, or "scrub," images and videos for the same reasons. Unlike images of child pornography produced years earlier in which the offender and victim are prominently visible, in many recent images and videos, the offenders' goal is to make the setting "sterile"; the total focus is centered on the rape of the child victim, a focus which has mass appeal to the prurient interests of many other offenders.

3. Organized Criminal Groups Are Involved In The Production And Distribution Of Child Pornography

Organized criminal groups are becoming more prevalent in child exploitation investigations. Such groups include commercial enterprises that produce and distribute child pornography material for profit as well as non-commercial enterprises that produce and distribute child pornography images not for material gain, but to fuel the group members' common sexual interest in minors.

A. Many Organized Commercial Enterprises That Advertise And Distribute Child Pornography Do So For Profit

Such enterprises are responsible for extremely large-scale distribution of child exploitation material, and, as a result, have netted significant profits. From a profit perspective, commercial distribution of child exploitation material over the Internet can be safer, less expensive, and more lucrative that many other criminal enterprises. For example, as compared with traditional drug trafficking enterprises, selling child pornography over the Internet: (1) provides greater anonymity, (2) eliminates risks associated with having to physically transport contraband to buyers, and (3) involves an intangible product, an image, which can be sold millions of times over without having to replenish supply.

Groups engaged in the online business of advertising and distributing child pornography typically operate largely outside of the United States, but have an international customer base. These groups present significant investigative challenges for U.S. law enforcement. The primary challenges U.S. law enforcement face in investigating the commercial distribution of child pornography over the Internet are: (1) identifying who is involved in the commercial enterprise and (2) obtaining information and assistance from other countries, which is critical to investigating such cases. These groups are able to capitalize on the lack of regulation of Internet activity in many countries, as well as the fact that many countries lack strong legislation banning the sale of child pornography. Because these groups operate over the Internet, they are able to reach a huge market while employing various technological means to hide their tracks, such as the use of proxy servers and payment sites that do not maintain transactional records.

The Internet Watch Foundation (IWF) reports, during a one year period, identifying 1,536 domains that carry child pornographic content. According to the IWF, 74 percent of those domains are commercial[43] However, many of these domains are short lived, often less than 100 days, with limited activity. Immigration and Customs Enforcement (ICE) estimates the number of commercial web sites closer to 250 that actively maintain and display child pornography at a given moment.[44]

As illustrated by case examples,[45] organized commercial enterprises engaged in the advertisement and distribution of child pornography images pose significant threats to society as well as challenges to law enforcement. These groups have the ability to operate virtually and anonymously from anywhere in the world, thus facilitating the ongoing dissemination of child exploitation material. By using the Internet as their means of distribution, these groups are able to engage in mass distribution of child pornography images to a customer base that far exceeds law enforcement resources. In addition, because of the transnational nature of many of these groups, even multiple arrests of individuals who play roles in running the enterprises in one country do not necessarily end the enterprises' operations. For all of these reasons, organized commercial enterprises present a significant threat to the safety of children in that, with virtual anonymity, they facilitate the continued dissemination of child exploitation images and fuel the demand of those who seek such material.

Commercial child pornography is not limited to the Internet model discussed. Frequently, USPIS uncovers U.S.-based offenders using simple mail order catalogs either mailed or e-mailed to customers, to advertise child pornography and then fulfill orders by mail shipments. These offenders, reluctant to use computers, often have been involved in collecting child pornography for years—many before the advent of the Internet—and often are contact offenders.[46]

B. Some Organized Criminal Groups Seek Child Exploitation Material For Reasons Other Than Profit

Unlike an organized commercial enterprise, whose sole motivation is to profit from the continued dissemination of child pornography images rather than any particular interest in the content, organized groups of individuals who seek and trade such material for no material gain are, arguably, more dangerous because they are solely motivated by a sexual interest in minors. This sexual interest fuels such groups' desire not only to build their own collection of images, but also to obtain new images of recent abuse and, in some instances, to share their own acts of molestation with other group members either through discussion or, worse, through transmission of live video showing the abuse. Typically, these groups set specific criteria for who may join. One criteria often used is a demonstration that a prospective member has a genuine interest in engaging in sexual conduct with minors, such as requiring a prospective member to transmit child pornography to the group to gain membership. In addition, such groups often employ multiple layers of security in an attempt to evade law enforcement. Because members of such groups frequently are driven to commit contact offenses against children and take extraordinary efforts to go undetected, investigations into such groups' activities are very challenging and resource intensive.[47]

As law enforcement investigations illustrate,[48] these criminal enterprises typically go to great lengths to evade law enforcement and, ultimately, are identified only when an individual member's computer is seized for unrelated conduct and law enforcement, posing as the member, observes the group activity on the computer and can infiltrate the group. While investigations into these groups can yield the arrest of multiple child molesters, identification of the members and cooperation with foreign law enforcement, which may be required, can frustrate efforts to identify specific suspects.

4. Law enforcement agencies are focusing on factors that may help predict child pornographers who pose a greater risk to children.

Due to limited resources, law enforcement officers often are tasked with determining the ultimate targets of law enforcement operations; namely, who among the vast numbers of potential targets pose the greatest risk to children. While such determinations are difficult, certain characteristics tend to suggest an offender may pose a great risk to children, while other offenders may pose less of a threat.

Certain factors or characteristics, or combinations thereof, can signal that a particular child pornography offender poses a higher risk of being or becoming a contact offender. Interviews of law enforcement officers in this field, along with a review of research studies, suggest that the following factors or characteristics, alone or in combination, may signal such a risk:

- The offender has a prior history of sex offenses.

- The offender demonstrates a certain commitment to the collection or trade or both of child pornography.
    - The offender has been involved in the collection or trade of child pornographic images for a relatively long time.
    - The offender participates in online child pornography communities.
    - The offender uses more than one technology to collect or trade child pornography.
    - The offender uses advanced technologies to collect, or trade, or both, child pornography.
    - The offender uses sophisticated technologies or practices to avoid detection.
    - The offender shows an interest in images depicting extreme sexual conduct or very young victims.
    - The offender exhibits extreme care building, maintaining, and categorizing his collection of child pornography.
- The offender communicates with other offenders in online communities about his sexual interest in children.

The presence of any of these factors should alert law enforcement officers to the possibility that an offender, particularly one with ready access to children, could be a contact offender. Law enforcement, however, cannot summarily dismiss as a priority target an offender who appears only to be possessing images. In many instances, when law enforcement officers execute search warrants for a computer and premises of an offender who appears only to be possessing images, evidence of molestation is uncovered.[49]

An offender who purchases child pornography from a commercial web site, however, is not necessarily high-risk and may even be an entry-level offender. Paying for child pornography has not been shown to be an indicator of risk, and offenders buy child pornography for a variety of reasons. The fact that an offender resorts to paying for images may or may not signal a relative lack of sophistication. In addition, while some commercial sites have freshly produced sex abuse images, many simply recycle old images that are otherwise available elsewhere on the Internet. By contrast, some private trading groups[50] have more extreme and new material and membership in some of these groups is strictly vetted by the offenders operating the groups. Individuals must actively seek these groups to gain access, create usernames and passwords to gain entry, and often dedicate significant amounts of time to a particular group to maintain membership.

Similarly, an offender using pure P2P technology may signal less of a risk than an offender using a technology that combines P2P file sharing with the ability to interact with like-minded offenders. This is because pure P2P technology only requires a blind search of the network for images and videos using a search term; it does not require much personal investment or any personal contact to acquire images. Of course, these observations are not universal and those who trade on basic peer-to-peer can pose the same risk to a child as an offender using an encrypted message board to trade images. Similarly, an offender who does not use encryption or other evasive technologies can always pose the same or greater risk to a child than one who does.

B. Online Enticement

Online offenders use the Internet to entice and manipulate children into situations in which they become vulnerable to sexual exploitation, particularly child pornography, sexual contact, and abduction. From 2004 through 2008, ICAC task force officers processed 20,562 documented online enticement complaints, including 7,879 documented complaints of suspected *travelers*[51]—aggressive and dangerous online child predators who travel to the location of a child for the purpose of establishing physical contact.[52]

From 2004 through 2008, ICAC task force officers processed 20,562 documented online enticement complaints, including 7,879 documented complaints of suspected travelers[1]—aggressive and dangerous online child predators who travel to the location of a child for the purpose of establishing physical contact.

Online enticement can lead to offenders' grooming victims to self-produce child pornography, which then becomes part of the child pornography market and forever harms the child. Recent case examples have shown offenders using web cams to entice the minor to perform a sex act in front of the camera that he then records. Often, the offender will blackmail the minor into engaging in these acts through threats to reveal a less explicit recorded image to friends and family. NCMEC data show that approximately 28 percent of identified child victims seen in child pornography produced the images of themselves, whether by inducement or not, and this segment of child pornography has been increasing.[53]

In addition, another possible consequence of online enticement is *abduction*. According to National Incidence Studies on Missing, Abducted, Runaway and Throwaway Children, the primary motive in non-family abductions is sexual. Since the inception of the Child Abduction Rapid Deployment (CARD) teams in October 2005, the FBI has developed 10 CARD teams to combat this risk by aiding state and local law enforcement in child abduction investigations. 64 percent of non-family abduction deployments have resulted in the child victim being sexually victimized by their abductor. Moreover, in 36 percent of non-family abductions, the child victim was murdered by their abductor.

1. Online Enticement Complaints Are Increasing, Drawing More Law Enforcement Resources Into Complex And Time-Consuming Investigations.

Children are increasingly targeted for sexual exploitation by individuals who monitor Internet forums for potential victims. From 2004 through 2008 there were sharp increases in the number of online enticement incidents reported to the NCMEC CyberTipline[54] and the number of documented enticement complaints processed by ICAC investigators.[55] However, there is no actual measurement of online enticement. NCMEC acknowledges that increased public awareness has contributed to the increased number of incidents reported to the CyberTipline. Still, recent publicity has highlighted the fact that two prominent social networking sites had to delete the accounts of thousands of registered sex offenders using their sites.

Investigating the rising number of online enticement complaints poses a relatively new strain on law enforcement resources because online enticement cases require specialized technical training for investigators, coordination with Internet providers, and, often, the support of computer forensic examiners to recover digital evidence from computers and other electronic storage devices. Depending on the technical ability of the offender and the complexity of the case, child sexual exploitation investigations involving computer forensic evidence may be resolved in a few days or take years. Officers pursuing individual online predator suspects may monitor a suspect's Internet activity across several online forums, aliases, and communication devices.

2. Online Predators Demonstrate Great Patience In Manipulating Children Into Vulnerable Situations

Online predators gradually manipulate or "groom" children until they voluntarily provide sexual images online or agree to meet predators for sex. Grooming is the predators for sex. Grooming is the psychological process predators always have used to encourage children to engage in sexual activity, but it is now being applied to online enticement.[56] Grooming typically begins with the selection of a child who exhibits desired behaviors or psychological characteristics such low self-esteem or family problems. The victim frequently is shown increasing levels of attention, affection, empathy, and generosity. Online predators often relate to children through mastering music, movies, and games that appeal to the children. Predators often act in a patient and manipulative manner, listening to children's problems and becoming indispensable with advice. They prey on what makes children susceptible to manipulation, intimidation, and victimization—children's naïveté. Predators promote intra-familial rifts, alienate children from others in their lives, assume the parental role, and then declare their love, creating emotional dependence and infatuation simultaneously. Predators send children sex toys, demonstrate their uses, and indoctrinate children through the familiar medium of toys. At some point, the children provide compromising information about or images of themselves, perhaps using webcams presented to them as gifts. Predators then threaten exposure of the victims to friends and family and may even threaten lives. Ultimately, many predators coerce victims into sexual abuse, and many digitally memorialize their crimes for trading purposes and to ensure silence, essentially producing child pornography that will victimize children beyond the moment of sexual abuse.

Throughout the grooming process, predators[57] gradually introduce child pornography into their seduction methodology. As instructions for desired behaviors, children are shown suggestive images, nudity is introduced, and then actual sexual abuse is carried out. Gradually the idea of sex between adults and children is normalized. Alarmingly, predators are coaxing graphic images from victims, thereby accelerating the grooming process.

VIDEO GAME CHAT

In January 2008, a 27-year-old Missouri man allegedly traveled to California to meet a 15-year-old girl with the intention of engaging in sex. He initially made contact with the girl while playing video games on the Internet and developed the relationship by using social networking sites, text messaging, and a cell phone he sent to her as a birthday present. He was charged with using interstate commerce to entice or coerce a minor to engage in sexual activity and traveling in interstate commerce to engage in illicit sexual activity.

Source: ICE, News Release, "Missouri Man Charged with Traveling to California to Engage in Sex with Minor He Met on Xbox LIVE," February 6, 2009.

Grooming may occur using methods varying from those previously discussed, but in most cases the grooming process incorporates many of the aforementioned steps.

C. The Domestic Prostitution of Children

The domestic prostitution of children may be increasing as more criminals have discovered the high profitability and relatively low risk of commercial child sexual exploitation. In fact, those who profit from the sexual abuse of children are far less likely to be arrested or prosecuted than are the children they are exploiting. There are insufficient support and recovery programs for the victims. The combination of inadequate resources and the powerful psychological hold the defendants have over the victims makes it very difficult to end the cycle of exploitation as victims often repeatedly return to their abusers either voluntarily or forcibly.

1. Pimps Prey On Vulnerable Children, Manipulating Them And Then Trapping Them In Child Prostitution

Pimps, who are commercial sex traffickers,[58] manipulate children into a life of prostitution and then use physical and emotional abuse to keep their victims trapped in that way of life. Pimps target children who are vulnerable to exploitation, including those with low self-esteem, who are runaways or throwaways, and who have histories of physical and sexual abuse. Pimps typically recruit a vulnerable child by first showing affection and attention and promising a stable relationship. After the child has gained an emotional and psychological attachment to the pimp, he introduces the idea of prostitution to her[59] as something she can do to contribute financially to their "street family."

After the child has been manipulated into a relationship with the pimp, the pimp begins training or "seasoning" her by normalizing the life of prostitution and making her completely dependent on him. The child may be given a sexual education or be exposed to pornography to desensitize her to sexual images and terms. To solidify his control, the pimp or someone acting at his direction, will beat, torture, or starve the child[60] to force her into obedience. Some pimps use alcohol or drugs to control their victims. To manipulate the child, the pimp also uses emotional tactics such as renaming her to break down her identity and telling her that she has no value except as a prostitute. The pimp also separates the child from biological family and friends as well as anything familiar. Additionally, the pimp keeps all of the profit earned by the child and delivers violent punishment if the child withholds any money. The pimp uses a combination of praise and abuse that causes the child to constantly work for his affection. The child becomes completely dependent on the pimp for food, clothing, shelter, and attention. The pimp's control often is so complete that victims are incapable of leaving.

2. There Is Steady Demand And Profit In The Prostitution Of Children

Since 2003, the FBI, NCMEC, and CEOS have partnered on the Innocence Lost National Initiative, which targets the victimization of children through prostitution here in the United States. This effort has resulted in recovering 918 children and 554 state and federal convictions of those who prostitute our children. Moreover, from 2004 through 2008, ICAC Task Forces saw a 914 percent increase in the number of child victims of prostitution[61] complaints processed by their members (see Appendix D, OJJDP); a 31 percent increase in ICAC Task Forces (45 to 59) during that period accounts for some of the increase. It is not known to what extent that increase is explained by increased awareness as opposed to increased frequency of the crime. ICAC Task Forces are responsible primarily for investigating Internet-based crimes against children; therefore, the increase in ICAC complaints could reflect an increase in the use of the Internet to facilitate the prostitution of children that had already been occurring. During that same period, the number of child victims of prostitution incidents reported to the NCMEC Cyber Tipline increased as well. (See Appendix D, NCMEC.)

Some criminals have turned away from illicit activities such as drug dealing and robbery toward child sex trafficking, from which they can generate potentially several thousand dollars per day, as a single child can generate as much as $1,000 on a weekend night.[62] Simply, it is cheaper for a criminal to prostitute a child (which involves supplying the child with her primary needs of food, clothes, and shelter) than to commit other crimes such as drug dealing (which require a large capital investment up front to acquire the contraband). In fact, the profitability of child prostitutes to the pimp has increased as Internet advertising and web-enabled cell phones have aided pimps in reaching a larger client base; they can schedule more sexual encounters per child.

Many pimps increase their profits by working in loose affiliation with each other, sharing information about "hot spots" where there is higher demand; the traffickers transport the children to those locations. Pimps increase their profits by transporting prostituted children to host cities for major sporting events and conventions and to cities with consistent tourist populations, such as Las Vegas. For example, Internet advertisements for child victims of prostitution rose sharply in February 2009 in advance of the Super Bowl. The various locales where children are transported for prostitution collectively are known as circuits. Traveling through an established circuit of cities allows pimps to provide children to a fresh set of clients for a short period before continuing to the next city. The transitory nature of the crime also adds to the law enforcement challenge. Because pimps and their child victims are constantly on the move, it can be difficult for local law enforcement to begin building a case. It can also be difficult for law enforcement to make the necessary connections: for example, that the same victim has come into contact with law enforcement in cities on opposite sides of the country.

Determining the number of child prostitution-related prosecutions simply based on case statistics is difficult because at both the federal and state levels, certain criminal provisions could be applied both to cases involving a prostituted child and to cases involving the noncommercial sexual exploitation of a child. For example, at the state level, a customer could be charged with the statutory rape of a child rather than soliciting sex from a child. Under federal law, transporting a child for any illegal sexual activity, which could be prostitution but also could be molestation, is a crime. While it is possible to determine the number of prosecutions under a given statute, that data does not indicate which of the cases involved commercial sex acts; therefore, the statistical data based on prosecutions is unavoidably imprecise.

Officials report that prosecutions are very resource-intensive, requiring a large investment in investigative, prosecutorial, and victim-service resources. Nevertheless, law enforcement pressure on pimps is increasing. For example, since its inception in 2003, the Innocence Lost National Initiative (ILNI)[63] has located and recovered 918 children, resulting in 369 indictments and 554 convictions of traffickers in the federal and state criminal justice systems, disruption of 92 criminal enterprises disrupted, and dismantling of 44 criminal enterprises. When prosecuted federally, pimps face serious charges such as violation of the Mann Act[64], the Racketeer Influenced and Corrupt Organization Act (RICO)[65], or the Trafficking Victims Protection Act of 2000 (TVPA), and may receive lengthy sentences.[66] For example, four life sentences and several sentences ranging from 30 to 45 years have been awarded to pimps convicted through ILNI investigations.

The shortage of adequate resources for victims has an impact on the number of prosecutions. While obtaining a conviction against a pimp if the victim does not testify is possible, it is certainly much more difficult. The lack of adequate resources is a problem in its own right as it means the victims are not provided the treatment they need to begin the recovery process. In addition, if victims are not stabilized, they are much less likely to be able to participate effectively in the criminal justice process. If they cannot testify and the defendant is acquitted or is not prosecuted in the first instance, the defendant will be able to continue his exploitation of that child or of other children. Services are needed to ensure the victim can be involved in the prosecution, and the prosecution is needed to eliminate the defendant's ability to keep hurting the child, so she can further her recovery.

3. Child Victims Of Prostitution—The Victims Of Commercial Sexual Exploitation—Are More Likely To Be Arrested Than Are The Child Sex Traffickers Or Client Sex Offenders

Clients of child victims of prostitution are, in fact, child sex offenders; however, this form of child sexual exploitation often goes unpunished. In fact, the exploited child victim of prostitution is much more likely to be arrested for prostitution offenses than is the offender. For example, a 2005 study for Congress showed that in Boston, 11 female prostitutes (adult and child) were arrested for each male client arrest; in Chicago, the ratio was 9 to 1; and, in New York City, the ratio was 6 to 1. Part of the disproportionate arrest ratios are attributed to misinformation provided to officers by the children; that is, the children will represent themselves to be adults, and may provide false identification. Pimps typically provide child victims of prostitution with false identification that indicates an adult age and the pimps instruct the children to lie about their ages if arrested.

Similar to client offenders, pimps usually evade arrest and prosecution, primarily by avoiding detection altogether. When they are arrested, they often serve a minimum amount of time in prison or have their cases reduced to misdemeanors. Pimps typically operate within insular groups, supported by a network of independent but cooperative pimps. The transitory nature of their crime reduces the likelihood that a local law enforcement agency will be able to build enough investigative intelligence to make the case. Pimps share information regarding law enforcement operations, and if a pimp is arrested, other pimps often provide support by maintaining the arrestee's operations. Moreover, a child victim of prostitution, if arrested or rescued from prostitution, rarely reports the identity of her trafficker or testifies against an arrested trafficker, because she often has become dependent on the trafficker or is fearful of retaliation. Although convicting a defendant without the victim's cooperation is possible, cases are much stronger if the victim testifies. Traffickers know this and count on victims to refuse to testify, to recant, or to minimize the degree of criminal conduct.

4. Child Victims Of Prostitution Suffer Extreme Forms Of Exploitation And Often Are Unable, Even If Rescued, To Permanently Escape The Influence Of Traffickers

According to leading treatment and recovery providers, between 60 and 90 percent of child victims of prostitution in their programs were victims of child sexual abuse prior to being victimized through prostitution.[67] In fact, the Standing Against Global Exploitation organization (SAGE) reported that most of the children it supports were raped prior to adolescence. The trauma of early sexual abuse creates confusion in the minds of children and renders them vulnerable to exploitation by child sex traffickers. The prostitution of children takes place in a variety of different venues such as street prostitution, adult night clubs, sex parties, or motel rooms where traffickers will direct individual client offenders.

Children victimized by prostitution require specialized recovery programs[68] including shelter, nutrition, and appropriate medical treatment, as well as psychological evaluation; counseling, alcohol and drug treatment programs, education programs, and life skills training. Also, because traffickers often try to reclaim girls who have been rescued, the trafficker's presence could expose other children to being recruited for prostitution. In fact, traffickers often recruit children outside of recovery centers or send children into centers to recruit; in some cases, traffickers simply enter the facilities and remove the children. Traffickers often are successful in reclaiming child victims of prostitution, particularly those in short-term programs (less than 18 months), juvenile detention facilities, or jail. The stigma victims feel when placed in such facilities with other children who have no history of prostitution often causes them to return to the familiarity of the trafficker and prostitution.

There is a dearth of these specialized recovery programs, and the ones that do exist are often only for children who are under the age of 18. If they were prostituted as children but are now adults, they cannot be admitted into those programs. Often, the services provided to these victims are provided through the state, such as Child Protective Services, Temporary Assistance for Needy Families (TANF), or Medicaid.

D. Child Sex Tourism

Child sex tourists[69] prey on the most vulnerable children in the most impoverished areas of the world. Many of these predators are Americans, but the identification and prosecution of offenders is very difficult. Despite the great challenges, U.S. law enforcement officials continue to pursue, often successfully, the growing number of American sex tourists, attempting to stem the tremendous damage that these offenders are inflicting.

1. U.S. Citizens Account For A Large Portion Of International Child Sex Tourists And Their Numbers Are Growing

American sex tourists commonly travel to Southeast Asian countries (Cambodia, Laos, Philippines, Thailand) and, increasingly, to Mexico, Central and South America (Brazil, Costa Rica, and Honduras), and, to a lesser extent, Eastern European nations (Lithuania, and Russia.) Some reporting indicates that as many as 80 percent of the child sex tourists in Latin America and 25 percent of those in Southeast Asia[70] Sex tourists travel to certain countries primarily because gaining access to children frequently is aided by parents or organized crime groups and because many predators believe their anonymity, transient status, and, oftentimes, the limited attention to such crimes by local law enforcement officials makes their discovery unlikely. Within these countries, predators typically travel to very impoverished areas where they are more likely to be able to pay for access to children. In fact, some child sex tourists volunteer with foreign aid organizations or charities, particularly orphanages, to gain access to children in impoverished areas.

Although there is no estimate for the number of Americans who travel overseas for the purpose of sexually assaulting children, their ranks appear to be increasing. Since 2004, the number of child sex tourism incidents reported to the NCMEC CyberTipline has increased significantly overall.[71] However, the number of reported incidents declined sharply in 2008 (392) and again in 2009 (247), most likely reflecting an improved ability of child sex tourists to operate online in a less detectable fashion. Previously, law enforcement agencies were quite successful in identifying predators that planned travel through sex tour providers, but now most predators avoid such companies and instead make their own travel arrangements and wait until they arrive in the country to begin coordinating their illicit activity.

Finding Local Children in a Foreign Country

Predators often obtain information about brothels that offer children for sex or other available children from local taxi drivers, hotel concierges, restaurant wait staff, or newspaper advertisements. Sex tourists also solicit children independently in foreign destinations at beaches or on the street, particularly if the sex tourist is seeking boys. Some predators also contact foreign children through the Internet and arrange to meet them on the trip. Child sex tourists also gain information about local children through Internet chat rooms, message boards, and online forums. These Internet forums provide locations of child brothels, prices, accounts of child sexual abuse by other sex tourists, and sites for trading child pornography.

2. Child Sex Tourists Often Engage In Many Forms Of Child Exploitation, Causing Extreme And Lasting Damage To Victims

Sex tourists are increasingly creating child pornography by recording their acts of child sexual abuse to bring home as souvenirs. After returning home, child sex tourists may share or sell their images and videos with other child predators. Images of the child's abuse are permanently memorialized and impossible to remove from circulation once they enter the Internet stream. Some sex tourists also write graphic online accounts of their experiences and share information on how to find and abuse children in foreign locations. These accounts may entice other predators to engage in sex tourism.

The children abused by sex tourists suffer not only sexual abuse but also physical abuse and lasting health problems. Sex tourists often are violent in abusing children in foreign countries because they believe their victims will not report the offenses. Children sold in brothels often suffer from illnesses, exhaustion, malnourishment, infections, physical injuries, and sexually transmitted diseases. Living conditions are poor and medical treatment is rarely available to them. Children who fail to earn enough income generally are subject to severe punishment such as beatings and starvation.

3. Investigating And Prosecuting American Child Sex Tourists Is Very Difficult; However, A Change In Child Exploitation Laws Has Aided Prosecutors

Child sex tourists usually travel alone to foreign countries and operate in secret. Identifying victims and finding locations where abuse occurred is difficult, and evidence of the crime often is not preserved. Compounding the difficulties are differences in investigation and conflicts of law. Some investigative techniques such as wiretaps, covert recordings, and closed circuit television surveillance are prohibited in certain countries, and procedures for obtaining evidence must follow U.S. standards to be admissible in a U.S. prosecution. Moreover, the time and expense of sending investigators abroad and bringing witnesses to the United States for trial is significant and, for state or local agencies, the cost often is prohibitive. Prosecutors also face extradition challenges and considerable administrative obstacles when securing witnesses. Additionally, it is difficult for foreign victims to come to the United States and live in an unfamiliar environment for several weeks, often without family members, while they await testifying. Also, victims may be ostracized by their family and within their communities when they return home. Document translation also is time consuming and costly.

Despite the obstacles, many American child sex tourists are arrested and, in fact, prosecution has become easier. Since the enactment of the Prosecutorial Remedies and Other Tools to end the Exploitation of Children Today (PROTECT) Act of 2003, prosecutors are no longer required to prove that the offender traveled to a foreign country with the intent of having sex with a minor. Prosecutors only need to show that the offender in fact traveled to a foreign country and engaged in sexual conduct with a minor.

E. Child Exploitation in Indian Country

Child sexual abuse crime rates in Indian Country[72] are high according to anecdotal Assistant U.S. Attorney (AUSA) information, and child sexual assault cases comprise the overwhelming majority of child exploitation cases on tribal lands. Several AUSAs who prosecute crimes on Indian Country report prosecuting more sex crimes than physical assaults involving American Indian child victims. Most cases do not involve the use of computers or the Internet.

Prosecutors report their belief that the rate of child sexual abuse is higher in Indian Country than in the general U.S. population, but there is a dearth of reliable data regarding physical and sexual abuse—among children and adults—in Indian Country. Because no formal system currently is in place that provides for coordination in the collection and reporting of crime and justice data by the various federal, state, local, and tribal agencies responsible for law enforcement in Indian Country, the rates of specific violent crime categories are not available. Data that do exist—the National Institute of Justice (NIJ) reports that 34.1 percent of American Indian women are raped in their lifetimes as compared to 18.2 percent of all U.S. women—show that the rate of sexual abuse is higher among American Indian women than all U.S. women. Further, according to available data from the Bureau of Justice Statistics (BJS), American Indians experience per capita rates of violence that are more than twice those of the U.S. resident population. Rates of violence in every age group and for both males and females are higher among American Indians than among all other races.

Law enforcement officers and prosecutors often encounter unique obstacles when investigating and prosecuting child sexual abuse cases in Indian Country including the following:

- The remoteness of some reservations, compounded by extremely poor traveling conditions in inclement weather, may contribute to multiday delays for FBI personnel travelling to crime scenes to begin investigations and interviewing witnesses. Some victims and witnesses must travel more than 500 miles to attend federal court proceedings. Further, some areas lack roads, legal street addresses, and telephones.
- Many reservations have fairly small populations—sometimes numbering 100 or fewer residents. Victims and families, in general, are reluctant to report crimes when assailants are family members or people with status in their communities. In extremely small communities, victims and families may be far less likely to report crimes committed by someone with a close relationship to the victim or, in Indian Country, by an elder, spiritual leader, or tribal council member.
- Some American Indians who speak traditional languages may experience difficulty communicating in English with federal law enforcement and in federal court.
- Some American Indians who are unfamiliar with Anglo customs may be uncomfortable interacting with law enforcement, prosecutorial, and court personnel during investigations and trials. In some cases, victims and witnesses may have a tendency to distrust outsiders.

Child sexual abuse potentially has many short-and long-term impacts on American Indian victims and these potential problems frequently are exacerbated in Indian Country, where remote reservations result in isolation of the victims and their families and insufficient social services to assist victims with the effects of the abuse. Frequently reported short-term impacts include anger, hostility, low self-esteem, conduct disorders, delinquency, inappropriate sexual behavior, teen pregnancy, truancy, poor performance in school, substance abuse, and running away. Potential long-term impacts include sexual disturbance, depression, suicide, alcoholism, drug abuse, chronic unemployment, violence, and sexual abuse of others.

The Department has authority to prosecute child exploitation crimes in Indian Country predicated on two main federal statutes that govern federal criminal jurisdiction in Indian Country—18 U.S.C. § 1152 and § 1153. Section 1153, known as the Major Crimes Act, gives the federal government jurisdiction to prosecute certain enumerated serious offenses, such as murder, manslaughter, rape, aggravated assault, and child sexual abuse, when they are committed by Indians in Indian Country. Section 1152, known as the General Crimes Act, gives the Federal Government exclusive jurisdiction to prosecute all crimes committed by non-Indians against Indian victims. Section 1152 also grants the federal government jurisdiction to prosecute minor crimes by Indians against non-Indians, although that jurisdiction is shared with tribes, and provides that the federal government may not prosecute an Indian who has been punished by the local tribe for a minor offense. To protect tribal self-government, section 1152 also specifically excludes minor crimes between Indians, which fall under exclusive tribal jurisdiction. The federal government also has jurisdiction to prosecute federal crimes of general application, such as drug and financial crimes, when they occur in Indian Country. On a limited number of reservations, the federal criminal responsibilities under Sections 1152 and 1153 have been ceded to the states[73]

The Department's response to violent crime in Indian Country is informed by the circumstances of a tribe and the criminal justice issues confronting a particular reservation. The Department is focused on the prosecution of cases, but also recognizes that prevention, training, and other grassroots intervention efforts are vital for an effective solution to crime in Indian Country. These other efforts are important in Indian Country where financial resources may be limited and an adequate support system is not in place.

A task force model often is employed that allows the federal government to supplement tribal resources when possible. In these cases, the Department looks to the tribes' criminal justice systems as partners. Tribal law enforcement frequently is the first responder, collecting evidence and interviewing witnesses who will be critical to the success of federal prosecution. Moreover, a case may be prosecuted simultaneously in tribal and federal court; personnel in both systems engage in ongoing dialogue so that justice in both systems can be achieved. Sometimes this cooperation results in the tribe deferring to a U.S. Attorney's Office, while other times the U.S. Attorney's Office will defer to the tribe. In still other cases, it may be determined that the state, in fact, is where jurisdiction properly rests.

III. The Nation's Approach to Combatting Child Exploitation

For many years, the Department and many federal, state, and local agencies, and non-government organizations have fought against the sexual exploitation of our nation's children on many fronts. The Act requires the Department to report to Congress on a variety of these efforts, including: (A) a review of the Department's work to prevent, investigate, and prosecute child exploitation crimes;[74] (B) a review of the Internet Crimes Against Children Task Force Program;[75] (C) a review of other Federal programs efforts relating to child exploitation and education;[76] (D) a review of other efforts by private sector and nonprofit entities that promote child safety;[77] (E) a description of the Department's actions to help coordinate the various efforts that are underway, including efforts to coordinate internationally;[78] (F) a review of federal programs focused on Internet safety;[79] (G) a report on the Project Safe Childhood Conference;[80] and (H) an assessment of the technological assistance available to state and local law enforcement agencies and review of the backlog of the forensic analysis at Regional Computer Forensic Labs.[81]

This section of the Report provides information on all of the areas identified above by providing a brief review of the myriad groups and coordination efforts underway. The combined efforts of these groups represent the work of thousands of individuals and hundreds of thousands of hours of work, resulting in countless crimes not being committed, victims being rescued, and crimes being prosecuted. Due to the significance of all of these efforts, it would be impossible to detail all of the work performed by each group. Instead, this chapter attempts to provide a comprehensive overview of the number of agencies, organizations, and task forces that exist to address this issue and to provide Congress information about the extent to which the Department is assisting in coordinating and collaborating with these groups.

A. A Review of the Department of Justice's Offices Involved in the Fight to Prevent, Investigate, and Prosecute Child Exploitation Crimes

The Department has a number of components, offices, and agencies that devote personnel, resources, and time to the issue of preventing, investigating, and prosecuting child exploitation. These components include: the Office of the Deputy Attorney General (ODAG), FBI, the U.S. Marshals Service, the U.S. Attorneys Offices, the Criminal Division's Child Exploitation and Obscenity Section (CEOS) and the Office of International Affairs (OIA), the Office of Justice Programs (OJP), and the Office of Legal Policy (OLP). For example, the FBI is one of the premier law enforcement agencies in the world. It has fought the exploitation of children through major initiatives like the Innocent Images National Initiative (IINI), the Innocence Lost National Initiative (ILNI), and the Child Abduction Rapid Deployment (CARD) teams. The Marshals Service takes a lead role in locating and investigating unregistered sex offenders.

The United States Attorney's offices lead Project Safe Childhood, a program designed to marshal federal, state and local investigative and prosecution resources to combat the technology-facilitated sexual exploitation of children. CEOS is an office within the Criminal Division of the Department that is staffed by highly trained specialists who lead nationwide investigations, provide advice and training to the nation's prosecutors, and develop legislative and policy initiatives. OIA is another section within the Criminal Division, which is responsible for coordination with federal, state, and foreign authorities to obtain the international extradition of fugitives and the exchange of evidence and other legal assistance in support of investigations and prosecutions, including those for child exploitation crimes, in the United States and abroad. OJP provides funding and coordination for dozens of state and local programs for research projects, community outreach, and Internet safety training, and investigative agencies, including the 61 ICAC task forces. The Office of Legal Policy has aided in gathering information for this chapter, and in reviewing legislation in the area of child exploitation. The Office of the Deputy Attorney General houses the newly appointed National Coordinator for Child Exploitation Prevention and Interdiction.

1. Office of the Deputy Attorney General

The Act required the Department to appoint a "high official" to coordinate the formulation and implementation of the National Strategy, and to liaise with federal, state, local, and international groups to foster further cooperation in this area. The Department has appointed the National Coordinator for Child Exploitation Prevention and Interdiction, who is housed in the Office of the Deputy Attorney General. The National Coordinator has worked as a state and federal prosecutor specializing in crimes against children since 1996, and brings a wealth of substantive experience to the position.

2. The Federal Bureau of Investigation

The FBI is a leader in investigating child exploitation through several important initiatives. Agents working in Innocent Images focus on technology-facilitated crimes against children. This initiative has also been launched internationally, with investigators from many countries invited to train with agents from Innocent Images to foster cooperation and coordination. The FBI also leads 34 local task forces as part of the Innocence Lost initiative, which focuses on the forced domestic prostitution of our children, and has lead to the conviction of more than 500 pimps and madams. In 2006, the FBI formed Child Abduction Rapid Deployment (CARD) teams to aid state and local law enforcement in child abduction investigations. These teams have deployed in more than 55 cases since their creation.

a. Innocent Images National Initiative

The Innocent Images National Initiative (IINI) is a national FBI initiative that addresses crimes related to child pornography and the sexual exploitation of children through the use of online computers and related media. IINI investigations involve the use of highly sophisticated methods to identify subjects trying to evade law enforcement detection by the use of multiple layers of encryption and proxy servers in other countries. As such, IINI investigators and analysts have specific training requirements which include IINI online undercover and advance cyber crime courses. Agents are enrolled in a Cyber Career Path to specialize in these cyber crimes.

The Innocent Images National Initiative Unit (IINIU) is an intelligence-driven, proactive, multi-agency investigative initiative to combat the proliferation of child pornography/child sexual exploitation facilitated by online predators. The mission of IINIU is to reduce the vulnerability of children to acts of sexual exploitation and abuse, which are facilitated through the use of computers and digital media; to support FBI field offices in their efforts to identify and rescue child victims; to support others in their efforts to investigate and prosecute sexual predators who use the Internet and other online services to sexually exploit children for personal or financial gain; and to strengthen the capabilities of federal, state, local, and international law enforcement through training programs and investigative assistance. IINIU is responsible for all IINI program management and policy development, the training of all IINI investigators, research and development of emerging technologies, outreach initiatives and facilitates the forensic analysis of computer-related media. The Innocent Images International Task Force, an initiative and training program focused on coordination and cooperation with our allies, is described more fully in Section F(1)(d)(10)(i) below.

The FBI recently opened a new facility which is dedicated exclusively to the forensic analysis of digital evidence in the most significant child exploitation cases nationwide and conducts research in support of the investigative and forensic operations for IINI. The facility is located in Linthicum, MD and is a cooperative effort between the Cyber Division Innocent Images National Initiative and the Operational Technology Division's Computer Analysis Response Team (CART). The facility was formed to address the growing need for dedicated resources in the area of computer forensic analysis for child exploitation investigations. The dedication of the facility to a specific mission allows for examiners to specialize in this discipline and provide detailed content analysis to investigators. The facility is capable of providing large scale forensic support and analysis to enterprise investigations containing multiple terabytes of data. The facility supports forensic examination services on a wide variety of operating system platforms as well as other forms of digital media, including digital cameras and cell phones. The facility includes a research component that is actively engaged in developing tools and resources to better identify and conduct operations against the most egregious offenders. Efforts are continuing to develop an automated system capable of identifying new trends in relation to how offenders use the internet to conduct illegal activities.

IINI also takes the lead in Internet safety training on behalf of the FBI. The FBI's Safe Online Street (S.O.S.) Internet Challenge is a national Internet safety program designed to help students recognize potential dangers associated with the Internet, email, chat rooms and social networking sites. This initiative was launched nationally in the Fall of 2009. The program addresses and defines topics serious in nature such as seduction, child pornography, solicitation, exploitation, obscenity and online predators. Students take web-based quizzes and review specific web sites aimed at promoting online safety. Approximately 60,000 students have participated throughout the United States in the program. More information can be found at: http://www.fbi-sos.org /.

FBI and CEOS, in conjunction with NCMEC, operate the Endangered Child Alert Program (ECAP). In this program, FBI investigators select images of child pornography in which the perpetrator is at least partially visible. If all investigative efforts to identify the abuser have been exhausted, the FBI agents will then turn to the media and other public means to try to locate the individual. Working with CEOS trial attorneys, agents will obtain a "John Doe" or "Jane Doe" indictment against the offender. Once that is accomplished, the defendant's image will be displayed on the FBI website. If, after two weeks, the offender still has not been identified, the case will be featured on America's Most Wanted, the O'Reilly Factor, the Oprah Winfrey Show, and AOL. As of April 2010, this program has led to the recovery of over 31 victims of child sexual abuse and the location of 10 defendants. In a sister initiative, Operation Rescue Me, FBI, CEOS, and NCMEC work to identify child victims in series of child pornography images who have not been rescued. NCMEC provides FBI with the series, and the agents and analysts review the series for clues that will lead to the location of the child victims. As of April 2010, the initiative has identified seven child victims in four series of child pornography images.

B. FBI Crimes Against Children Unit

In June 2003, the FBI's Crimes Against Children Unit, in conjunction with the Department's Child Exploitation and Obscenity Section and the National Center for Missing & Exploited Children, launched the Innocence Lost National Initiative. Their combined efforts were aimed at addressing the growing problem of domestic sex trafficking of children in the United States. In the six years since its inception, the Initiative has resulted in the development of 38 dedicated task forces and working groups throughout the U.S. involving federal, state and local law enforcement agencies working in tandem with U.S. Attorney's Offices. These task forces and working groups have recovered 918 children and obtained state and federal convictions against 554 pimps, madams, and their associates who exploit children through forced prostitution.

On June 16, 2008, the FBI's Crimes Against Children Unit deployed the Innocence Lost Database (ILD) to users in all FBI Field Offices, Innocence Lost Task Forces, and local law enforcement agencies. The ILD was developed to assist law enforcement to identify domestic child victims of prostitution; collect and track intelligence regarding suspected pimps; and build intelligence driven enterprise level investigations. The ILD currently maintains over

20,000 entries from agencies such as the Las Vegas Metropolitan PD, Boston PD, Dallas PD, Oakland PD, Los Angeles PD, Toledo PD, FBI, and NCMEC. Over the course of a year, these records now number 25% more than the initial 16,000 records entered into the system. Currently, over 2,100 entries pertain to identified child victims of prostitution.

Criminal organizations are fluid and traffic victims interstate, i.e., to profitable locations, making it difficult to address the crime problem by local law enforcement alone. The focus of the FBI is to offer a task force approach employing the enterprise theory of investigation. The ILD offers a centralized, comprehensive electronic file, accessible to law enforcement 24/7. The ILD is an intelligence driven database that houses information on suspected pimps, child victims and adult prostitutes in an effort to connect enterprises and share intelligence. The ILD is hosted on the Law Enforcement On-line (LEO) Network and accessible through the Innocence Lost Special Interest Group.

Since 2006, the Child Abduction Rapid Deployment Team (CARD) has deployed in 55 cases involving 58 children. In sixty-one percent (61%) of these cases, the abductor had a known relationship to the child. Persons with known relationships to the child could seem like unlikely suspects. However, in 2009, the FBI's CARD Team has had the most deployments since being established in 2006. This is an indication that child abductions are an increasing problem and poses a threat to families. The motive behind some abductors with a known relationship to a child include; sexual intentions, divorce, ransom, a vicious act of retaliation.

Of the cases in which the CARD Team was deployed, there were 32 female child victims, and 26 male child victims. A majority of these reported abductions were committed by family members (35%), or persons with a known relationship to the child (29%), totaling 64 % of reported abductions were committed by persons with a known relationship to the child. Of 54 cases the CARD Team has deployed on only 6% were registered sex offenders. Abductions committed by family members are sometimes initially reported as an abduction and later discovered to be a false allegation. For example, a parent will claim their child was abducted, when in fact they have murdered the child.

Of the 55 CARD Team deployments, the motive of the abductor was determined in 27 cases: 58% (15) of the deployments were sexually motivated, 24% (7) of the deployments were motivated by family issues, and 8% (2) of the deployments were motivated by ransom/money. While more than half of the deployments have been sexually motivated it is important to note that does **not** mean the suspects were registered sex offenders at the time of the abduction. Of the 58% of sexually motivated cases, 34% (9) of the suspects had a known relationship with the child.

Although child abduction is a reactive threat, the FBI remains proactive by conducting research on new and continuing trends in child abduction. Moreover, the FBI will strive to maintain updated statistics, in order report trends and best practices that law enforcement can use in an effort to reduce the risk of child abduction.

The FBI's Child Sex Tourism (CST) Initiative was developed to address the numerous child sex offenders in the US who travel abroad to procure children in other countries for sexual purposes. These offenders believe that they can commit a crime against a child with impunity abroad because they feel they are no longer subject to US law, that they are "anonymous" while traveling abroad, that they can claim ignorance of local laws, and that the local population would be reluctant to report such crimes to law enforcement. Some offenders even rationalize that they are "helping" prostituted children by providing them with a source of income, and that sex between adults and children is socially acceptable in the victim child's culture. The victims of this crime are generally impoverished children who must join the workforce at an early age to help support their families.

Numerous countries in Southeast Asia are so well-known for child sex tourism that there are entire neighborhoods which are considered brothels, and there are open-air markets where children can be purchased for sex. Children are sometimes sold to pimps by their own families because of extreme poverty, and sex acts between adults and children can be witnessed in public places such as bars and restaurants.

The effects of child sex tourism reach beyond the shattered lives of children overseas. In countries like Cambodia, Thailand, the Philippines, Costa Rica and Mexico, where the largest child sex tourism crime problem exist, the plurality of perpetrators are from the U.S. The prominence of child sexual abuse by U.S. citizens paints a despicable portrait of American tourists among local populations in those countries, and fosters anti-American sentiment in general.

The FBI's CST Initiative employs a proactive investigative strategy to identify and disrupt the activities of child sexual predators before they are able to victimize additional minors. Intelligence sharing with both host country authorities and interested non-governmental organizations has led to the identification of offenders and predicated areas where child sexual exploitation is rampant. The FBI utilizes these partnerships to collect evidence against predicated targets and facilitate the arrest and prosecution of subjects by host country authorities and/or in the U.S. The FBI has implemented a three-step approach to addressing the CST threat. These steps include assessing the scope of the problem, identify training needs, and the implementation of in-country operations.

3. United States Marshals Service

The United States Marshals Service has a long history of recovering fugitives. In 2006, the Adam Walsh Act tasked them with primary responsibility for locating and apprehending sex offenders who fail to register as required on state sex offender registries as well as initiating federal investigations into sex offender registration violations and related offenses in noncompliance of the Act. Since July 2006, the USMS has apprehended approximately 40,000 fugitives wanted for sexual assaults, sex offender registration violations and other sex crimes. Additionally, investigators have opened more than 2,200 investigations on convicted sex offenders for violations of the Act and arrested more than 770 individuals who have been federally charged.

The Marshals Service conducts sex offender specific special operations in conjunction with their state and local counterparts to increase sex offender registry compliance and to identify, locate, and arrest those that are non-compliant. Since October 2008, the Marshals Service has conducted 161 such operations, partnering with 566 state and local jurisdictions to conduct more than 15,000 compliance checks resulting in the arrest of approximately 1,500 non registered sex offenders. The compliance checks are designed to detect registry non-compliance and have led to the discovery of and subsequent referral to FBI/ICE/ICAC and/or state authorities' evidence of possession of child pornography and other child exploitation crimes. This multi-pronged departmental approach maintains a consistent level of focus across the broadest spectrum enhancing the overall impact on those who offend.

The Marshals Service works with NCMEC in recovering missing and exploited children through its Operation Pickup program. There is a USMS case manager assigned to NCMEC who pursues the Services' efforts on behalf of abducted children. Operation Pickup has been instrumental in recovering more than 129 children since its inception in 2005. In recent years, the number of recoveries has increased. In 2006, 16 children were recovered while in 2009, 77 children were successfully recovered through Operation Pickup.

4. United States Attorney's Offices

Recognizing that our nation faced an epidemic of technology-assisted child exploitation crimes, the Department launched Project Safe Childhood (PSC) in 2006. Through a network of federal, state and local law enforcement agencies and advocacy organizations, PSC coordinates efforts to protect our children by investigating and prosecuting online sexual predators. PSC is implemented through a partnership of U.S. Attorneys; the Child Exploitation and Obscenity Section of the Department's Criminal Division; Internet Crimes Against Children task forces; federal partners, including the FBI, U.S. Postal Inspection Service, Immigration and Customs Enforcement and the U.S. Marshals Service; non-governmental organizations such as the National Center for Missing & Exploited Children (NCMEC); and state and local law enforcement officials.

Under PSC, the number of federal child exploitation prosecutions has increased significantly, along with the number of federal, state and local investigations and convictions, and more and more victims are being identified. PSC's education and awareness efforts complement this focus on enforcement. In FY 2009, the 93 U.S. Attorneys' Offices filed 2,315 indictments against 2,427 defendants, representing a 40 percent increase over FY 2006. A total of 2,877 victims of child pornography crimes have been identified and many rescued, 1,973 of them since the launch of PSC, through enhanced law enforcement coordination and the efforts of NCMEC.

5. Criminal Division's Child Exploitation and Obscenity Section (CEOS)

The Justice Department's Child Exploitation and Obscenity Section ("CEOS"), situated within the Department's Criminal Division, consists of approximately twenty attorneys and a six-person High Technology Investigative Unit ("HTIU"). CEOS leads the Criminal Division's campaign against the sexual exploitation of children, using its experience in investigating and prosecuting the most challenging child sexual exploitation cases to shape domestic and international policy, launch nationwide investigations against the worst offenders, and provide guidance and training to other prosecutors and agents, both within and outside the federal government. CEOS is able to leverage a small amount of resources into extraordinary results. For example, in the last three years CEOS has spearheaded 18 national operations that have resulted in the investigation of over 2000 individuals. CEOS targets, among other crimes, (1) the production, advertising, distribution, receipt and possession of images depicting the sexual assault of children (child pornography); (2) the online inducement of children for sexually predatory purposes; (3) the travel of offenders, or transportation of children by offenders, across state lines for sexually predatory purposes; (4) the sex trafficking of children, including the prostitution of children on our city streets; and (5) child sex tourism involving offenders who travel to foreign, often impoverished countries to prey sexually on vulnerable children.

Since FY 2001, the caseload of CEOS attorneys has increased every year, and has increased cumulatively by over 1100 percent. At the end of FY 2009, CEOS's Trial Attorneys, who also handle national policy, legislation, training and outreach, collectively had an active caseload of 352 investigations and 162 charged cases. CEOS's HTIU – consisting of a handful of computer forensic specialists – was instrumental in nearly every investigation and case, often discovering key evidence that meant the difference between the conviction or acquittal of a dangerous sex offender, or conviction for a higher or more serious offense. The large number of cases and investigations generated results primarily from resources dedicated to national operations and the significant involvement of CEOS' High Tech Investigative Unit in undertaking the forensic investigation necessary to identify the targets. This upward trend can be expected to continue based on CEOS' deep expertise, single-mission focus, along with its position as a headquarters unit—unrestricted by jurisdictional boundaries.

CEOS' nationwide focus also positions it to develop strategic partnerships outside of law enforcement circles in order to expand the effectiveness of the Department's overall enforcement efforts. CEOS again takes full advantage of this unique ability -- having developed critical partnerships with key Non-Governmental Organizations, foreign governments (through bilateral and multilateral efforts, and through international police organizations such as INTERPOL and EUROPOL) and foreign entities such as the G8, the Council of Europe, and the United Nations Crime Commission. CEOS also engages the private sector in order to find ways for technology companies to fight the trafficking of child pornography over the Internet.

CEOS also has helped shape legislation in a number of ways. In some instances, CEOS attorneys drafted legislative proposals in order to make the laws more effective. In other instances, CEOS is also called upon to provide Congress with technical assistance concerning pending legislation. Coordinated through the Department's Office of Legislative Affairs, CEOS attorneys will analyze and comment on pending legislation, or will meet with staffers for informal briefings to share their expertise and perspective on a specific crime problem. Whenever new legislation is passed, CEOS then provides critical guidance to the field on how to implement the new laws. This guidance takes many forms: formal memoranda, advice provided to prosecutors who call CEOS' duty line, and sample indictments or briefs responding to defense challenges to the new provision.

CEOS also partners with all United States Attorney's Offices, all federal law enforcement agencies, as well as foreign law enforcement, to operate nationally and trans-nationally targeting offenders that almost invariably are unburdened by geographical boundaries. This affords CEOS a unique view of the global threat and provides a firm basis of knowledge with which to aid in the development of a focused and coordinated response.

Many prosecutors and agents find child sexual exploitation cases to be technically and emotionally challenging, if not something to avoid altogether. Thus, CEOS considers it a critical part of its mission to provide extensive guidance and training to AUSAs and agents who are working these cases. This guidance, which takes the various forms described below, covers a wide range of topics such as (1) developing and presenting computer forensic evidence at trial; (2) addressing recurring defense strategies, and handling well-known defense experts; (3) how to effectively use the specialized statutes and Rules of Evidence that apply to child sexual exploitation cases; (4) the novel issue of victim restitution in non-contact child pornography cases; and many other topics. In just over a year, CEOS provided training more than 170 times in various domestic and international venues, to more than 1,000 federal, state, and local prosecutors and investigators, including many foreign officials.

CEOS also maintains and updates an intranet site, accessible by all United States Attorney's Offices and Main Justice components, that provides links to the current and previous newsletters, topical indices for the newsletter articles, the case digest, a library of go-by motions, jury instructions, memoranda, and other useful documents. Since September 2007, over 32,000 items have been downloaded from this website. Moreover, agents and AUSAs who need immediate assistance can also call the CEOS duty line, staffed by CEOS Trial Attorneys who can provide particularized, on-the-spot guidance. CEOS has fielded over 1,700 duty calls during the past 15 months.

Examples of CEOS's work include:

- CEOS worked with the FBI and National Center for Missing & Exploited Children to develop a national initiative to combat the domestic prostitution of children (the *Innocence Lost Initiative*) at a time when no one recognized this as a crime. Today, this is a growing area of enforcement and recognized widely as a vexing crime problem. *Innocence Lost* currently operates in 34 task forces and working groups.
- CEOS played an instrumental role in the design and implementation of Project Safe Childhood, which was conceived to enhance the government's response to Internet-facilitated child exploitation crimes.
- CEOS partnered with the National Center for Missing & Exploited Children, the FBI, and other federal partners to develop a mechanism to identify offenders, as well as victimized children depicted in the images of sexual abuse through the Endangered Child Alert Program and Operation Rescue Me. CEOS also worked with these partners to ensure that these victims' rights are upheld.
- CEOS recognized the challenges posed to Assistant United States Attorneys (AUSAs) by the technological sophistication of child pornography offenders and the complexities of online crime. CEOS responded by creating the High Technology Investigative Unit ("HTIU"), which now employs six computer forensic specialists. The HTIU was the first ever forensic unit co-located in a federal prosecutorial office. This synergy considerably enhances the Department's capacity to prosecute cutting-edge, technologically complex child exploitation crimes.
- CEOS has been assisting the Department to devise a strategy to address severe forensic shortfalls and challenges to effective information-sharing among law enforcement agencies.
- To address a lack of consensus concerning the danger posed by child pornography collectors to children, CEOS proposed, developed and delivered, through the G8 Law Enforcement Projects Sub-Group, an International Symposium of experts to identify the correlation between child pornography offenders and child molesters.
- CEOS worked closely with NDIC in developing the Threat Assessment contained in this chapter.
- Federal law enforcement partners from 2 out of the 3 key agencies involved in protecting children from sexual predators have agents co-located with CEOS to ensure maximum coordination.

6. Office of Justice Programs (OJP)

The Office of Justice Programs (OJP) works in partnership with federal, state, local and tribal government officials to support the justice system. The OJPs' partnerships provide actionable plans to all levels of government to improve the administration of justice.

Achieving the mission requires coordination and cooperation among its components, to include, the Bureau of Justice Assistance (BJA), the Bureau of Justice Statistics (BJS), the Community Capacity Development Office, the National Institute of Justice (NIJ), the Office for Victims of Crime, the Office of Juvenile Justice and Delinquency Prevention (OJJDP), and the Office of Sex Offender Sentencing, Monitoring, Apprehending, Registering and Tracking.

a. Office of Juvenile Justice and Delinquency Prevention (OJJDP)

OJP's Office of Juvenile Justice and Delinquency Prevention (OJJDP) provides national leadership, coordination, and resources to prevent and respond to juvenile delinquency and victimization. OJJDP supports states and communities in their efforts to develop and implement effective and coordinated prevention and intervention programs. OJJDP provides extensive training and technical assistance to state and local law enforcement regarding children's issues. Additionally, OJJDP provides funding and training support for the Internet Crimes Against Children (ICAC) Task Forces. As noted above, these task forces play a significant role in addressing exploitation of children on the internet. Other programs supported by OJJDP are listed below.

i. AMBER Alert Program

Since 1996 the Department has supported states and communities in developing their AMBER Alert response teams to respond to incidences of missing children before those children are victimized or exploited. AMBER Alert is a partnership among State and local governments, the media, and the U.S. Department. There are currently 120 regional and local AMBER Alert plans covering all 50 States and the District of Columbia. Special AMBER Alert initiatives help tribal governments develop capacity to implement AMBER Alert responses in Indian Country and to increase international law enforcement cooperation across the U.S. borders with Mexico and Canada. To date, 492 children have been recovered by Federal, State, and local law enforcement through the AMBER Alert program.

ii. Preventing Commercial Sexual Exploitation of Children (CSEC) Initiative

The CSEC Initiative is a grant program administered by the Department, through OJJDP, to provide communities with resources to develop a better understanding of the CSEC problem and the ability to implement local plans involving law enforcement, court officials, and human service personnel, along with state and municipal decision makers in combating sexual exploitation juveniles. The initiative includes demonstration, direct service, and training and technical programs, as well as research and evaluation initiatives.

In the past, demonstration and direct service programs have included the New York City Coalition Against the Commercial Sexual Exploitation of Children, the Fulton County, Georgia based Juvenile Justice Fund and Girls Educational and Mentoring Services (GEMS), based in Harlem, NY. In New York City and in Fulton County, Georgia each effort received funding to design and develop programs that strengthen the effective collaboration between government and nongovernment agencies addressing CSEC issues. As a direct service effort, GEMS provides short and long residential services and counseling to girls ages 12 – 21 who have experienced sexual exploitation and domestic trafficking to exit the commercial sex industry.

Training and technical assistance resources were provide to The Salvation Army in order to develop a multi-site training and technical assistance program to assist communities in aligning investigative, prosecutorial, and victim service resources to reduce the impact of commercial sexual exploitation of children and youth. Five target communities were selected, to include: Atlantic City, New Jersey; Chicago, Illinois; Denver, Colorado; San Diego, California; and Washington DC.

In FY 2009 OJJDP expanded training and technical assistance efforts and CSEC research. The new initiative, titled "Improving Community Response to CSEC" provided $500,000 to three communities in order to strengthen effective collaboration between stakeholder organizations and, ultimately, develop an effective community response to child victims of exploitation.

The expanded training and technical assistance effort, which is based on the curriculum designed under the initiative, will provide the training to the three communities funded under the Improving Community Response to CSEC initiative, as well as providing training to the ICAC Task Force Program.

iii. Services for Victimized Children Through Child Advocacy Centers

The Department, through OJJDP, provides grants to Local Children's Advocacy Centers (CACs) to aid in coordinating the investigation, treatment, and prosecution of child sexual abuse cases by utilizing multidisciplinary teams of professionals involved in child protective and victim advocacy services, law enforcement and prosecution, and physical and mental health. One of the primary goals of the CAC Program is to ensure that child abuse victims are not further traumatized by the systems designed to protect them. OJJDP provides financial support through grants and cooperative agreements to the following regional, State, and local child advocacy centers:

- Alameda County, CA, Children's Assessment Center
- CASA of Los Angeles County
- Children's Advocacy Centers of OK, Inc
- Children's Health Care
- Children's Hospitals of the King's Daughters
- National Children's Alliance
- DC Children's Advocacy Center -Safe Shores, Washington, DC
- Denver Children's Advocacy Center
- EAC Child Advocacy Center, Central Islip, NY
- Eau Claire, WI Child Advocacy Center
- Friends of CASA Los Angeles County
- National Children's Advocacy Center Inc.
- Philadelphia Children's Alliance
- Putnam County CAC
- SOWEGA CASA
- Stepping Stones Child Advocacy, La Crosse WI
- Children's Advocacy Center For The Pikes Peak Region Inc
- Young Women's Christian Association of Northcentral PA

iv. The Association of Missing and Exploited Children's Organizations (AMECO)

The Department, through OJJDP, provides annual grants to AMECO which is an association of member organizations in the United States and Canada who provide services to families with missing and exploited children. AMECO's mission as an international association of nonprofit organizations, is to provide a voice on issues related to missing and exploited children and their families and to nurture credible, ethical and effective nonprofit member organizations. AMECO members are national, regional and local non-profit organizations that provide direct services to the families of missing and exploited children and community education programs to enhance community safety.

b. Bureau of Justice Assistance

The Bureau of Justice Assistance (BJA) supports law enforcement, courts, corrections, victim services, technology, and prevention initiatives that strengthen the nation's criminal justice system. The BJA currently provides funding to 42 human trafficking task forces across the United States. Since effectively combating trafficking requires a multidisciplinary approach, the human trafficking task forces include members of state and local law enforcement, prosecutors, immigration and customs enforcement officers, and victim assistance coordinators. These task forces are focused on the identification, rescue, and restoration of victims as well as prosecution of the perpetrators of trafficking for forced labor and sexual exploitation. Although these task forces do not focus exclusively on child victims, operations conducted by these human trafficking task forces sometimes result in the identification of child victims.

c. National Institute of Justice

The National Institute of Justice (NIJ) is the research, development and evaluation agency of the Department and is dedicated to researching crime control and justice issues. NIJ provides objective, independent, evidence-based knowledge and tools to meet the challenges of crime and justice, particularly at the state and local levels. NIJ's principal authorities are derived from the Omnibus Crime Control and Safe Streets Act of 1968, as amended (see 42 USC § 3721-3723) and Title II of the Homeland Security Act of 2002. NIJ supports a variety of research in the area of child exploitation, which is summarized in Section G, below.

d. Office for Victims of Crime

The Office for Victims of Crime (OVC) oversees diverse programs that benefit victims of crime. The agency supports training programs designed to educate criminal justice and allied professionals regarding the rights and needs of crime victims. Since 2003, the Office for Victims of Crime has provided over $37 million to serve human tracking victims and responding service provides, training over 90,000 practitioners in communities across the United States about the dynamics of human trafficking, to include sex trafficking of minor children.

e. Bureau of Justice Statistics

The Bureau of Justice Statistics (BJS) is the primary source for criminal justice statistics in the United States. In 2007, the BJS released *Federal Prosecution of Child Sex Exploitation Offenders, 2006,* which presents federal criminal case processing statistics on child pornography, sex abuse, and sex transportation status in the U.S. criminal code for 2006. This includes national data on the number as well as type of offenders referred to and prosecuted by the U.S. Attorneys and describes the sentences they receive. Additionally, the BJS collects federal criminal case processing data as part of the Federal Justice Statistics Programs. This database compiles comprehensive information on individuals processed through the federal justice system.

Further, the BJS is conducting a project through Northeastern University and the Urban Institute to create and maintain an online reporting system for human trafficking cases. The primary users are the human trafficking task forces funded by the Department through the Bureau of Justice Assistance.

The project has been a success, and at this moment the system – called the Human Trafficking Reporting System (HTRS) – is online and receiving data. Pursuant to the goal of accurately reporting statistics on human trafficking, the following has been achieved:

- A common definition and reporting protocol has been developed based on the TVPA.
- Retrospective data from 2007 have been entered into the HTRS by almost all of the task forces and internal reports have been submitted to BJS. On-site technical assistance has been provided to those task forces experiencing difficulties with the system.
- Additional data have been submitted to BJS, bringing the data up to date through the 2nd quarter of 2008.

The data captured by the HTRS will be used to support the Department's reporting requirements under the 2005 TVPRA. Overall, these data will provide a detailed look at the characteristics of human trafficking cases identified by the Task Forces, including, when available, characteristics of offenders and victims and the circumstances surrounding each case.

f. Office of Sex Offender Sentencing, Monitoring, Apprehending, Registering, and Tracking (SMART)

The SMART Office was authorized by the Adam Walsh Child Protection and Safety Act of 2006 to administer the standards for the Sex Offender Registration and Notification Program set forth in Title I of the Adam Walsh Act. The responsibilities of the SMART Office include providing jurisdictions with guidance regarding the implementation of the Adam Walsh Act.

The SMART Office also tracks important legislative and legal developments related to sex offenders. The SMART Office is involved in all issues related to sex offenders and offending including child sexual exploitation and adult victimization. One key role the SMART Office plays is providing technical assistance to territories, Indian tribes, federal, state, and local governments, and to public and private organizations. This includes but is not limited to sex offender registration and violations, research, juvenile sex offenders, child sexual exploitation and abuse, sexual assault prosecutions including state and local, tribal, federal and military cases. The SMART Office also responds to concerns from the public about sex offenders in their communities. The SMART Office has handled more than 1300 technical assistance calls since its implementation in 2007.

The SMART Office has supported the development of a number of tools to assist the registration jurisdictions to implement SORNA's requirements. The Tribe and Territory Sex Offender Registry System (TTSORS) was developed by the Department of Justice and the SMART Office to assist the tribes and territories in implementing Sex Offender Registration and Notification Act (SORNA) registry system requirements. Management and update access to this system is restricted—only tribe and territory agencies responsible for the management and registration of sex offenders have access to TTSORS. A similar program has also been developed for states -- the Sex Offender Registry Tool (SORT). Both TTSORS and SORT are offered at no cost to SORNA registration jurisdictions.

7. Bureau of Prisons

The Bureau of Prison's (BOP) Sex Offender Management Program (SOMP) is responsible for the treatment of incarcerated sexual predators. SOMP is a multi-component program that includes treatment (SOTP), assessment, specialized correctional management, and population management.

Treatment: The Bureau's sex offender treatment programs are stratified into two levels: the high-intensity Residential (SOTP-R) and the moderate intensity Non-residential Sex Offender Treatment Programs (SOTP-NR). Currently, Federal Medical Center (FMC) Devens, Massachusetts is the only institution with the SOTP-R. Five SOMP institutions offer the SOTPNR.

The **Residential Sex Offender Treatment Program (SOTP-R):** is a high intensity program designed for high risk sexual offenders (ordinarily, inmates with multiple sex offenses, or a history of contact sexual offenses). The SOTP-R is a unit-based program with a cognitive-behavioral emphasis. The cohousing of SOTP-R participants permits the implementation of a modified therapeutic community. The SOTP-R is offered at FMC Devens. The program is designed to be 12 to 18 months in duration.

The **Non-residential Sex Offender Treatment Program (SOTP-NR):** is a moderate intensity program designed for low to moderate risk sexual offenders. A significant number of inmates who volunteer for SOTP-NR are first-time offenders serving a sentence for an Internet sex crime. The SOTP-NR shares the SOTP-R's treatment philosophy and program materials, but lacks the frequency of treatment groups and the program duration of the SOTP-R. In addition, because SOTP-NR participants reside in the general population, there is no modified therapeutic community. All SOMP institutions offer the SOTP-NR. The typical duration of the SOTP-NR is 9-12 months.

Community Treatment Services: Inmates completing the SOTP-NR and the SOTP-R are expected to participate in community treatment services (if they receive community placement). Community treatment services are group or individual sessions provided on an outpatient basis by a contracted treatment provider. Participants will be expected to attend these services while in RRC and on home confinement. Inmates with a requirement to participate in sex offender treatment while on Supervised Release will ordinarily continue with the same treatment vendor upon transition to USPO supervision.

SOMP Evaluations: SOMP staff conduct intake screenings on all arriving sex offenders. They also conduct Initial Risk Assessments and Discharge Reports on inmates releasing to the community.

Specialized Correctional Management: SOMP institutions may impose Correctional Management Plans (CMP) on sex offenders who engage in risk relevant behavior. Risk relevant behavior refers to conduct related to a sexual offender's history that indicates a risk of future sexual offending upon release (e.g., collecting sexual pictures of children; attempting to contact potential child victims).

Population Management: To encourage voluntary participation in treatment and minimize protective custody lockups, at least 40% of the inmates in the general population at SOMP institutions have a history of sexual offense. SOMP institutions may accommodate referrals of inmates who are unable to remain in general population due to their sexual offense.

Commitment and Treatment Program (CTP): The Adam Walsh Child Protection and Safety Act requires the Bureau to review releasing sex offenders for possible certification as sexually dangerous persons. The Bureau has designated FCI Butner as the facility where certified, postsentence persons and civilly committed sex offenders will be transferred for treatment. To accommodate the CTP mission, the Sex Offender Treatment Program at FCI Butner was transferred to FMC Devens in 2006.

8. Office of Community Oriented Policing Services (COPS)

The Department of Justice's Office of Community Oriented Policing Services (COPS) has announced $11.4 million in grants to support partnerships between state or local government agencies and their U.S. Attorney's and U.S. Marshal's offices that focus on reducing child endangerment. The funds were awarded to 26 state and local agencies under the Child Sexual Predator Program and will help officials locate, arrest, and prosecute child sexual predators, as well as enforce state sex offender registration laws.

In addition to the grants, COPS will fund the National Center for Missing & Exploited Children to provide approximately $600,000 in technical assistance to grant recipients. The technical assistance will include training on establishing effective anti-child endangerment programs, and on-site guidance for the grant recipients. The COPS Office will also develop a "best practices" publication that documents the experience of the grantees and will benefit other municipalities and states that pursue similar anti-child endangerment partnerships.

9. Office of International Affairs (OIA)

The Office of International Affairs (OIA) serves as the central authority for the United States under more than 50 bilateral mutual legal assistance treaties (MLATs) and several multilateral conventions relating to international legal assistance and evidence gathering. OIA also functions as a central coordinating office for international extradition matters. In its role as central authority, OIA handles hundreds of cases involving requests for evidence and fugitives wanted on child exploitation charges in the United States and abroad. OIA supports fugitive retrieval efforts by lending its expertise to extradition cases, assisting in the preparation of extradition requests, providing legal advice on extradition matters, and assisting U.S. prosecutors in litigating extradition proceedings for foreign fugitives who are located in the United States and who, often, must be removed from an environment in which they pose a continuing threat to U.S. children. OIA also works directly or with Assistant U.S. Attorneys to execute requests from foreign governments seeking evidence located in the United States to support foreign criminal proceedings. Finally, in administering the MLATs and other conventions, OIA also assists state and federal prosecutors in the United states to obtain evidence located abroad to support all types of crimes, including child pornography, child prostitution, child molestation/rape, child sex tourism, luring of children using the internet, sexual assaults of minors and trafficking in persons (including minors).

10. Office of Legal Policy (OLP)

The Office of Legal Policy (OLP) has played an important role in coordinating the Department's efforts to combat child exploitation, such as by participating in developing the Department's views on key pieces of legislation, assisting the SMART Office in drafting regulations concerning the Sex Offender Registration and Notification Act, and drafting regulations implementing the Adam Walsh Act's amendment to 18 U.S.C. § 2257 and enactment of 18 U.S.C. § 2257A. In addition, OLP assisted in the development of this chapter by coordinating with various Department components to obtain information on enforcement and other activities.

11. Interpol Washington

INTERPOL Washington, a component of the Department, is designated by the Attorney General as the official U.S. representative to the International Criminal Police Organization (INTERPOL). As the national point of contact for INTERPOL in the United States, INTERPOL Washington routinely exchanges criminal investigative data with international counterparts on behalf of the more than 18,000 federal, state, local and tribal law enforcement agencies in the United States. INTERPOL Washington is uniquely positioned within the interagency to facilitate secure and immediate international communications and information sharing between domestic and foreign law enforcement agencies which is critical in the global fight against child exploitation. In this role, INTERPOL Washington is capable of instantly providing criminal intelligence and investigative leads from worldwide sources to all U.S. agencies assigned to INTERPOL Washington, which includes the Department, DHS, Department of State (DOS), FBI, ICE, USMS, and all relevant state and local liaison offices. Key child protection programs at INTERPOL Washington include:

- Providing support to the USMS and other federal, state, local and tribal law enforcement agencies charged with locating and apprehending fugitive and non-compliant sex offenders;
- Tracking convicted sex offenders who relocate, visit, or are deported to foreign countries;
- Tracking convicted sex offenders who relocate or visit the U.S. from foreign countries;
- Utilizing the INTERPOL Notice System and I-24/7 Global Communications System, a secure messaging system, to exchange investigative information and requests for

assistance, locate and identify victims and witnesses, combat sex tourism, and locate missing and abducted children;

- Providing ICE, FBI, and other law enforcement agencies with international investigative assistance, which includes combating the distribution of child sex abuse images via the Internet and identifying known victims; and
- Supporting NCMEC in locating missing children, publishing international alerts on missing children, and collaborating with DOS, domestic and foreign law enforcement to return these children.

B. A Review of the Internet Crimes Against Children Task Force Program

In the Act, Congress requested that the Department thoroughly review all aspects of the ICAC Task Force Program.[82] Specifically, Congress requested information on the number of task forces, the number of trained personnel, the amount of grants that fund the program, the number of arrests by each task force, the number of criminal referrals, the number of prosecutions, the level of coordination of the task forces, an assessment of training conducted, and a review of technical tools available to the task forces. Below, the Department provides this information. This review, and the data contained herein, show the robust efforts underway at the state and local level, funded by the Department, in fighting child exploitation. Since 1998, ICACs have arrested more than 17,000 people suspected of sexually exploiting children.

The data in this chapter come from monthly and quarterly required data submissions from the State and local Internet Crimes Against Children (ICAC) Task Forces and other ICAC program grantees to the Office of Juvenile Justice and Delinquency Prevention (OJJDP). Data are presented for the FY 2008, and for the first six months of calendar 2009, as these are the most current data available at the time of writing. Other sources, including the National Center for Missing & Exploited Children, also contributed data to this chapter.

The PROTECT our Children Act calls for a number of variables to be included in the review of the ICAC program. Some of the variables outlined in the Act were not available for FY 2009, as they were not required ICAC program data submissions prior to the passage of the Act. Beginning in January 2009, OJJDP implemented new data collection requirements for the (then 59) ICAC Task Forces. These data will be available for reporting in 2011.[83]

1. Background on the ICAC Program

The ICAC Task Force Program has been protecting American children since 1998. The ICAC program is a national network of 61 coordinated Task Forces representing over 2,000 federal, state, local and tribal law enforcement and prosecutorial agencies. These agencies are engaged in investigations, forensic examinations, and prosecutions related to Internet crimes against children. Additionally, the Task Forces provide forensic and investigative technical assistance to law enforcement and prosecutorial officials, as well as community education information to parents, educators, prosecutors, law enforcement, and others concerned with child victimization. By helping state, local, and tribal law enforcement agencies develop effective and sustainable responses to online child victimization and child pornography,

OJJDP and the ICAC program have built capacity at the local level to address ICAC related offenses. Program accomplishments include:

- Since the program's inception in 1998, the ICAC Task Forces have reviewed over 180,000 complaints of alleged child sexual victimization resulting in the arrest of nearly 17,000 individuals.
- In fiscal year 2008, ICAC investigations led to more than 3,108 arrests, over 14,339 forensic examinations, and the identification of over 1,000 real children who were victims of some form of abuse and neglect.
- In the first three quarters of FY 2009, the ICAC's have arrested nearly 3,300 individuals, with almost one-third of those arrests (1,275) resulting in the acceptance of a plea agreement by the defendant in lieu of a trial.
- ICAC has always included a robust training component. Since the ICAC program's beginning in 1998, nearly 100,000 law enforcement officers, prosecutors, and other professionals have been trained throughout the United States and in 17 countries around the world on techniques to investigative and effectively prosecute ICAC related cases.
- In fiscal year 2008, the ICAC program trained over 26,000 law enforcement personnel, over 2,200 prosecutors, and more than 8,000 other professional working in the ICAC field. In first three quarters of fiscal year 2009, the number of trained law enforcement personnel increased to over 28,000, while 1,832 prosecutors have been trained.[84]

The Act statutorily authorized the ICAC Task Force Program for the first time. Pursuant to the authorizing legislation, the ICAC Program seeks to maintain and expand state and regional ICAC Task Forces to address technology-facilitated child exploitation. These Task Forces work collaboratively as a national network of law enforcement and prosecutorial agencies that prevent, interdict, and investigate Internet crimes against children. The program requires existing Task Forces to develop multijurisdictional, multiagency responses to such offenses by providing funding and other support to state and local law enforcement agencies as a means to help them acquire the necessary knowledge, personnel, and equipment. In 2009 the Office of Justice Programs/ Office of Juvenile Justice and Delinquency Prevention issued the first continuation funding solicitation for the ICAC Task Forces as a program authorized by the PROTECT Act. The 2009 solicitation included language from the Act describing the functions and responsibilities of the ICAC Task Forces and their data reporting responsibilities.

As provided for in Section 103 of the Act, ICAC Task Forces are dedicated to the following:

- Increasing the investigative capabilities of state and local law enforcement officers in the detection, investigation, and apprehension of Internet crimes against children offenses or offenders, including technology-facilitated child exploitation offenses.
- Conducting proactive and reactive Internet crimes against children investigations.
- Providing training and technical assistance to ICAC Task Forces and other Federal, state, and local law enforcement agencies in the areas of investigations, forensics,

prosecution, community outreach, and capacity-building, using recognized experts to assist in the development and delivery of training programs.

- Increasing the number of Internet crimes against children offenses being investigated and prosecuted in both Federal and State courts.
- Creating a multiagency Task Force response to Internet crimes against children offenses within each State.
- Participating in the Department's Project Safe Childhood initiative, the purpose of which is to combat technology-facilitated sexual exploitation crimes against children.
- Enhancing nationwide responses to Internet crimes against children offenses, including assisting other ICAC Task Forces, as well as other Federal, State, and local agencies with Internet crimes against children investigations and prosecutions.
- Developing and delivering Internet crimes against children public awareness and prevention programs.
- Participating in such other activities, both proactive and reactive, that will enhance investigations and prosecutions of Internet crimes against children.

2. Number and Location of ICAC Task Forces

At the time the Act was passed, there were 59 ICAC Task Forces covering all fifty States and the District of Columbia. Each of these Task Forces was selected through a series of competitive requests for proposals issued between 1998 and 2007. In May 2009 OJP released a competitive solicitation for two more ICAC Task Forces to be created in the New York City metropolitan area and in the Houston, Texas metropolitan area. These two new awards were made in August, 2009, bringing the total number of Task Forces to 61.

Table 1. ICAC Task Force Agencies (N=61)

State	Task Force Agency	State	Task Force Agency
AK	Anchorage Police Department	MS	Mississippi Attorney General
AL	State of Alabama	MT	City of Billings
AR	Arkansas State Police	NC	North Carolina Department of Justice
AZ	Phoenix Police Department	ND	Office of Attorney General - ND
CA	City of San Jose	NE	Nebraska State Patrol
CA	City of San Diego	NH	City of Portsmouth
CA	City of Los Angeles	NJ	New Jersey DPS
CA	County of Sacramento	NM	New Mexico Attorney General's Office
CA	County of Fresno	NV	Las Vegas Metropolitan Police
CO	City of Colorado Springs	NY	New York State Police
CT	Connecticut DPS	NY	New York City Police Department[85]
DE	Delaware Department of Justice	OH	Cuyahoga County Prosecutors Office
FL	Broward County Sheriff Office	OK	Oklahoma SBI
FL	County of Polk	OR	Oregon Department of Justice
FL	City of Gainesville	PA	Delaware County, PA

GA	Georgia Bureau of Investigation	RI	Rhode Island State Police
HI	State of Hawaii	SC	South Carolina Attorney General
IA	Iowa Department of Public Safety	SD	Office of the Attorney General- SD
ID	Idaho Office of Attorney General	TN	City of Knoxville
IL	County of Cook	TX	Texas Office of the AG
IL	Illinois Attorney General's	TX	Pasadena Independent School District [86]
IN	Indiana State Police	TX	City of Dallas
KS	Sedgwick County Sheriff's Department	UT	Utah Attorney General
KY	Kentucky State Police	VA	County of Bedford
LA	LA Department of Justice	VA	Virginia State Police
MA	Massachusetts State Police	VT	Burlington VT Police Department
MD	Maryland State Police	WA	Seattle Police Department
ME	Maine State Police	WI	Wisconsin Department of Justice
MI	Michigan State Police	WV	West Virginia State Police
MN	Saint Paul Police Department	WY	Wyoming Attorney General
MO	City of Glendale		

Source: Office of Juvenile Justice and Delinquency Prevention

3. Number of Trained Personnel at Each ICAC Task Force

Due to the Task Force structure, affiliate agency personnel working ICAC-related cases fluctuate based on a number of circumstances including amount of pass-through funding to the affiliate and the volume of ICAC-related complaints. For this period, ICAC Task Forces reported the following dedicated full-time equivalents (FTEs) working ICAC-related cases: approximately 954 investigators; 156 prosecutors; 394 forensic specialists (includes forensic examiners and on-scene preview personnel); and 153 community education specialists.

In an effort to build the capacity to respond to internet crimes against children, each ICAC Task Force provides training to State and local law enforcement, prosecutors, and other personnel. This Table reports the number of personnel attending training by Task Force for FY 2008 and the first six months of 2009.

4. Federal Grants Awarded to Each Task Force

In FY 2009, pursuant to the Act, OJJDP changed the ICAC program from a 24-month funding cycle to a 12-month funding cycle. Also pursuant to the Act, in FY 2009 a budget formula was developed to allocate funding to each of the Task Forces.

Number of Trained Personnel (N=59)

State	Task Force Agency	Number of Trained Personnel	
		FY 2008	Jan-Jun 2009
AK	Anchorage Police Department	599	280
AL	Alabama Bureau of Investigation	111	245
AR	Arkansas State Police	761	59

(Continued)

AZ	Phoenix Police Department	1461	369
CA	Fresno County Sheriff's Office	66	60
CA	Los Angeles Police Department	182	216
CA	Sacramento County Sheriff's Office	483	77
CA	San Diego Police Department	275	126
CA	San Jose Police Department	1,098	6
CO	Colorado Springs Police Department	94	41
CT	Connecticut State Police	171	338
DE	Delaware Department of Justice	163	2
FL	Broward County Sheriff's Office	19	16
FL	Gainesville Police Department	484	157
FL	Polk County Sheriff's Office	662	392
GA	Georgia Bureau of Investigation	485	534
HI	Hawaii Department of Attorney General	1,001	270
IA	Iowa Division of Criminal Investigation	35	281
ID	Idaho Office of Attorney General	50	166
IL	Cook County State's Attorney's Office	1,201	248
IL	Illinois Office of Attorney General	48	2,422
IN	Indiana State Police	947	1,188
KS	Sedgwick County Sheriff's Office	239	149
KY	Kentucky State Police	327	545
LA	Louisiana Department of Justice	29	55
MA	Massachusetts State Police	1,736	4,907
MD	Maryland State Police	981	504
ME	Maine State Police	284	196
MI	Michigan State Police	32	285
MN	St. Paul Police Department	1,275	1,490
MO	Glendale Police Department	4,630	1,180
MS	Mississippi Office of Attorney General	903	170
MT	Billings Police Department	113	1,209
NC	North Carolina State Bureau of Investigation	2,285	743
ND	North Dakota Bureau of Criminal Investigation	65	1
NE	Nebraska State Patrol	61	126
NH	Portsmouth Police Department	48	185
NJ	New Jersey State Police	1,308	732
NM	New Mexico Attorney General's Office	306	304
NV	Las Vegas Metropolitan Police Department	7	3
NY	New York State Police	40	560
OH	Cuyahoga County Prosecutor's	163	11
OK	Oklahoma State Bureau of Investigation	615	52
OR	Oregon Department of Justice	618	471
PA	Delaware County District Attorney's Office	619	109
RI	Rhode Island State Police	6	9
SC	South Carolina Attorney General's Office	402	251

SD	South Dakota Division of Criminal Investigation	564	29
TN	Knoxville Police Department	1,836	334
TX	Dallas Police Department	1	3
TX	Office of the Attorney General of Texas	67	57
UT	Utah Office of Attorney General	111	3
VA	Bedford County Sheriff's Office	739	82
VA	Virginia State Police	277	260
VT	Burlington Police Department	678	546
WA	Seattle Police Department	391	120
WI	Wisconsin Department of Justice	421	1,410
WV	West Virginia State Police	20	0
WY	Wyoming Division of Criminal Investigation	1	599
	TOTAL	32,594	25,183

Source: Reports from ICAC Task Forces

In addition, because of funds made available to the ICAC program through the American Reinvestment and Recovery Act (ARRA) (Public Law 111-5) OJJDP made two grant awards to each of the Task Forces.[87] The Table below shows the FY 2009 ARRA Award and the FY 2009 Continuation Grant made to each Task Force.

Federal Grants Awarded to ICAC Task Forces in FY 2009 (N=61)

State	Agency	FY 2009 Funding	FY 2009 ARRA	FY 2009 Total
Alabama	Alabama Bureau of Investigation	$318,423.00	$652,884.00	$971,307.00
Alaska	Anchorage Police Department	$200,000.00	$437,265.00	$637,265.00
Arizona	Phoenix Police Department	$427,898.00	$824,004.00	$1,251,902.00
Arkansas	Arkansas State Police	$298,451.00	$580,983.00	$879,434.00
California	San Jose Police Department	$437,594.00	$863,930.00	$1,301,524.00
California	San Diego Police Department	$348,774.00	$708,238.00	$1,057,012.00
California	Fresno County Sheriff's Office	$297,488.00	$607,097.00	$904,585.00
California	Los Angeles Police Department	$709,836.00	$1,350,900.00	$2,060,736.00
California	Sacramento County Sheriff's Office	$344,321.00	$702,838.00	$1,047,159.00
Colorado	Colorado Springs Police Department	$332,111.00	$675,991.00	$1,008,102.00
Connecticut	Connecticut State Police	$283,345.00	$584,975.00	$868,320.00

(Continued)

Delaware	Delaware Department of Justice	$200,000.00	$437,109.00	$637,109.00
Florida	Broward County Sheriff's Office	$474,066.00	$881,389.00	$1,355,455.00
Florida	Gainesville Police Department	$371,537.00	$729,688.00	$1,101,225.00
Florida	Polk County Sheriff's Office	$448,962.00	$837,551.00	$1,286,513.00
Georgia	Georgia Bureau of Investigation	$491,879.00	$947,058.00	$1,438,937.00
Hawaii	Hawaii Department of Attorney General	$250,000.00	$463,917.00	$713,917.00
Idaho	Idaho Office of Attorney General	$205,000.00	$454,294.00	$659,294.00
Illinois	Illinois Office of Attorney General	$426,569.00	$832,822.00	$1,259,391.00
Illinois	Cook County State's Attorney's Office	$341,689.00	$696,224.00	$1,037,913.00
Indiana	Indiana State Police	$405,491.00	$793,329.00	$1,198,820.00
Iowa	Iowa Division of Criminal Investigation	$295,980.00	$574,077.00	$870,057.00
Kansas	Sedgwick County Sheriff's Office	$267,889.00	$557,551.00	$825,440.00
Kentucky	Kentucky State Police	$329,569.00	$652,491.00	$982,060.00
Louisiana	Louisiana Depart-ment of Justice	$300,523.00	$623,474.00	$923,997.00
Maine	Maine State Police	$205,000.00	$455,239.00	$660,239.00
Maryland	Maryland State Police	$340,226.00	$688,800.00	$1,029,026.00
Massachusetts	Massachusetts State Police	$397,831.00	$774,492.00	$1,172,323.00
Michigan	Michigan State Police	$567,228.00	$1,094,876.00	$1,662,104.00
Minnesota	St. Paul Police Department	$355,826.00	$701,346.00	$1,057,172.00
Mississippi	Mississippi Office of Attorney General	$238,389.00	$514,677.00	$753,066.00
Missouri	Glendale Police Department	$385,454.00	$733,895.00	$1,119,349.00
Montana	Billings Police Department	$200,000.00	$422,046.00	$622,046.00
Nebraska	Nebraska State Patrol	$219,969.00	$481,092.00	$701,061.00
Nevada	Las Vegas Metro-politan Police Department	$274,276.00	$566,519.00	$840,795.00
New Hampshire	Portsmouth Police Department	$215,000.00	$475,306.00	$690,306.00
New Jersey	New Jersey State Police	$463,399.00	$901,077.00	$1,364,476.00
New Mexico	New Mexico Attorney General's Office	$228,550.00	$488,527.00	$717,077.00
New York	New York State Police	$373,050.00	$1,618,399.00	$1,991,449.00
New York	New York City Police	$500,000.00	$0.00	$500,000.00

	Department			
North Carolina	North Carolina State Bureau of Investigation	$458,299.00	$879,040.00	$1,337,339.00
North Dakota	North Dakota Bureau of Criminal Investigation	$200,000.00	$413,449.00	$613,449.00
Ohio	Cuyahoga County Prosecutor's Office	$586,566.00	$1,122,272.00	$1,708,838.00
Oklahoma	Oklahoma State Bureau of Investigation	$318,221.00	$635,360.00	$953,581.00
Oregon	Oregon Department of Justice	$327,108.00	$655,983.00	$983,091.00
Pennsylvania	Delaware County District Attorney's Office	$596,512.00	$1,084,541.00	$1,681,053.00
Rhode Island	Rhode Island State Police	$205,000.00	$452,438.00	$657,438.00
South Carolina	South Carolina Attorney General's Office	$357,072.00	$687,278.00	$1,044,350.00
South Dakota	South Dakota Division of Criminal Investigation	$210,000.00	$444,133.00	$654,133.00
Tennessee	Knoxville Police Department	$384,286.00	$748,510.00	$1,132,796.00
Texas	Dallas Police Department	$392,624.00	$776,503.00	$1,169,127.00
Texas	Pasadena Independent School District PD	$500,000.00	$0.00	$500,000.00
Texas	Office of the Attorney General of Texas	$343,321.00	$1,479,163.00	$1,822,484.00
Utah	Utah Office of Attorney General	$268,806.00	$539,879.00	$808,685.00
Vermont	Burlington Police Department	$200,000.00	$437,282.00	$637,282.00
Virginia	Bedford County Sheriff's Office	$349,038.00	$681,572.00	$1,030,610.00
Virginia	Virginia State Police	$280,831.00	$581,935.00	$862,766.00
Washington	Seattle Police Department	$431,941.00	$848,038.00	$1,279,979.00
West Virginia	West Virginia State Police	$233,026.00	$485,386.00	$718,412.00
Wisconsin	Wisconsin Depart-ment of Justice	$381,647.00	$735,622.00	$1,117,269.00
Wyoming	Wyoming Division of Criminal Investigation	$200,000.00	$424,573.00	$624,573.00
	TOTAL	**$20,995,891.00**	**$41,499,327.00**	**$62,495,218.00**

Source: Office of Juvenile Justice and Delinquency Prevention

5. Assessment of Federal, State, and Local Cooperation

The Act called for an assessment of ICAC Task Force activities including the following factors:

(a) the number of arrests made by each Task Force;
(b) the number of criminal referrals to United States attorneys for prosecution;
(c) the number of prosecutions and convictions from the referrals to United States attorneys for prosecution;
(d) the number, if available, of local prosecutions and convictions based on ICAC Task Force investigations; and
(e) other information demonstrating Federal, State, and local coordination.

As provided for in Section 106(d) of the Act, each funded State or local ICAC Task Force reported on the following data elements for last 12-month period. For certain data elements, no mechanism was in place to capture the indicated data; however, a full year of data is provided unless otherwise noted.

a. Number of Arrests

For FY 2008, ICAC Task Forces reported 3,108 arrests; 2,408 arrests were reported for the first six months of 2009.[88] This Table shows the number of arrests for the 59 Task Forces.

Number of Arrests Reported by ICAC Task Forces (N=59)

State	Agency	FY 2008 # Arrests	Jan.-June 2009 # Arrests
AK	Anchorage Police Department	24	10
AL	Alabama Bureau of Investigation	35	9
AR	Arkansas State Police	36	21
AZ	Phoenix Police Department	57	34
CA	Fresno County Sheriff's Office	80	26
CA	Los Angeles Police Department	12	51
CA	Sacramento County Sheriff's Office	34	30
CA	San Diego Police Department	33	22
CA	San Jose Police Department	12	13
CO	Colorado Springs Police Department	68	80
CT	Connecticut State Police	21	4
DE	Delaware Department of Justice	52	17
FL	Broward County Sheriff's Office	132	66
FL	Gainesville Police Department	45	43
FL	Polk County Sheriff's Office	96	147
GA	Georgia Bureau of Investigation	77	96
HI	Hawaii Department of Attorney General	17	18
IA	Iowa Division of Criminal Investigation	21	9
ID	Idaho Office of Attorney General	15	9
IL	Cook County State's Attorney's Office	26	24
IL	Illinois Office of Attorney General	65	37
IN	Indiana State Police	51	54
KS	Sedgwick County Sheriff's Office	36	17
KY	Kentucky State Police	66	49

LA	Louisiana Department of Justice	63	140
MA	Massachusetts State Police	30	16
MD	Maryland State Police	42	42
ME	Maine State Police	6	6
MI	Michigan State Police	26	41
MN	St. Paul Police Department	19	21
MO	Glendale Police Department	188	149
MS	Mississippi Office of Attorney General	0	2
MT	Billings Police Department	9	59
NC	North Carolina State Bureau of Investigation	45	17
ND	North Dakota Bureau of Criminal Investigation	8	2
NE	Nebraska State Patrol	33	39
NH	Portsmouth Police Department	16	13
NJ	New Jersey State Police	66	72
NM	New Mexico Attorney General's Office	13	19
NV	Las Vegas Metropolitan Police Department	51	38
NY	New York State Police	157	118
OH	Cuyahoga County Prosecutor's Office	334	72
OK	Oklahoma State Bureau of Investigation	70	18
OR	Oregon Department of Justice	44	18
PA	Delaware County District Attorney's Office	92	52
RI	Rhode Island State Police	3	20
SC	South Carolina Attorney General's Office	73	23
SD	South Dakota Division of Criminal Investigation	21	22
TN	Knoxville Police Department	26	43
TX	Dallas Police Department	6	21
TX	Office of the Attorney General of Texas	98	105
UT	Utah Office of Attorney General	98	72
VA	Bedford County Sheriff's Office	58	55
VA	Virginia State Police	92	104
VT	Burlington Police Department	41	14
WA	Seattle Police Department	31	7
WI	Wisconsin Department of Justice	80	62
WV	West Virginia State Police	20	16
WY	Wyoming Division of Criminal Investigation	38	4
	TOTAL	**3,108**	**2,408**

Source: Reports from ICAC Task Forces

b. Number of Criminal Referrals to United States Attorneys for Prosecution

During FY 2008, ICAC Task Forces reported 1,139 referrals to U.S. Attorneys; of those cases, 757 cases (66%) were accepted for federal prosecution. For the first six months of 2009, 681 cases were referred to Unites States Attorneys; of those, 537 cases (79%) were accepted for federal prosecution. The Table below shows the number of referrals by ICAC Task Forces to United States Attorneys and the number of cases accepted for federal prosecution.

Number of Criminal Referrals to United States Attorneys for Prosecution (N=59)

State	Agency	FY 2008 Submitted	FY 2008 Accepted	Jan.-June 2009 Submitted	Jan.- June 2009 Accepted
AK	Anchorage Police Department	5	3	2	2
AL	Alabama Bureau of Investigation	30	10	17	15
AR	Arkansas State Police	18	18	7	6
AZ	Phoenix Police Department	0	0	0	0
CA	Fresno County Sheriff's Office	51	39	16	15
CA	Los Angeles Police Department	2	0	14	4
CA	Sacramento County Sheriff's Office	7	7	14	11
CA	San Diego Police Department	16	11	19	17
CA	San Jose Police Department	2	1	0	0
CO	Colorado Springs Police Department	11	7	6	5
CT	Connecticut State Police	0	0	0	0
DE	Delaware Department of Justice	12	12	4	4
FL	Broward County Sheriff's Office	10	4	22	22
FL	Gainesville Police Department	30	27	16	14
FL	Polk County Sheriff's Office	17	18	8	7
GA	Georgia Bureau of Investigation	8	8	5	3
HI	Hawaii Department of Attorney General	19	15	6	5
IA	Iowa Division of Criminal Investigation	37	31	16	12
ID	Idaho Office of Attorney General	5	4	3	3
IL	Cook County State's Attorney's Office	1	1	0	0
IL	Illinois Office of Attorney General	17	17	12	10
IN	Indiana State Police	73	59	21	21
KS	Sedgwick County Sheriff's	5	4	4	4
KY	Kentucky State Police	51	36	28	24
LA	Louisiana Department of Justice	13	5	8	7
MA	Massachusetts State Police	16	3	10	9

(Continued)

State	Agency	FY 2008 Submitted	FY 2008 Accepted	Jan.-June 2009 Submitted	Jan.- June 2009 Accepted
MD	Maryland State Police	4	3	9	13
ME	Maine State Police	6	7	4	4
MI	Michigan State Police	4	4	1	10
MN	St. Paul Police Department	6	6	3	5
MO	Glendale Police Department	59	31	67	48
MS	Mississippi Office of Attorney General	0	0	0	0
MT	Billings Police Department	29	25	54	44
NC	North Carolina State Bureau of Investigation	32	24	23	28
ND	North Dakota Bureau of Criminal Investigation	12	11	4	3
NE	Nebraska State Patrol	20	19	4	3
NH	Portsmouth Police Department	9	4	3	3
NJ	New Jersey State Police	11	3	1	1
NM	New Mexico Attorney General's Office	2	1	1	2
NV	Las Vegas Metropolitan Police Department	28	27	12	14
NY	New York State Police	31	22	9	8
OH	Cuyahoga County Prosecutor's Office	0	0	0	0
OK	Oklahoma State Bureau of Investigation	17	11	13	7
OR	Oregon Department of Justice	23	23	8	8
PA	Delaware County District Attorney's Office	30	25	19	20
RI	Rhode Island State Police	2	1	3	4
SC	South Carolina Attorney General's Office	13	0	5	3
SD	South Dakota Division of Criminal Investigation	17	11	10	8
TN	Knoxville Police Department	30	25	27	25
TX	Dallas Police Department	1	1	3	2
TX	Office of the Attorney General of Texas	22	19	6	6
UT	Utah Office of Attorney General	10	8	0	0
VA	Bedford County Sheriff's Office	121	17	74	10
VA	Virginia State Police	66	43	29	21

Table. (Continued)

State	Agency	FY 2008 Submitted	FY 2008 Accepted	Jan.-June 2009 Submitted	Jan.- June 2009 Accepted
VT	Burlington Police Department	12	9	1	1
WA	Seattle Police Department	3	2	12	5
WI	Wisconsin Department of Justice	18	14	9	4
WV	West Virginia State Police	43	15	8	6
WY	Wyoming Division of Criminal Investigation	2	6	1	1
	TOTAL	**1,139**	**757**	**681**	**537**

Source: Reports from ICAC Task Forces

C. Number Of Prosecutions And Convictions From Referrals To United States Atto-Rneys

Prior to passage of the Act these data were not collected by OJJDP. Beginning in January, 2009 OJJDP implemented new data collection requirements for the ICAC Task Forces. These data will be available for reporting in 2011.

D. Number Of Local Prosecutions And Convictions Based On ICAC Task Force Invest-Tigations

Prior to passage of the Act these data were not collected by OJJDP. Beginning in January, 2009 OJJDP implemented new data collection requirements for the ICAC Task Forces. These data will be available for reporting in 2011.

E. Cases Referred By The Icac Task Forces To Federal, State Or Local Law Enfor-cement For Further Review And Investigation

In FY 2008, ICAC Task Forces referred 6,387 complaints to Federal, State, and local law enforcement agencies for further review and investigation; in the first six months of calendar year 2009, 4,255 complaints were referred out for further review and investigation shows the number of cases referred by the ICAC Task Forces to Federal, State, or local partners for further investigation.

Cases Referred for Further Review and Investigation by ICAC Task Forces (N=59)

State	Agency	FY 2008 # of Cases Referred			Jan.-June 2009 # of Cases Referred		
		Federal	State	Local	Federal	State	Local
AK	Anchorage Police Department	5	24	5	8	10	1
AL	Alabama Bureau of Investigation	14	78	21	15	36	10
AR	Arkansas State Police	9	32	11	1	14	12
AZ	Phoenix Police Department	29	157	98	15	60	111

(Continued)

State	Agency	FY 2008 # of Cases Referred			Jan.-June 2009 # of Cases Referred		
		Federal	State	Local	Federal	State	Local
CA	Fresno County Sheriff's Office	67	11	5	14	9	4
CA	Los Angeles Police Department	1	3	9	40	49	30
CA	Sacramento County Sheriff's	9	22	25	12	13	14
CA	San Diego Police Department	37	8	8	42	0	12
CA	San Jose Police Department	11	8	3	3	11	74
CO	Colorado Springs Police Department	33	64	29	12	11	13
CT	Connecticut State Police	9	12	4	0	8	17
DE	Delaware Department of Justice	7	10	9	4	4	13
FL	Broward County Sheriff's Office	9	6	424	2	1	212
FL	Gainesville Police Department	21	0	0	13	20	11
FL	Polk County Sheriff's Office	14	18	1	10	30	25
GA	Georgia Bureau of Investigation	11	60	70	3	38	38
HI	Hawaii Department of Attorney General	17	1	4	3	2	0
IA	Iowa Division of Criminal Investigation	17	11	6	7	3	3
ID	Idaho Office of Attorney General	12	15	14	9	12	4
IL	Cook County State's Attorney's Office	5	17	3	0	1	0
IL	Illinois Office of Attorney General	26	32	16	5	9	8
IN	Indiana State Police	33	5	30	16	40	44
KS	Sedgwick County Sheriff's Office	8	29	24	6	8	16
KY	Kentucky State Police	18	133	11	8	14	3
LA	Louisiana Department of Justice	13	26	47	21	85	56
MA	Massachusetts State Police	11	55	20	8	27	3
MD	Maryland State Police	4	7	27	4	1	6
ME	Maine State Police	11	72	40	9	92	44
MI	Michigan State Police	2	12	2	10	0	30
MN	St. Paul Police Department	0	29	64	3	17	114

Table. (Continued)

State	Agency	FY 2008 # of Cases Referred			Jan.-June 2009 # of Cases Referred		
		Federal	State	Local	Federal	State	Local
MO	Glendale Police Department	42	51	246	196	32	108
MS	Mississippi Office of Attorney General	0	7	1	0	3	0
MT	Billings Police Department	88	393	233	24	15	17
NC	North Carolina State Bureau of Investigation	23	36	147	48	14	120
ND	North Dakota Bureau of Criminal Investigation	8	11	1	0	3	0
NE	Nebraska State Patrol	17	42	3	8	31	3
NH	Portsmouth Police Department	9	18	2	3	8	2
NJ	New Jersey State Police	25	39	50	4	0	11
NM	New Mexico Attorney General's Office	1	8	7	4	28	6
NV	Las Vegas Metropolitan Police Department	24	33	13	9	52	15
NY	New York State Police	15	190	76	5	51	66
OH	Cuyahoga County Prosecutor's Office	82	98	91	19	7	33
OK	Oklahoma State Bureau of Investigation	34	59	30	15	19	11
OR	Oregon Department of Justice	21	37	56	11	21	26
PA	Delaware County District Attorney's Office	75	146	113	21	68	50
RI	Rhode Island State Police	3	4	1	0	2	0
SC	South Carolina Attorney General's Office	11	14	37	2	5	2
SD	South Dakota Division of Criminal Investigation	22	11	6	23	21	5
TN	Knoxville Police Department	8	13	6	14	32	56
TX	Dallas Police Department	5	222	41	9	372	102
TX	Office of the Attorney General of Texas	19	21	56	14	28	136
UT	Utah Office of Attorney General	23	71	10	2	41	3
VA	Bedford County Sheriff's Office	24	76	194	13	41	71
VA	Virginia State Police	41	15	10	25	37	4
VT	Burlington Police Department	19	49	4	2	3	7
WA	Seattle Police Department	5	17	6	10	9	18

(Continued)

State	Agency	FY 2008 # of Cases Referred			Jan.-June 2009 # of Cases Referred		
		Federal	State	Local	Federal	State	Local
WI	Wisconsin Department of Justice	14	36	71	3	31	40
WV	West Virginia State Police	11	21	5	3	12	4
WY	Wyoming Division of Criminal Investigation	4	2	8	1	7	2
	TOTAL	**1,136**	**2,697**	**2,554**	**791**	**1,618**	**1,846**

Source: Reports from ICAC Task Forces

6. Investigative Technical Assistance Provided By ICAC Task Forces

ICAC Task Forces reported 11,976 investigative technical assists for FY 2008; 8,227 investigative technical assists were reported for the first six months of 2009. The ICAC Task Forces provide investigative technical assistance in a variety of ways, including reviewing sample affidavit and search warrant language; providing advice and guidance in the development and execution of both small and large scale undercover operations; and participating in the arrest and interview of an individual suspected of engaging in child sexual exploitation. Other examples of investigative technical assistance include providing contact information and direction in communicating with Internet Service Providers or common approaches to extracting information from an online search engine to corroborate a suspect's Internet activity. The shows the number of investigative assists by ICAC Task Forces.

Number of Investigative Technical Assists Provided by ICAC Task Forces (N=59)

State	Agency	FY 2008 Technical Assists	Jan.-June 2009 Technical Assists
AK	Anchorage Police Department	31	130
AL	Alabama Bureau of Investigation	48	37
AR	Arkansas State Police	333	200
AZ	Phoenix Police Department	401	205
CA	Fresno County Sheriff's Office	183	94
CA	Los Angeles Police Department	55	213
CA	Sacramento County Sheriff's Office	39	35
CA	San Diego Police Department	92	92
CA	San Jose Police Department	68	61
CO	Colorado Springs Police Department	74	82
CT	Connecticut State Police	227	123
DE	Delaware Department of Justice	32	7
FL	Broward County Sheriff's Office	591	174
FL	Gainesville Police Department	345	140
FL	Polk County Sheriff's Office	45	48
GA	Georgia Bureau of Investigation	155	60

(Continued)

State	Agency	FY 2008 Technical Assists	Jan.-June 2009 Technical Assists
HI	Hawaii Department of Attorney General	37	20
IA	Iowa Division of Criminal Investigation	314	200
ID	Idaho Office of Attorney General	70	49
IL	Cook County State's Attorney's Office	64	8
IL	Illinois Office of Attorney General	102	63
IN	Indiana State Police	186	182
KS	Sedgwick County Sheriff's Office	142	90
KY	Kentucky State Police	384	296
LA	Louisiana Department of Justice	24	93
MA	Massachusetts State Police	256	186
MD	Maryland State Police	80	33
ME	Maine State Police	71	102
MI	Michigan State Police	47	99
MN	St. Paul Police Department	295	204
MO	Glendale Police Department	303	264
MS	Mississippi Office of Attorney General	35	33
MT	Billings Police Department	33	538
NC	North Carolina State Bureau of Investigation	401	156
ND	North Dakota Bureau of Criminal Investigation	158	78
NE	Nebraska State Patrol	191	362
NH	Portsmouth Police Department	32	58
NJ	New Jersey State Police	121	124
NM	New Mexico Attorney General's Office	207	112
NV	Las Vegas Metropolitan Police Department	194	121
NY	New York State Police	457	188
OH	Cuyahoga County Prosecutor's Office	114	31
OK	Oklahoma State Bureau of Investigation	336	89
OR	Oregon Department of Justice	193	97
PA	Delaware County District Office	1006	448
RI	Rhode Island State Police	87	88
SC	South Carolina Attorney General's	609	227
SD	South Dakota Division of Criminal Investigation	225	114
TN	Knoxville Police Department	422	331
TX	Dallas Police Department	97	148
TX	Office of the Attorney General of Texas	172	140
UT	Utah Office of Attorney General	282	173
VA	Bedford County Sheriff's Office	311	208
VA	Virginia State Police	112	127
VT	Burlington Police Department	129	40
WA	Seattle Police Department	208	131

(Continued)

State	Agency	FY 2008 Technical Assists	Jan.-June 2009 Technical Assists
WI	Wisconsin Department of Justice	348	244
WV	West Virginia State Police	52	47
WY	Wyoming Division of Criminal Investigation	350	184
	TOTAL	**11,976**	**8,227**

Source: Reports from ICAC Task Forces

7. Computer Forensic Examinations By ICAC Task Forces

In FY 2008, 14,339 computer forensic examinations were reported; 19,269 computer forensic exams were reported in 2009. The goal of a forensic examination is to indentify files that contain child sexual abuse images. Forensic exams may include examination of video, text, or picture files; examination of chat logs, e-mails, or other communication programs; and / or examination of file storage and structure. The level of effort required for a forensic exam varies greatly by the size and type of device being examined. Investigators commonly seize multiple media in one investigation, including: internal and external hard drives, flash drives, DVDs and CDs, cells phones and other digital media devices containing terabytes of data in an effort to identify contraband files. The below shows the number of forensic examinations completed by ICAC Task Forces.

Number of Computer Forensic Examinations by ICAC Task Forces (N=59)

State	Agency	FY 2008 # Forensic Exams	Jan.-June 2009 # Forensic Exams
AK	Anchorage Police Department	121	216
AL	Alabama Bureau of Investigation	240	193
AR	Arkansas State Police	361	271
AZ	Phoenix Police Department	274	95
CA	Fresno County Sheriff's Office	97	71
CA	Los Angeles Police Department	64	205
CA	Sacramento County Sheriff's	250	165
CA	San Diego Police Department	82	88
CA	San Jose Police Department	60	44
CO	Colorado Springs Police Department	116	183
CT	Connecticut State Police	45	119
DE	Delaware Department of Justice	175	75
FL	Broward County Sheriff's	107	132
FL	Gainesville Police Department	202	267
FL	Polk County Sheriff's Office	79	144
GA	Georgia Bureau of Investigation	278	188
HI	Hawaii Department of Attorney General	57	31
IA	Iowa Division of Criminal Investigation	308	244

(Continued)

State	Agency	FY 2008 # Forensic Exams	Jan.-June 2009 # Forensic Exams
ID	Idaho Office of Attorney General	65	71
IL	Cook County State's Attorney's Office	36	16
IL	Illinois Office of Attorney General	433	191
IN	Indiana State Police	386	318
KS	Sedgwick County Sheriff's Office	118	28
KY	Kentucky State Police	297	150
LA	Louisiana Department of Justice	153	91
MA	Massachusetts State Police	224	193
MD	Maryland State Police	235	119
ME	Maine State Police	121	71
MI	Michigan State Police	187	107
MN	St. Paul Police Department	356	217
MO	Glendale Police Department	813	628
MS	Mississippi Office of Attorney General	67	47
MT	Billings Police Department	39	762
NC	North Carolina State Bureau of Investigation	433	234
ND	North Dakota Bureau of Criminal Investigation	178	55
NE	Nebraska State Patrol	307	343
NH	Portsmouth Police Department	64	72
NJ	New Jersey State Police	65	124
NM	New Mexico Attorney General's Office	168	200
NV	Las Vegas Metropolitan Police Department	292	182
NY	New York State Police	881	495
OH	Cuyahoga County Prosecutor's Office	176	149
OK	Oklahoma State Bureau of Investigation	222	91
OR	Oregon Department of Justice	358	126
PA	Delaware County District	924	495
RI	Rhode Island State Police	34	74
SC	South Carolina Attorney General's Office	497	235
SD	South Dakota Division of Criminal Investigation	305	212
TN	Knoxville Police Department	524	270
TX	Dallas Police Department	26	91
TX	Office of the Attorney General of Texas	602	345
UT	Utah Office of Attorney General	190	195
VA	Bedford County Sheriff's Office	216	152
VA	Virginia State Police	43	105
VT	Burlington Police Department	273	55
WA	Seattle Police Department	180	94
WI	Wisconsin Department of Justice	679	514
WV	West Virginia State Police	120	104

(Continued)

State	Agency	FY 2008 # Forensic Exams	Jan.-June 2009 # Forensic Exams
WY	Wyoming Division of Criminal Investigation	136	37
	TOTAL	**14,339**	**10,789**

Source: Reports from ICAC Task Forces

8. Number And Type Of ICAC Task Force Affiliate Agencies

An affiliate is defined as a law enforcement agency that is working in partnership with a Task Force and has agreed in writing to adhere to ICAC Operational and Investigative Standards. The below shows the number of law enforcement agencies participating in the program standards established by the ICAC Task Force Program as of August 30, 2009.

ICAC Task Forces report 199 affiliate agencies added to the program during the first six months of 2009. Additionally, ICAC Task Forces report relationships with law enforcement agencies without a signed agreement (MOU). The below shows the number of agencies cooperating with ICAC Task Forces who have not yet signed an MOU.

Number and Type of ICAC Task Force Affiliate Agencies (N=59)

Agency Type	Number of Affiliate Law Enforcement Agencies
TF Lead Agencies	59
State	139
County	986
City/Local	1,330
Tribal	8
Federal	124
TOTAL	**2,646**

Source: Reports from ICAC Task Forces (As reported on August 30, 2009)

Number and Type of ICAC Task Force Partner Agencies (N=59)

Agency Type	Number of Law Enforcement Partnerships
State	20
County	43
City/Local	33
Tribal	1
Federal	41
TOTAL	**138**

Source: Reports from ICAC Task Forces (As reported on August 30, 2009)

9. Assessment Of Training And Technical Assistance To Support ICAC Grantees

The purpose of the ICAC Training and Technical Assistance (ICAC T&TA) program is to provide law enforcement officers, computer forensic investigators and prosecutors with the tools necessary to effectively investigate and prosecute computer facilitated crimes against children. Since 2005, OJJDP awarded funding to Fox Valley Technical College (FVTC) to design and implement cutting-edge training and technical assistance focused on investigative techniques and best practices for undercover operations to combat Internet crimes against children.

In FY 2008, the ICAC T&TA Program delivered 34 T&TA sessions and 1 national conference, reaching nearly 5,700 participants. The below highlights the courses offered and the average evaluation rating by type of event.

From October 2008 to June 2009, the ICAC T&TA Program delivered 39 T&TA sessions and 1 regional conference, reaching over 2,700 participants. The below highlights the courses offered and the average evaluation rating by type of event.

FY 2008 ICAC T&TA Course Offerings and Evaluation Data

Program	Sessions Offered	# Participants	Regional Training or TA	Average Evaluation Score (Scale 1-10)
CyberTips Management	1	21	Regional	8.71
ICAC Investigative Techniques	10	299	Regional	9.34
ICAC Investigative Techniques	4	88	TA	8.92
ICAC Peer-to-Peer	2	83	Regional	9.08
Project Safe Childhood	6	319	Regional	8.55
Project Safe Childhood	1	33	TA	9.47
ICAC Trial Advocacy for Prosecutors	1	17	Regional	8.75
ICAC Undercover Chat Investigations	6	179	Regional	9.28
ICAC Undercover Chat Investigations	2	57	TA	9.37
ICAC Unit Supervisor	1	31	Regional	9.4
ICAC National Conference	1	2,280	National	-

Source: Reports from ICAC Training & Technical Assistance Program

ICAC T&TA Course Offerings and Evaluation Data (October 2008 – June 2009)

Program	# Sessions Offered	# Participants	Regional Training or TA	Average Evaluation Score (Scale 1-10)
CyberTips Management	1	19	Regional	9.33
ICAC First Responder	9	573	Regional	9.02
ICAC Investigative Techniques	5	150	Regional	9.08

(Continued)

Program	# Sessions Offered	# Participants	Regional Training or TA	Average Evaluation Score (Scale 1-10)
ICAC Investigative Techniques	3	106	TA	9.20
ICAC Peer-to-Peer	2	58	Regional	8.87
ICAC Peer-to-Peer	2	58	TA	9.17
Project Safe Childhood	3	117	Regional	9.20
ICAC Trial Advocacy for Prosecutors	2	60	Regional	9.09
ICAC Instructor Development Train the Trainer	1	41	TA	9.7
ICAC Undercover Chat Investigations	4	119	Regional	9.22
ICAC Undercover Chat Investigations	3	70	TA	9.07
ICAC Unit Supervisor	1	66	Regional	8.78
SVICAC Conference	1	642	Regional	-

Source: Reports from ICAC Training & Technical Assistance Program

With funds provided by the American Recovery and Reinvestment Act of 2009 (the "Recovery Act") (Public Law 111-5), OJJDP has increased its capacity to deliver training and technical assistance to the ICAC Task Force. Starting in FY 2010, OJJDP will fund the following training providers:

- Girls Educational and Mentoring Services, Inc. (GEMS) – to deliver training and technical assistance to the ICAC Task Forces to increase the capacity of members toeffectively combat interrelated forms of the commercial sexual exploitation of children (CSEC).
- The SEARCH Group, Inc. - to provide highly specialized training related to social networking sites, peer to peer file sharing, wireless networks, and cell phone technology.
- The National District Attorneys Association (NDAA) – to deliver national training courses for prosecutors, including their two-part Unsafe Havens class (Part I focuses on pre-trial and investigation, while Part II is an advanced trial advocacy course addressing jury selection through sentencing).
- The University of Mississippi and the National Judicial College – to develop high quality educational programming for State judges on the investigation and prosecution of technology-assisted crimes against children.
- The National White Collar Crime Center (NW3C) - to deliver an innovative training program for law enforcement, prosecutors, and other stakeholders in the ICAC program to improve investigative, prosecutorial and forensic capabilities; create and distribute guidelines, best practices and investigative methodologies; and coordinate meetings with grantees and practitioners.

- The Innocent Justice Foundation – to develop a comprehensive mental health and wellness program for ICAC Task Force personnel to address negative effects and trauma for individuals exposed to child pornography through their work.

In addition to funds provided by the Recovery Act, OJJDP will provide funding to the Fox Valley Technical College (FVTC) to support the core ICAC Training and Technical assistance program that includes training focused on investigative techniques and best practices for undercover operations to combat Internet crimes against children.

FVTC will also coordinate with OJJDP to provide site-specific technical assistance to the ICAC Task Forces, meeting logistics for the quarterly ICAC Commanders' meetings, the National ICAC Conference, Missing Children's Day ceremony, and other tasks.

10. Assessment Of Leveraging State And Local Funds

In addition to bi-annual federal grants to support the work of the ICAC Task Forces[89], most Task Forces also receive cash or in-kind support from State and local authorities. The State and local funds are leveraged through the federal support for the ICAC program. Data from a sample of ICAC Task Forces reflecting leveraged State and local funds are shown in the Table below, along with the average annual OJJDP funding awarded to the ICAC Task Forces during each of the three fiscal years. These data are reported over three fiscal years, FY 2006, 2007 and 2008.

OJJDP is taking steps to collect annual data on State and local funds from all Task Forces. These data will be available in 2011.

C. Other Federal Agencies' Efforts

1. Department of Homeland Security's Efforts

The Department of Homeland Security (DHS) leverages resources within federal, state, and local governments, coordinating the transition of multiple agencies and programs into a single, integrated agency. More than 87,000 different governmental jurisdictions at the federal, state, and local level have homeland security responsibilities. The comprehensive national strategy seeks to develop a complementary system connecting all levels of government without duplicating effort.

Created in March 2003, Immigration and Customs Enforcement (ICE) is the largest investigative branch of the Department of Homeland Security. The agency combines the law enforcement arms of the former Immigration and Naturalization Service (INS) and the former U.S. Customs Service to more effectively enforce our immigration and customs laws and to protect the United States against terrorist attacks. In the fight against child exploitation and human trafficking, ICE has developed highly successful initiatives that focus on identifying, investigating, and arresting child predators and sexual offenders, as well as attacking the infrastructure that supports smuggling and trafficking organizations and the assets that are derived from these criminal activities. This might include seizing currency, property, weapons, and vehicles.

Average Total and Percentage of Leveraged Local and State Funds to ICAC Task Forces (N=19)

Funding Source	*Fiscal Year*		
	2006	*2007*	*2008*
Average Local Contribution	$ 488,526	$ 604,107	$ 665,877
OJJDP Average Award	$ 424,993	$ 458,333	$ 462,873
Average Annual Operational Cost	$ 915,525	$ 1,064,447	$ 1,130,758
Percent of ICAC Operations Supported with Leveraged State and Local Funds	53%	56%	58%

Source: Reports from ICAC Task Forces and OJJDP

ICE plays a significant role in combating the sexual exploitation of children. ICE accomplishes this mission through the Office of Investigations (OI), the Office of International Affairs (OIA), the Office of Intelligence, and the Office of Detention and Removal (DRO).

During FY 2010, the Federal Law Enforcement Training Center (FLETC) led a team of subject matter experts from various DHS components to develop computer/web based training (CBT) for Federal, state, local and tribal law enforcement officers to increase awareness of indicators of human trafficking. There are four video training scenarios, one of which addresses trafficking of minors who are sexually exploited. This interactive, web-based training also includes resource information from ICE

a. Office of Investigations

i. Cyber Crimes Center (C3) Child Exploitation Section

Initiated in 1997, the Cyber Crimes Center (C3) Child Exploitation Section (CES) investigates large-scale producers and distributors of child pornography as well as individuals who travel in foreign commerce for the purpose of engaging in sex with minors. The CES employs the latest technology to collect evidence and track the activities of individuals and organized groups who sexually exploit children through the use of websites, chat rooms, newsgroups and peer-to-peer trading. The CES also conducts clandestine operations throughout the world to identify and apprehend violators. The CES assists the field offices and routinely coordinates major investigations. The CES works closely with law enforcement agencies from around the world because the exploitation of children is a matter of global importance. The CES manages the entire ICE Child Exploitation Program to include: Operation Predator.

Operation Predator is a program designed to identify, investigate, and as appropriate, administratively remove child predators through the efforts of four principal entities of ICE: the Office of Investigations, the Office of International Affairs, the Office of Detention and Removal, and the Federal Protective Service. Officially launched by ICE on July 9, 2003, Operation Predator combines immigration investigative and administrative initiatives that target foreign nationals, undocumented aliens, and previously deported criminal aliens involved in child exploitation crimes and investigate the importation and exportation of images associated with child exploitation. Operation Predator works in partnership with the Justice's Project Safe Childhood, a comprehensive program to integrate the efforts of federal, state, and local law enforcement, non-government organizations, industry, and communities to counter the issue of child exploitation. ICE, through Operation Predator, maintains relationships with the National Center for Missing & Exploited Children, the Federal Bureau of Investigation (FBI), U.S. Postal Inspection Service, U.S. Secret Service, the Department of Justice, and the Internet Crimes Against Children Task Forces. ICE focuses on the international, trans-border dimension of child exploitation and integrates this enforcement with the national and local efforts of other law enforcement agencies in the United States. ICE routinely coordinates and integrates investigative efforts with foreign law enforcement, in order to identify, arrest and prosecute the principals who are involved in international pedophilic groups or who travel internationally for the purpose of having sex with children. As of February 28, 2010, 12,854 sexual predators have been arrested as a result of this initiatives conducted under the auspice of Operation Predator. Of those, 6,342 have been removed from the United States.

The following programs are primary initiatives of the CES and fall under the Operation Predator umbrella:

- **National and International Operations**
  The CES initiates national and international investigations involving large-scale production and/or distribution of child pornography by individuals and/or groups. These operations seek to dismantle and prosecute the individuals and/or groups while disseminating the downstream leads to ICE offices, both domestic and international, for further investigation. The CES coordinates these operations with the U.S. Department of Justice, Child Exploitation and Obscenity Section (CEOS). The CES also provides support and guidance to ICE field offices, both domestic and international, that are engaged in large scale child exploitation investigations.
- **Virtual Global Task Force**
  The Virtual Global Task Force (VGT) is a collaboration of international law enforcement agencies with the common goal of protecting children from sexual exploitation. The mission of the VGT is to make the Internet a safer place, to identify, locate and help children at risk, and to hold predators accountable for their actions. The VGT was established in 2003 and includes the U.S. (ICE), United Kingdom (Child Exploitation and Online Protection Centre), Canada (Royal Canadian Mounted Police), Australia (Australian Federal Police), Italy (Postal and Communication Police), the Ministry of Interior for the United Arab Emirates, and The International Criminal Police Organization (INTERPOL) as its current members. The VGT is intended to augment, not supplant, existing law enforcement initiatives and international relationships related to child exploitation issues. ICE is the exclusive U.S. representative to the VGT; the Section Chief CES serves as the senior practitioner to the VGT.
- **Child Sex Tourism**
  The Child Sex Tourism (CST) program originated in 1997 and became a major initiative after the passage of the 2003 Prosecutorial Remedies and Other Tools to end the Exploitation of Children Today Act, or PROTECT Act. Child sex tourism is a pervasive international problem. These predators often have a long history of abusing children, both in the United States and abroad. The CES investigates U.S. citizens and/or lawful permanent residents who are arrested in, or traveled to, a

foreign country for the purpose of engaging in sexual acts with children. The CES is responsible for and the coordinating point for ICE's National Child Sex Tourism Strategy. The CES also provides support to ICE field offices, both domestic and foreign, engaged in child sex tourism investigations.

- **Lead Intake and Dissemination**
  The CES is the central point within OI for the receipt and dissemination of child exploitation and child sex tourism leads. The CES receives leads from INTERPOL, European Union law enforcement Agency (EUROPOL), the National Center for Missing and Exploited Children (NCMEC), the U.S. Department of State (DOS), the DOJ, various federal, state, and local government agencies, various non-governmental agencies, both domestic and international, and the ICE field offices, both domestic and international. The CES is responsible for assessing the referrals and identifying the appropriate office for dissemination. This assessment involves identifying the specific violations and issuing legal process.
- **National Child Victim Identification System**
  Following the April 2002 Supreme Court decision in *Ashcroft v. Free Speech Coalition,* 535 U.S. 234 (2002), a case striking down as overbroad, a ban on "virtually" created child pornography under the Child Pornography Prevention Act of 1996, the need for a single national repository for all known child pornographic images became critically important. ICE recognized this vulnerability and developed the National Child Victim Identification System (NCVIS). NCVIS is an ICE-led initiative in partnership with the U.S. Secret Service, the U.S. Postal Inspection Service, the Department of Justice funded Internet Crimes Against Children Task Forces, the Department's Child Exploitation and Obscenity Section, the FBI, and the National Center for Missing & Exploited Children to facilitate the identification of child pornography produced utilizing real children. The system is dynamic in nature, and contains known and unique digital child pornographic images. NCVIS, operated and managed by C3, supports child exploitation investigations and prosecutions conducted by federal, state, local and foreign law enforcement entities.
- **National Center for Missing and Exploited Children**
  The CES maintains a full time liaison position at the NCMEC. This liaison position is responsible for receiving ICE field office submissions to the NCMEC Child Victim Identification Program (CVIP), coordinating ICE field office technical assistance requests to NCMEC, and providing additional support as required to NCMEC. The CES liaison also receives leads from NCMEC and facilitates the dissemination to the appropriate ICE field office, both domestic and international. The CES liaison assists ICE Attaché offices in setting up virtual private network connections to NCMEC's Cybertipline so the Attaché may receive reports for their area of responsibility directly from NCMEC.
- **U.S. Department of Justice, Child Exploitation and Obscenity Section**
  The CES maintains a part-time liaison position within DOJ CEOS. The liaison position facilitates ICE international/national child exploitation operations. The liaison position also provides guidance, in coordination with DOJ CEOS, to ICE field offices, both domestic and international.

ii. Victim Assistance Program

ICE's Victim Assistance Program (VAP) plays a key role in assisting victims of trafficking in persons and sexual exploitation. ICE has over 300 collateral duty victim witness coordinators who are trained to recognize indicators of human trafficking and sexual exploitation, and to provide victims with direct support and assistance. These coordinators ensure that victims are aware of their rights under federal law, and make referrals to appropriate local services.

b. Office of Intelligence

The ICE Office of Intelligence (Intel) supports ICE efforts to combat child exploitation through a number of programs.

- **Human Smuggling**
  Intel supports OI and OIA with both tactical and strategic intelligence regarding child smuggling/child trafficking investigations and operations. At the strategic level, Intel Analysts prepare threat assessments to support the accurate deployment of our agency resources. At the tactical level, analysts support significant investigations and operations both domestically and with international law enforcement allies abroad. Via the Secure Communities initiative, ICE Intel identifies aliens illegally present who have reentered the country after deportation for serious sexual offenses against children; Intel identifies and prioritizes those aliens illegally present who pose a significant threat to reoffend against children and a danger to our communities.
- **Forced Child Labor (FCL)**
  Intel supports OI and OIA with both tactical and strategic intelligence surrounding FCL investigations and operations. At the strategic level, Intel Analysts prepare threat assessments to support the accurate deployment of our agency resources. At the tactical level, analysts support significant investigations and operations both domestically and with international law enforcement allies abroad to prevent the illegal importation of goods produced as a result of the exploitation of children.
- **Child Sex Tourism**
  In furtherance of ICE's overall mission to combat Child Sex Tourism, ICE Intel launched Operation Angel Watch, an intelligence-driven effort to combat child sex tourism by identifying registered sex offenders traveling internationally who demonstrate behavior indicative of travel to gain access to children for sexual exploitation.

2. Department of Defense's Efforts

The Department of Defense Education Activity (DoDEA) provides instruction covering the topics of Internet safety and Internet predators as a necessary component of their technology integration program. This instruction is provided to students within the DoD schools by Information Specialists (librarians) and Education Technologists. All of the DoDEA schools are additionally equipped with commercial Internet Filtering devices designed to restrict access to inappropriate sites while, at the same time, allowing the necessary flow of information to and from DoDEA's student population.

DoD has dedicated a Military Criminal Investigation Officer (MCIO) Representative position that will rotate among the Military Services (currently held by NCIS) at the National Center for Missing and Exploited Children. The MCIO representative will primarily serve as a liaison to NCMEC's Exploited Children Division assisting with the Child Victim Identification Program (CVIP) and CyberTipline, and will also assist the Missing Children Division as the opportunities arise.

DoD also implements zero tolerance for trafficking in persons and runs a campaign to raise awareness of trafficking in persons. Training on trafficking in persons is mandatory for all military and civilian personnel. On October 14, 2005, President Bush signed E.O. 13387 "2005 Amendments to the Manual for Courts-Martial, United States" that enumerates the Article 134, UCMJ, offense of "Patronizing a Prostitute." A Public Service Announcement is aired on Armed Forces Networks and the Pentagon channel to reinforce this chargeable offense. Moreover, a new Federal Acquisition Regulation was promulgated in February, 2009 ensuring government contractor companies now must include a trafficking clause in their employment contracts which stipulates that they are responsible for: complying with United States law and local theater regulations on trafficking in persons; providing information to their employees to ensure compliance; and that they are subject to contract penalties for non-compliance. These responsibilities also flow down to all the subcontractors of a given company. In compliance with the Congressionally-mandated "William Wilberforce Trafficking Victims Protection Reauthorization Act", DoD IG is required to submit a report investigating contracts or subcontracts in which there is a "heightened risk" that a contractor may engage in trafficking in persons. In a report released on January 2010, DOD IG found that 93% of their private contracts included a clause on trafficking in persons.[90] In addition to this, DoD Instruction 2200.01 mandates that an annual trafficking in persons briefing requirement applies to all military personnel. The Secretaries of the Military Departments are responsible for the requirement for annual trafficking in persons general awareness training for all military and civilians in their departments, while the Commanders of the Combatant Commands are responsible for combating trafficking in persons policy within their respective areas of responsibility. These briefings will be required both as a part of theater/country in processing orientation and then as refresher training in these briefings.

DoD is currently revising the DoD trafficking in persons training modules to add more information about child soldiers to make members aware of the Optional Protocol to the United Nations Convention on the Rights of the Child in the involvement of children in armed conflict.

3. U.S. Postal Inspection Service Efforts

Postal Inspectors, since the enactment of the Sexual Exploitation of Children Act of 1977, have aggressively pursued and brought to justice over 5,200 child pornographers who relied upon the mail to traffic in this illegal material and/or sexually exploit a child. Postal Inspectors specializing in child exploitation investigations are in constant demand to provide their guidance and assistance to law enforcement agencies throughout the United States and abroad. Since 1997, Postal Inspectors have arrested over 2,700 offenders; 931 of those offenders were child molesters who were directly responsible for the sexual abuse of a child.

The Postal Inspection Service has held a position at the National Center for Missing & Exploited Children (NCMEC), a private, nonprofit, 501(c)(3) organization, for approximately 5 years. The inspector is responsible for handling all evidence submissions by law enforcement agencies under NCMEC's Child Victim Identification Program (CVIP); coordinating all activities related to the Deliver Me Home program; serving as the primary point of contact between NCMEC and postal inspectors throughout the country; and performing other duties as assigned. In CVIP, the inspector assigned to NCMEC receives and coordinates the thousands of requests by law enforcement for a review of images for known and identified victims. In the past five months, the inspector assigned to NCMEC has processed more than 1,250 requests for review of images, destroyed 1,105 disks containing child pornography, and returned 104 disks to submitting law enforcement. Since October 1, 2004, the USPSIS representative has received, logged, and returned in excess of 13,900 separate submissions from law enforcement agencies. CVIP's policy of not returning submissions unless specifically requested by the submitting agency is still in effect.

a. Deliver Me Home Program

Deliver Me Home is a joint program of NCMEC, the Postal Inspection Service, and the United States Postal Service. Postal Inspectors coordinate activities with NCMEC and Postal Service groups to share resources in locating abducted or missing children. Since the program began in September 2004, a total of 54 children have been located. Integral to the Deliver Me Home program are the missing children flyers Postal Inspectors dispatch to targeted ZIP Codes to alert communities and collect information about a missing or abducted child. Postal Inspectors have distributed 750,000 flyers. Deliver Me Home was enhanced in FY 2007 by the lobby poster program, which allowed managers at NCMEC's Missing Children's Division to request displays of Missing and Abducted Children posters in the lobbies of all Post Offices within a given geographic area. More than 100 posters have been distributed since the program's inspection in August 2007.

ADVO, a leading marketing services company that offers newspaper-delivered promotions, direct mail, coupons, and other services, operates "*Have You Seen Me?*" which contains pictures of missing children, which are delivered regularly to more than 90% of American homes as part of a mail circular. Since the program's inception in 1984, ADVO has mailed more than 80 billion photos profiling over 1,500 of America's missing children. A newly designed mail circular improves the program's visibility and overall cost-effectiveness. After a 22-year partnership, NCMEC, USPS, and ADVO continue to work together to find ways to evolve and enhance the Missing Children's Program.

As a result of leads generated by the "Have You Seen Me?" program, 144 missing children to date have been safely recovered. According to NCMEC, photos are the number one tool parents and law enforcement officials have in their search for missing children. By featuring recent or age-progressed photos of missing children and their alleged abductors, the program empowers the American public to help safely recover missing children.

Postal Inspectors regularly make presentations and conduct training on various topics related to the investigation of child exploitation at regional, national, and international conferences. In addition, Postal Inspectors often lead workshops or training sessions at Department's Project Safe Childhood and NCMEC-sponsored training programs.

b. 2 SMRT 4U Campaign

The 2 SMRT 4U Campaign was developed by the Postal Inspection Service in conjunction with NCMEC and Teen Vogue magazine in support of the Attorney General's

Project Safe Childhood initiative. The campaign was launched in November 2006 and ran throughout FY 2007.

Its purpose was to encourage teens to practice safe, smart habits when posting information about themselves on social networking Web sites and blogs. Using a tagline of *"Type Smart. Post Wisely,"* the campaign offered teens a free "awareness" ring, similar in concept to the Lance Armstrong bracelet, to promote knowledge of Internet safety. Made of polished steel and engraved with the campaign slogan "2 SMRT 4U," the ring was promoted via the Website and magazine by 17-year-old actress Hayden Panettiere, star of NBC's *Heroes*, who served as the campaign spokesperson.

Nearly one-half million rings were ordered and distributed to teens in 82 countries. More importantly, 68 percent of teens who visited the 2 SMRT 4U Web site reported that they changed their behavior and practiced safer online habits. Additionally, the campaign tallied 17,591 calls to the NCMEC's Cyber Tipline, which allows teens to report child sexual exploitation 24/7.

The 2 SMRT 4U Internet Safety Awareness Campaign far exceeded expectations. The Smithsonian National Postal Museum created a Web page to promote the campaign through its exhibit, "Postal Inspectors: The Silent Service." The Postal Inspection Service was honored to receive the Department of Justice's 2007 Internet Safety Award for the achievements throughout the campaign. The campaign has now been transferred to the direction of the National Center for Missing & Exploited Children.

4. Department of Health and Human Services Efforts

At the federal level, the Department of Health and Human Services (HHS) is responsible for helping victims of human trafficking become eligible to receive benefits and services so they may rebuild their lives safely in the United States. It does this primarily through three offices within the Administration for Children and Families: the Anti-Trafficking in Persons Division within the Office of Refugee Resettlement; the Office on Child Abuse and Neglect's programs in the Children's Bureau; and the Family and Youth Services Bureau, which administers the Runaway and Homeless Youth program.

The Anti-Trafficking in Persons Division within the Office of Refugee Resettlement helps certify adult victims of "a severe form of trafficking" so that these individuals are able to receive federally funded benefits and services to the same extent as refugees. Though not required to be certified by HHS, minors who are determined to be victims receive "Eligibility Letters" for the same types of benefits, as well as the Unaccompanied Refugee Minor Program's therapeutic foster care services.

a. The Office on Child Abuse and Neglect

The Office on Child Abuse and Neglect provides leadership and direction on the issues of child maltreatment and the prevention of abuse and neglect under the Child Abuse Prevention and Treatment Act (CAPTA). They are the focal point for interagency collaborative efforts, national conferences, and special initiatives related to child abuse and neglect, and for coordinating activities related to the prevention of abuse and neglect and the protection of children at-risk. They support activities to build networks of community-based, prevention-focused family resource and support programs through the Community-Based Family Resource and Support Program. They also support improvement in the systems that handle child abuse and neglect cases, particularly child sexual abuse and exploitation and maltreatment related fatalities, and improvement in the investigation and prosecution of these cases through the Children's Justice Act.

The Runaway and Homeless Youth Program assists homeless youths, providing basic necessities, reuniting youths with their families when possible, and aiding the transition to adulthood for older homeless youths who cannot return home. The Runaway and Homeless Youth Program provides four primary services:

- The Basic Center Program provides financial assistance to establish or strengthen community-based programs addressing the immediate needs of runaway and homeless youth and their families.
- Transitional Living Program grantees provide long-term, supportive assistance to older homeless youth, ages 16 to 21, who cannot return to their families but are not yet equipped to live on their own.
- The Street Outreach Program funds local youth service providers that conduct street-based education and outreach, and that offer emergency shelter and related services to young people who have been, or who are at risk of being, sexually abused or exploited.
- The National Runaway Switchboard (1-800-RUNAWAY) is a national communications system that assists youth who have run away, or are considering running away, and their families.

b. Children's Bureau

The Children's Justice Act (CJA) provides grants to States to improve the investigation, prosecution and judicial handling of cases of child abuse and neglect, particularly child sexual abuse and exploitation, in a manner that limits additional trauma to the child victim. This also includes the handling of child fatality cases in which child abuse or neglect is suspected and some cases of children with disabilities and serious health problems who also are victims of abuse and neglect.

States direct these system improvement funds to a variety of projects, a few of the State CJA projects address child exploitation, human tracking and internet safety. Support is provided to State and local police, child welfare staff and others for training and the purchase of equipment and technology to support efforts to prevent child exploitation. http://www.acf.hhs.gov/programs/cb/programs_fund/state

The National Resource Center on Youth Development, a service of the Children's Bureau (CB) is part of CB's Training and Technical Assistance Network (T&TA Network). The purpose of the T&TA Network is to build the capacity of State, local, Tribal, and other publicly administered or publicly supported child welfare agencies and family and juvenile courts. T&TA Network members provide assistance to States and Tribes in improving child welfare systems and ensuring the safety, permanency, and well-being of children and families.

The NRC on Youth Development collaborates with several outside agencies and organizations to continuously improve their ability to offer appropriate technical assistance and training. Included in the workplan for the NRC is focus and work on the prevention of exploitation of youth. These efforts will continue collaboration between CB, the NRC, other

Resource Centers and the Family and Youth Services Bureau (and their Runaway and Homeless Youth Training and Technical Assistance Centers). http://www.nrcys.ou.edu/yd/default.html

c. Office of the Assistant Secretary for Planning and Evaluation

The Adam Walsh Child Protection and Safety Act of 2006 (P.L. 109-248) requires that HHS conduct a study to assess the feasibility of establishing a national child abuse and neglect registry and present the results in a Report to Congress.

About 45 states maintain child abuse registries, which are databases that allow child protective services investigators routine access to child abuse history information to inform better current investigations. Most states also use their registries to conduct pre-employment background checks on persons who work with children, such as day care providers. The Adam Walsh Child Protection and Safety Act of 2006 (P.L. 109-248) requires that HHS conduct a study to assess the feasibility of establishing a national child abuse and neglect registry and present the results in a Report to Congress. This interim report describes key issues regarding the feasibility of establishing a national child abuse registry and concludes that implementation is not feasible under the statutory limitations of the authorizing legislation. Further feasibility study activities are underway and will be described in a final report when results are available. Report: http://aspe.hhs.gov/hsp/09/ChildAbuseRegistryInterimReport/index.shtml

d. Office of Refugee Resettlement

The Children's Bureau (CB) works closely with the Office of Refugee Resettlement (ORR). CB's Office on Child Abuse and Neglect (OCAN) partnered with ORR's Division of Unaccompanied Children's Services (DUCS) to develop training materials to assist in the care and placement of unaccompanied alien children. Issues of exploitation and/or trafficking impact many of the children ORR serves. The BRYCS program, Bridging Refugee Youth and Children's Services (BRYCS) is a one of the initiatives of ORR to provide national technical assistance to organizations serving refugees and immigrants so that all newcomer children and youth can reach their potential.[91]

5. Military Criminal Investigative Organizations (MCIO) Efforts

a. General MCIO Collaboration and Coordination

The National Center for Missing & Exploited Children (NCMEC), along with the Naval Criminal Investigative Service (NCIS), United States Army Criminal Investigation Command (USACIDC), Air Force Office of Special Investigations (AFOSI), and the Coast Guard Investigative Service (CGIS), have proposed the creation of a MCIO billet at the NCMEC. The MCIO representative will primarily serve as a liaison to NCMEC's Exploited Children Division assisting with the Child Victim Identification Program (CVIP) and CyberTipline, and will also assist the Missing Children Division as the opportunities arise.

Effective April 20, 2009, this new rotating billet will align all MCIO procedures regarding the handling of child sexual exploitation cases where child exploitation images/videos exist. The MCIO representative will become the sole MCIO point of contact for the submission of images/videos to the NCMEC Child Victim Identification Program

(CVIP), Child Recognition and Identification System (CRIS). In addition, the representative will monitor the NCIS Child Pornography Image Index (CPII) to help de-conflict duplicate entries, and submit images/videos to the Armed Forces Center for Child Protection (AFCCP) to obtain a Sexual Maturity Rating (SMR).

Agents from all branches will be able to send copies of images/videos directly to the MCIO representative (badge-to-badge transfer) who will then coordinate with NCMEC, AFCCP, and the Defense Computer Forensic Laboratory (DCFL). This procedure will expedite results, ensure proper formatting, and eliminate unnecessary evaluations.

Additionally, the MCIO representative will have access to the NCMEC CyberTipline. The CyberTipline, often referred to as the "9-1-1 of the Internet," serves as the national clearinghouse for online reporting of tips regarding child sexual exploitation including child pornography, online enticement of children for sex acts, molestation of children outside the family, sex tourism of children, child victims of prostitution, and unsolicited obscene material sent to a child. The MCIO representative will be able to review and take action on reported leads by accessing the "Federal Matrix", a de- confliction tool within the CyberTipline. Access to this matrix is provided to agency representatives assigned to NCMEC, including the Federal Bureau of Investigation (FBI), Immigration and Customs Enforcement (ICE), United States Postal Inspection Service (USPIS), and United States Secret Service (USSS). The MCIO representative will be able to review submitted CyberTipline reports, conduct DoD database searches, and disseminate reports involving DoD assets to the proper jurisdiction. This will ensure MCIO involvement from the inception of the investigation which will help to protect DoD interests and eliminate late or after-the-fact notification.

The MCIO representative will work with local, state, and federal partners regarding on-going or large scale child exploitation operations, helping identify possible DoD targets and quickly disseminating this information to the field.

The MCIO representative will also provide guidance and training to the MCIO community with regard to child exploitation investigations and operations. The MCIO representative will assist agents and the JAG Corps community with obtaining Victim Impact Statements, ageregression/age-progression images, sanitized photographs for trial preparation, training related PowerPoint presentations, Internet safety materials, and published research studies. The MCIO representative will help to assist outside law enforcement agencies with DoD database checks, Service Record Book reviews, and any additional support with regard to child exploitation investigations.

Additionally, the MCIO Representative will sit on the NCMEC Law Enforcement Committee, Federal Agency Task Force on Missing and Exploited Children, and the Internet Crimes Against Children Advisory Group. Representation on these committees will enhance MCIO visibility and information sharing capabilities.

b. Department of Navy's Crime Reduction Program - Campaign to Prevent Child Abuse/Child Exploitation

The Department of the Navy (DON) Crime Reduction Program dedicated its third campaign to support child abuse/child exploitation prevention. From Apr-Jun 2009, the Naval Criminal Investigative Service (NCIS) and DON partners, like Fleet and Family Support Center and Marine Corps Community Services, joined forces to increase education and awareness on the subject of child abuse. Eighty-two briefings were conducted with 6,081 attendees. Community outreach events were held aboard installations, including Leadership

Breakfasts, Child Abuse Prevention Fairs, Information Booths, Distribution of Child Identification Kits, Distribution of Flyers/Posters/Brochures and Presentations by Guest Speakers.

D. Public-Private Coordination Efforts to Prevent and Interdict Child Exploitation

The Department of Justice also has relationships with private organizations focused on protecting children from exploitation, many of which it supports with grant funding. NCMEC is discussed in the preceding section, but the following is a more fulsome description of the program along with a brief description of several other partnerships.

1. The National Center for Missing & Exploited Children (NCMEC)

Twenty years ago, a tragic series of child abductions and murders made names like Adam Walsh of Hollywood, Florida and Etan Patz of New York household names. These tragedies exposed a fundamental weakness in our approach to investigating multi-jurisdictional crimes: the United States, with its 50 states and approximately 18,000 separate state and local law enforcement agencies, had no established protocol for inter-agency communication and cooperation around cases of missing and endangered children. Because these cases almost always cross jurisdictional boundaries, this was a fatal flaw in our response.

At a White House ceremony on June 13, 1984, President Ronald Reagan announced the creation of the National Center for Missing & Exploited Children (NCMEC) and challenged it to attack this difficult problem through a true public-private partnership. To assist in their work, NCMEC was granted online access to the FBI's national crime computer (NCIC) and other public databases. In 1997, the FBI Director created a new field in the police report form, so that when a child is abducted, NCMEC receives instant notification. During its first five years of operation, NCMEC's recovery rate for missing children was 62 percent. Since 1990, the recovery rate has climbed to 97 percent.

OJP provided the Department of Justice's ongoing support of NCMEC, awarding more than $24 million in FY 2008 to support the Center's operations. Among the missions of NCMEC are to help prevent child abduction and sexual exploitation, help find missing children, and assist victims of child exploitation, their families, and the professionals who serve them. OJP funds assist NCMEC in its mission, which is in part based on congressional mandates (*see* 42 U.S.C. §§ 5771 et seq.; 42 U.S.C. § 11606; 22 C.F.R. § 94.6):

- Serves as a clearinghouse of information about missing and exploited children;
- Operates a Cyber Tipline that the public may use to report Internet-related child sexual exploitation;
- Provides technical assistance to individuals and law-enforcement agencies in the prevention, investigation, prosecution, and treatment of cases involving missing and exploited children;

- Assists the U.S. Department of State in certain cases of international child abduction in accordance with the Hague Convention on the Civil Aspects of International Child Abduction;
- Offers training programs to law-enforcement and social-service professionals;
- Distributes photographs and descriptions of missing children worldwide;
- Coordinates child-protection efforts with the private sector;
- Networks with non-profit service providers and state clearinghouses about missing-persons cases; and
- Provides information about effective state legislation to help ensure the protection of children.

As noted above, the NCMEC is a private, nonprofit entity with particular statutory responsibilities. NCMEC works with many of the Department's components to advance child exploitation interdiction. For instance, pursuant to 42 U.S.C. § 5773(b)(1), NCMEC operates the Congressionally-mandated Cyber Tipline and the Child Victim Identification Program.

To date, NCMEC has received 753,590 reports to the CyberTipline from the public and electronic service providers on the following categories of crimes: possession, manufacture, and distribution of child pornography; online enticement of children for sexual acts; child prostitution; sex tourism involving children; extrafamilial child sexual molestation; unsolicited obscene material sent to a child; misleading domain names; and misleading words or digital images on the Internet. Analysts in NCMEC's Exploited Child Division intake the reports, analyze the content, add value, and forward the tip to the appropriate international, state, federal, or local law enforcement agency for investigation.

NCMEC's Child Victim Identification Program (CVIP) has a dual mission: (1) to help prosecutors obtain convictions by proving that a real child is depicted in child pornography images; and (2) to assist law enforcement in locating unidentified child victims. NCMECs Child Victim Identification Program has reviewed more than 28.5 million child pornography images and videos in order to identify and rescue child victims, and has disseminated 19,800 reports to prosecutors in support of their cases against child sexual predators. Because of the United States Supreme Court's holding in *Ashcroft v. Free Speech Coalition*, 535 U.S. 234 (2002), federal prosecutors need to prove that the children depicted in child pornography images are real children. Local and federal law enforcement agencies submit copies of seized child pornography to federal law enforcement agencies assigned to NCMEC, accompanied by a written request that the images be reviewed for apparent identified children. NCMEC then provides a report to the submitting law enforcement agency listing the files that contain identified child victims as well as detailed information about the law enforcement officer who identified each child victim; those officers can then provide any evidence needed in court. Essentially CVIP acts as a law enforcement pointer system. A critical function of CVIP is the effort to assist law enforcement agencies in rescuing the child victims depicted in these images from their abusers. While reviewing contraband, CVIP analysts closely examine the images and videos submitted by law enforcement and document any clues that may lead to the location of an unidentified child victim. Once a location has been determined, the appropriate law enforcement agency may begin an investigation to rescue the child(ren). CVIP requests notification and basic case information when a victim of child pornography is identified by law enforcement. Working with federal law enforcement partners, information about such investigations is added to NCMEC's system. The addition of this information increases the value of CVIP's reviews by assisting in the prosecution of other offenders.

NCMEC provides training to United States Attorneys and Project Safe Childhood Coordinators at national Project Safe Childhood Conferences. NCMEC's Exploited Child Division CVIP and CyberTipline staff provide resources and technical assistance to law enforcement. To prevent duplication of efforts, NCMEC provides monthly deconfliction reports to United States Attorneys and ICAC Task Forces describing all law enforcement efforts stemming from CyberTipline reports in their states.

Additionally, NCMEC provides information to the Office of Victims Assistance (OVA) about victims of child pornography who have been newly identified by law enforcement so that OVA can begin providing services.

2. Other Examples of Public-Private Coordination

Many private organizations receive financial support from the Department of Justice / Office of Justice Programs through earmark appropriations designated by Congress or through participation in competitive grant funding programs.

a. Child Help

Founded in 1959, Childhelp® is a national non-profit organization dedicated to helping victims of child abuse and neglect. Childhelp's approach focuses on prevention, intervention and treatment. The Childhelp® National Child Abuse Hotline, 1-800-4-A-CHILD operates 24 hours a day, seven days a week, and receives calls from throughout the United States, Canada, the U.S. Virgin Islands, Puerto Rico and Guam. Childhelp's programs and services also include residential treatment services (villages); children's advocacy centers; therapeutic foster care; group homes; child abuse prevention, education and training; and the National Day of Hope®, part of National Child Abuse Prevention Month every April.

i. Darkness to Light

Darkness to Light is a national nonprofit 501c3 organization and initiative located in Charleston, SC. The organizational mission is to diminish the incidence and impact of child sexual abuse, so that more children will grow up healthy and whole and to deliver programs that will raise awareness of the prevalence and consequences of child sexual abuse by educating adults about the steps they can take to prevent, recognize and react responsibly to the reality of child sexual abuse.

ii. Girls Educational and Mentoring Services Inc.

Girls Educational and Mentoring Services' (GEMS) mission is to empower young women, ages 12-21, who have experienced commercial sexual exploitation and domestic trafficking to exit the commercial sex industry and develop to their full potential. GEMS is committed to ending *commercial sexual exploitation and domestic trafficking of children* by changing individual lives, transforming public perception, and revolutionizing the systems and policies that impact sexually exploited youth.

iii. Enough Is Enough

Enough Is Enough (EIE), a non-partisan, 501(c)(3) non-profit organization, emerged in 1994 as the national leader on the front lines to make the Internet safer for children and families. Since then, EIE has pioneered and led the effort to confront online pornography, child pornography, child stalking and sexual predation with innovative initiatives and effective communications.

iv. i-SAFE

i-SAFE Inc. is a non-profit foundation dedicated to protecting the online experiences of youth everywhere. i-SAFE incorporates classroom curriculum with dynamic community outreach to empower students, teachers, parents, law enforcement, and concerned adults to make the Internet a safer place.

v. Kristi House, Inc.

Kristi House provides a healing environment for all child victims of sexual abuse and their families, regardless of income, through prevention, treatment and coordination of services with our community partners.

vi. Nevada Child Seekers

Nevada Child Seekers, a registered nonprofit organization, created in 1985, advocates for and engage in prevention, identification and location efforts on behalf of missing and exploited children.

vii. Paul and Lisa Program Inc

The organization strives to meet the changing needs of the community to help prevent sexual exploitation of children. Paul & Lisa raises awareness through media, attending conferences, writing newsletters, and applying for federal grants, and its Street Outreach and Prevention Education Programs.

viii. Web Wise Kids Inc.

Web Wise Kids offers fun, challenging and interactive simulations based on real-life criminal cases—*MISSING, Mirror Image* and *Airdog* to teach children about Internet risks.

ix. San Diego Police Foundation

The Foundation is an independent 501 (c) (3) nonprofit organization providing support for efforts that enhance police/community relations, crime prevention and public safety through grant funding for specialized equipment, training, and cooperative community programs.

x. Self Reliance Foundation

The ultimate goal of "Self Reliance" guides all of SRF's activities. Our programs seek to empower individuals and communities to make well-informed decisions that improve their lives, by providing information and opportunities for self-reliance and empowerment.

xi. Washtenaw Area Council for Children

The Washtenaw Area Council for Children (WACC) is the Michigan Children's Trust Fund designated agency for the prevention of child abuse and neglect in Washtenaw County. The mission of the Council is to prevent child abuse and neglect through educational services and programs to children, parents, community members and youth-serving professional throughout Washtenaw County.

xii. INOBTR

In partnership with government and private citizens, INOBTR ("I Know Better") promotes awareness and educates children, parents and teachers to reduce the chance of children becoming victims of Internet crimes.

xiii. TechMission Youth Program

In 2005, a Department of Justice grant enabled TechMission to start its Safe Families Program, which promotes online safety through providing free training and web-filtering software.

E. A Review of the Department's Cooperation and Coordination Efforts

The Act required the Department to review its efforts to cooperate and coordinate with other agencies and private sector entities. This cooperation and coordination are crucial to the success of this effort to prevent and interdict child exploitation. Examples of activities provided here include interactions involving States, local, and tribal government agencies and Federal programs. The efforts included in this section include interagency working groups to facilitate cooperation and coordination of programs and policy; public-private groups intended to bring private industry and federal agencies together to work on specific issues; efforts to coordinate with the judicial branch; and federally funded programs that provide resources and other support to State, local, and tribal government agencies private and non-profit organizations.

The program descriptions included in the section were collected by surveying the members of the Federal Inter-Agency Task Force on Missing and Exploited Children and other agencies and components about their programs and by reviewing programs recently funded by the Department addressed in the websites maintained by the Department's components and offices.

1. Overarching Efforts to Coordinate Child Exploitation, Prevention, and Interdiction

a. The Federal Inter-Agency Task Force on Missing and Exploited Children

Title IV of the Juvenile Justice and Delinquency Prevention Act of 1974, as amended, the Missing Children's Assistance Act of 1984, authorizes the Administrator of the Office of Juvenile Justice and Delinquency Prevention (OJJDP) to coordinate the Federal Government's response to missing and exploited children. From this role, the Federal Inter-Agency Task Force on Missing and Exploited Children was created in 1995. The Task Force has met quarterly for more than ten years, and is chaired by the OJJDP Associate

Administrator for the Child Protection Division. Members include the Department of Justice, Department of Defense, Department of Education, Department of Homeland Security, Department of Health and Human Services, Department of State, Department of the Interior, and the U.S. Postal Service. The Task Force meets to discuss programs and policy that affect efforts to protect children.

b. Online Safety and Technology Working Group (OSTWG)

The Online Safety and Technology Working Group (Working Group) was established pursuant to the "Protecting Children in the 21st Century Act." Participants, including federal agencies, evaluate industry efforts and are developing recommendations to promote online safety for children through education, labeling, and parental control technology. The Working Group also evaluates and develops recommendations on industry efforts to prevent and respond to criminal activity involving children and the Internet. The OSTWG will submit a report to Congress and the Assistant Secretary for Communications and Information of its findings and make recommendations on how to increase online safety measures.

c. Project Safe Childhood Initiative

While Project Safe Childhood was mentioned above, it is more fully described here. The Department's 93 U.S. Attorney's Offices lead Project Safe Childhood. Project Safe Childhood (PSC) is a Department of Justice initiative launched in 2006 that aims to combat the proliferation of technology-facilitated sexual exploitation crimes against children. OJJDP's Project Safe Childhood public education and community awareness program is a critical part of current law enforcement efforts to combat the sexual exploitation. PSC coordinates investigations and prosecutions of online sexual predators and is implemented through a partnership of U.S. Attorneys, CEOS, Internet Crimes Against Children (ICAC) task forces, FBI, U.S. Postal Inspection Service, ICE, Marshals Service, advocacy organizations such as the NCMEC and state and local law enforcement officials.

In FY 2007, OJJDP provided $4 million dollars in grants to further the goals of Project Safe Childhood. As part of that effort, OJJDP provided $ 2.5 million to fund a national public education and awareness campaign. This media campaign was unique in that various components could be adapted for continued use and distribution at the local, state, and regional levels by PSC Coordinators and other appropriate organizations. OJJDP also provided $1.5 million dollars in funding for projects at the local, state, or multi-state levels. These projects featured outreach efforts and innovative programming to schools, youth and community organizations, business entities, and various parent groups. These programs provided comprehensive training, curricula and online educational programming about online safety for children. The focus of OJJDP's Project Safe Childhood public education and community awareness program is prevention: public education and awareness about the online sexual exploitation of children helps to prevent the victimization of children through technology-facilitated means.

- The national media campaign was designed as a bilingual campaign (in English and Spanish) and featured four public service announcements, a three-part Webisode, Web banners, radio ads, movie theater ads and print materials. These materials are being used by appropriate law enforcement and advocacy groups to educate the public about the technology-facilitated victimization of children and about the importance of online safety.

- The PSAs titled "Know Where They Go" and "No Lo Harias" are a call to action to parents and ask them to learn about online safety and to supervise their children's online activities. The PSAs titled "Decisions" and "No Arruines Tu Vida" target potential and low-level online predators, informing them that downloading child pornography or enticing minors online are serious federal crimes with lifelong consequences and legal ramifications. Audience-specific websites were created to provide additional information.
- The PSC media campaign featured a national media launch, regional media events in four cities, and large scale public awareness events about Internet safety in designated markets. These events were supported by television, radio, online and movie theater placement of PSAs in these regions.
- The Department supported local events with U.S. Attorneys' Offices across the nation utilizing materials developed under the Project Safe Childhood initiative.
- Under PSC, the number of federal child exploitation prosecutions has increased significantly, along with the number of federal, state, and local investigations and convictions, and more victims are being identified.

d. ICACs

As discussed in depth above, the 61 ICAC Task Forces are funded and coordinated through the Department's OJP. These Task Forces are designed and have proven successful in collaboratively working with federal, state, and local offices.

2. FBI's Law Enforcement Coordination Efforts

As noted above, the FBI is engaged in many task forces and initiatives, including their Innocent Images National Initiative, the Innocence Lost National Initiative, and the Innocent Images International Task Force. All of these initiatives involve agents and investigators from all levels of the government.

The FBI has also stepped up its efforts to disrupt human trafficking operations worldwide and to free these organization's victims. The FBI works with other local, state, and federal law enforcement agencies and national victim-based advocacy groups in joint task forces that combine resources and expertise on the issue. Today, the FBI participates in approximately 30 law enforcement task forces and the 42 Bureau of Justice Assistance-sponsored task forces around the nation.

FBI Victim Specialists (along with victim specialists from the United States Attorneys' Offices and/or other non-government victim assistance providers) work with human trafficking victims to not only advise them of their rights as victims but also to assure they get the help they need to address their short-term and long-term needs—like legal and repatriation services, immigration relief, housing, employment, education, job training, and child care. In addition, FBI field offices continue to build relationships with civic and community groups and non-governmental organizations that can refer cases and provide valuable insights and information.

3. Efforts to Coordinate with the Judicial Branch

The Department is actively engaged with the Judicial Branch. Under the Sentencing Reform Act of 1984, the Attorney General serves as an *ex-officio* member of the United States Sentencing Commission. Each year, the Department submits to the Sentencing Commission a report commenting on the operation of the sentencing guidelines, suggesting changes that appear to be warranted, and otherwise assessing the Commission's work. 28 U.S.C. § 994(o). The Department participates in all Sentencing Commission meetings, testifies at Commission public hearings on all significant issues pending before the Commission, and participates in the Commission's annual training seminar. The Department also serves as an *ex-officio* member of the Advisory Committee on the Criminal Rules, the Judicial Conference Committee responsible for reviewing proposals to amend the Federal Rules of Criminal Procedure, as well as the Judicial Conference's Standing Committee on Rules of Practice and Procedure. The Department will be participating in a panel discussion on child exploitation sentencing at the Sentencing Commission's National Conference in June 2010.

4. International Coordination Efforts to Prevent and Interdict Child Exploitation

The circulation and collection of child pornography, child sex trafficking, and child sex tourism are crimes that necessarily cross international borders. Therefore, the United States regularly engages in bilateral and multilateral efforts to deter and prevent the sexual exploitation of children.

With respect to the international trafficking of children for sexual exploitation, the United States funds programs abroad to combat trafficking, exploitive child labor, commercial sexual exploitation of children, and child sex tourism. In 2003, President Bush launched a $50 million Initiative on Trafficking in Persons (POTUS Initiative) to support organizations that rescue, shelter, and provide services to women and children who are victims of trafficking. This initiative has funded projects in Brazil, Cambodia, India, Indonesia, Mexico, Moldova, Sierra Leone, and Tanzania. The Departments of State and Health and Human Services have also funded deterrence and public information campaigns abroad in countries such as Cambodia, Costa Rica, Brazil, Thailand, and Mexico targeted at U.S. child sex tourists.

As previously noted, pursuant to bilateral and multilateral legal assistance treaties with foreign governments, the United States regularly cooperates with law enforcement authorities of other countries to investigate and prosecute the prostitution of children, child pornography, and the sale of children, as well as child sex tourism. The United States funds training for law enforcement and consular officials of foreign countries in the areas of trafficking in persons, child sex tourism, and sexual exploitation of women and children. The United States also supports deterrence programs that encourage innovative partnerships among governments, labor, industry groups, and NGOs to end the employment of children in hazardous or abusive conditions. Examples of these innovative partnerships include: cooperation with the government of South Korea to replicate a San Francisco-based model offenders prevention program targeted at persons who are arrested for soliciting sexual services from prostituted persons; cooperation with travel and tourism companies both in the United States and abroad to support an ethical code of conduct to protect children from commercial sexual exploitation in travel and tourism; and cooperation between an international faith-based organization, UNICEF and the Madagascar ministries of Population, Tourism and Education to conduct a survey of the types of child labor and sexual exploitation that will lead to a nationwide anti-trafficking campaign.

The United States is also a Party to several relevant child protection treaties. In 1999, the United States was one of the first countries to ratify ILO Convention 182. This Convention calls on signatories to take immediate measures to eliminate, as a matter of urgency, the worst forms of child labor, which include all forms of slavery or practices similar to slavery, such as the sale and trafficking of children and forced labor; the use, procuring or offering of a child for prostitution or pornography; the use, procuring or offering of a child for illicit activities such as drug trafficking; and work which, by its nature of the circumstances in which it is carried out, is likely to harm the health, safety or morals of children.

In 2002, the United States ratified the Optional Protocol to the Convention on the Rights of the Child on the sale of children, child prostitution and child pornography. This treaty contains a broad range of protection for children, including requirements for states Parties to criminalize a broad range of acts and activities relating to sexual exploitation of children. The United States submitted its Initial Report on its implementation of the Optional Protocol to the UN Committee on the Rights of the Child in 2007. A U.S. delegation led by the State Department's Office to Monitor and Combat Trafficking in Persons took part in a vigorous, transparent discussion of obligations met, best practices, and areas for further intensity of effort on this protocol and its counterpart protocol on children in armed conflict in a regular review by the UN Committee on the Rights of the Child in May 2008 in Geneva. In January of this year, the United States submitted its second report to the UN Committee on the Rights of the Child regarding further implementation of the same two optional protocols. The United States is also a Party to the UN Protocol to Prevent, Suppress and Punish Trafficking in Persons, Especially Women and Children. The United States signed the Protocol on December 13, 2000, and it entered into force for the United States on December 3, 2005. The Protocol calls for information exchange in certain circumstances (Art. 10). The general provisions of the Transnational Organized Crime Convention, to which the United States is also a Party, apply to the Protocol and contain provisions on extradition (Art. 16) and mutual legal assistance (Art. 18).

Additionally, since the Trafficking Victims Protection Act (TVPA) was passed in 2000, the United States has submitted annual Trafficking in Persons Reports to the United States Congress on foreign governments' efforts to eliminate severe forms of trafficking in persons. The 2008 Report assessed the efforts of 170 countries to combat trafficking in persons, including their government's efforts to prosecute traffickers, protect victims, and prevent the crime. A government that fails to make significant efforts to bring itself into compliance with the minimum standards for eliminating trafficking, as established in the TVPA, receives a "Tier 3" assessment in the Report. Such an assessment may trigger the withholding of U.S. non-humanitarian, nontrade-related foreign assistance to that country. The TIP Report has also added greater emphasis on foreign government's efforts to combat demand and exploitation of children overseas by its citizens. Based on the minimum standards for fighting child sexual exploitation constituting trafficking in persons, it has been a useful vehicle to encourage other nations to adopt extraterritorial laws which allow for the prosecution of its citizens for victimizing children when engaging in sex tourism in other countries just as the United States enacted in the form of the PROTECT Act in 2003.

In 2007, the United States actively promoted the issue of confronting commercial sexual exploitation of children in multilateral fora. For the United Nations' annual Commission on

Crime Prevention and Criminal Justice ("Crime Commission"), the United States successfully pushed for the issue of commercial sexual exploitation of children to be one of two Commission themes. The United States introduced a resolution that was subsequently adopted titled: *Effective Crime Prevention and Criminal Justice Responses to Combat Sexual Exploitation of Children*. During the Crime Commission, the U.S. delegation also co-hosted a successful event for representatives of member states that included screening of the movie *Human Trafficking* and an expert panel discussion on child trafficking. The Department's CEOS and OIA worked closely with the Department of State on these efforts.

The G-8 Lyon-Roma Group finalized two U.S.-drafted documents in 2007 related to commercial sexual exploitation of children. The first document was a Justice and Home Affairs Ministers' statement *Reinforcing the International Fight Against Child Pornography*. All eight countries endorsed this document, which emphasizes the importance of having strong legislation against child pornography in all countries. The second document addressed *Experience in the Implementation of Extraterritorial Jurisdiction for Sex Crimes*. This document discusses the growing problem of international sex tourism and the need to be able to prosecute citizens in their home country for the sex crimes they commit against children abroad. CEOS and the Department of State collaborated on these efforts.

Also in 2007, the U.S. Department of State served as chair of the Regional Conference on Migration (RCM), an organization composed of Central and North American immigration and policy officials. Trafficking in persons was the theme of the 2007 ministerial meeting in New Orleans. At this meeting, the United States worked in tandem with other member countries to adopt a non-binding document "Regional Guidelines for Special Protection in Cases of the Repatriation of Child Victims of Trafficking." Through the RCM, ICE, and U.S. Customs and Border Protection (CBP) organized a training workshop on trafficking in persons and smuggling that included presentations by RCM members Honduras, Mexico, Canada, and El Salvador. Additionally, CEOS, NCMEC, FBI, and ICE helped to develop and implement the first-ever INHOPE International Law Enforcement Coordination Conference held in Helsinki, Finland, in 2009. This conference, attended by online child exploitation experts from around the world, is scheduled to occur again this year on September 28, 2010 in Madrid, Spain. Further, CEOS routinely presents on the subject of online child exploitation at other international conferences held annually by Europol, Interpol, and the European Commission.

In the area of child sex tourism, CEOS and ICE partner in ICE's sex tourism initiative to identify "hot spot" locations and send a team of investigators and prosecutors to those locations to partner with the foreign government and develop a proactive strategy to identify and prosecute offenders.

a. Department of Justice's International Efforts

Through various components of the Department of Justice, the United States has trained foreign law enforcement officials in numerous countries on investigating and prosecuting child sex trafficking and has worked with governments to develop model anti-trafficking legislation and has fostered international cooperation in hundreds of cases.

The FBI's Innocent Images International Task Force (IIITF) became operational on October 6, 2004, and includes law enforcement officers from countries such as: United Kingdom, Norway, Finland, Ukraine, Belarus, Australia, Thailand, the Philippines, Croatia, Latvia, Germany, the Netherlands, New Zealand, Canada, Sweden, Fiji, Cyprus, Iceland,

Denmark, Panama, and Europol. To date, more than 70 international officers have traveled to the United States from 33 different countries and worked side-by-side with Special Agents of the FBI at the Innocent Images Operations Unit. IIITF has allowed for the real-time transfer of information from and to the FBI, and between task force members and their countries. Task Force Officers stay in the United States for several weeks and they remain an integral part of the task force once they return to their home countries. The FBI's IIITF successfully brings together law enforcement from around the world to address the global crime problem of online child exploitation.

The FBI has implemented joint operations overseas with governments in two major child sex tourism (CST) destinations, Thailand and Cambodia. These operations target child sex tourists who do not plan their illegal activities from the United States, but rather seek to procure children once they arrive at their destination. The purpose of these operations is to coordinate with host country law enforcement to gather evidence against American offenders that is admissible in American courts, with the goal of extraditing those offenders back to the United States for prosecution. The FBI coordinates all efforts through its Legal Attachés in those countries to provide, training, equipment and logistical support to these joint operations.

FBI's CST Initiative employs a proactive investigative strategy to identify and disrupt the activities of sexual predators before they are able to victimize additional children. In conjunction with those country authorities, as well as interested NGOs, the CST Initiative employs the use of both undercover employees and confidential human sources to identify predatory individuals and groups operating in high threat areas for child sexual exploitation. Furthermore, its purpose is to collect evidence against these predicated targets and facilitate their arrest/prosecution by host country authorities as well as the United States.

CEOS has worked with foreign law enforcement agencies, such as Interpol, Europol, and Eurojust, to coordinate international investigations. Some of these investigations begin with the identification of an offender in the United States, while others begin with the identification of an offender in a foreign country. All, however, are complex cases requiring close international teamwork.

The Criminal Division's Office of Overseas Prosecutorial Development, Assistance and Training (OPDAT), drawing on the expertise of experienced prosecutors from CEOS, the Civil Rights Division and its Human Trafficking Prosecution Unit, and the United States Attorney's Offices, has designed and executed technical assistance and training programs overseas to strengthen international capacity to combat trafficking in persons, including child sex trafficking and child exploitation offenses. OPDAT assisted Brazil in the drafting of a child pornography law, enacted in November 2008, which makes possession of child pornography a felony, the first time it has been so criminalized in Brazil. OPDAT provided technical assistance and training to Russia in addressing its serious child exploitation and pornography problems. As a result, the Russian MVD (Interior Ministry) agreed to participate in the FBI's Innocent Images Global Task Force; Russian child pornography investigations increased tenfold; and in July 2009, Russia enacted legislation with severe penalties for crimes against minors, including sexual abuse.

Additionally, CEOS, in partnership with OPDAT and the State Department, regularly provides training for foreign delegates on child exploitation offenses as part of the State Department's International Visitor Program. These training sessions range from providing an overview of U.S. child exploitation laws, including child protection statutes, and how to investigate and prosecute human trafficking cases successfully.

From 2007 – 2009, CEOS discussed these issues with delegates from countries such as Albania, Algeria, Austria, Bosnia, Brazil, Cambodia, China, Colombia, Cyprus, Ecuador, Egypt, Finland, France, Germany, Ghana, Hungary, Iceland, India, Indonesia, Israel, Japan, Jordan, Kazakhstan, Kosovo and Bosnia, Laos, Latvia, Macedonia, Malta, Myanmar, Pakistan, the Philippines, Poland, Portugal, Romania, Russia, Serbia, Switzerland, Syria, Tajikistan, Thailand, Turkey, the Ukraine, and the United Arab Emirates.

Moreover, CEOS trial attorneys regularly perform extensive overseas training programs. For example, CEOS team members have travelled to several cities throughout Latvia to train an audience of Latvian judges, police, and prosecutors on numerous topics related to human trafficking. These topics included an overview of U.S. laws, a discussion of appropriate investigative techniques, and a primer on the international response to human trafficking, including a discussion of relevant international treaties. CEOS attorneys have conducted similar training programs in Cambodia, Nepal, Thailand, Morocco, Nigeria, Armenia, and Indonesia. In 2009 alone, CEOS attorneys went to the Philippines, Panama, Morocco, Brazil, Colombia, and the Dominican Republic for child sex tourism trainings.

As outlined above, CEOS contributes to policy developments at the international level, working with such bodies as the G8, the United Nations, and the Council of Europe. For example, to address a lack of consensus concerning the danger posed by child pornography collectors to children, CEOS proposed, developed and delivered, through the G8 Law Enforcement Projects Sub-Group, an International Symposium of experts to identify the correlation between child pornography offenders and child molesters. As outlined above, this symposium led to a May 30, 2009, declaration by the G8 Ministers of Justice and Home Affairs titled, *"The Risk to Children Posed by Child Pornography Offenders*" recognizing the findings made by the experts at the symposium. CEOS also contributes information and expertise to inform the U.S. Government's report on its implementation of the Optional Protocol on the sale of children, child prostitution and child pornography to the U.N.'s Convention on the Rights of the Child.

CEOS also attended the meetings at which the Council of Europe drafted its "Convention on the Protection of Children Against Sexual Exploitation and Sexual Abuse." The convention will require signatories to criminalize all child pornography crimes, including simple possession and intentionally accessing child pornography online, solicitation (grooming), child sex abuse, and child prostitution.

In November 2008, the Department led the U.S. Government's multidisciplinary delegation to the World Congress III Against Sexual Exploitation of Children and Adolescents, held in Rio de Janeiro, Brazil. The U.S. Government prepared and submitted to the Rapporteur of World Congress III a report reflecting the U.S. Government's efforts to combat sexual exploitation of children and adolescents since World Congress II in Yokohama in 2001. While in Rio, the U.S. Government was an active participant in negotiating and working on the Rio Declaration and Plan of Action to Prevent and Stop Sexual Exploitation of Children and Adolescents.

In 2008, INTERPOL Washington, the Department, and DOS joined with the G8 members to fund and create the INTERPOL International Child Sexual Exploitation Database (ICSE): Formerly known as the INTERPOL Child Abuse Images Database (ICAID), the database allows investigators to compare newly seized images of child pornography to those already known to the international law enforcement community in order to identify new victims and rescue them from ongoing abuse. INTERPOL's database currently contains over

550,000 images reported by 40 countries and has led to the identification of over 1,600 child victims. INTERPOL Washington facilitates participation in the ICSE by ICE and the FBI.

Within the INTERPOL member countries, INTERPOL Washington was the first to make the issuance of Green Notices against child sex offenders a priority. These notices serve as international warnings about subjects who are assessed by national law enforcement authorities as continuing threats to public safety or may commit other criminal offenses. The issuance of Green Notices is also based on previous criminal convictions or history of criminal activity (habitual offenders, sex offenders, violent gang members, child pornographers). To date, INTERPOL Washington has published 3,285 such notices on deported child sexual predators in support of ICE's Operation Predator.

Finally, by administering numerous MLATs and multilateral conventions for evidence gathering, other forms of legal assistance and extradition, OIA has supported numerous transnational investigations and foreign prosecutions.

b. Department of Homeland Security's International Efforts

ICE's Office of International Affairs maintains an active and aggressive overseas investigation program to combat the sexual exploitation of children. OIA's 63 offices in 44 countries are responsible for the coordination of international investigations with foreign counterparts and providing investigative support to domestic offices. ICE Attachés are DHS' primary liaison with host country governments, industries, and law enforcement. In addition to its investigative responsibilities, Attaché and OIA Headquarters offices conduct training and outreach to educate foreign government counterparts of the dangers child exploitation poses to their country's wellbeing. OIA helps facilitate capacity building in host nations by sharing best practices utilized by U.S. federal law enforcement.

ICE has been charged with investigating violations of the Tariff Act of 1930 (Title 19 USC 1307), which prohibits the importation of merchandise mined, produced, or manufactured wholly or in part in any foreign country by forced labor, including forced child labor (FCL). ICE also has a legislative mandate to conduct international FCL outreach and training. OIA fulfills these responsibilities by conducting continuous outreach and training to foreign law enforcement and non-governmental organizations (NGOs), thusly promoting investigative collaboration.

OIA hosts three major biennial regional training events to discuss the issues of FCL, Child Sex Tourism, and Human Trafficking. The events are hosted in three separate regions of the world to address not only international topics of concern, but also topics specific to each region (Asia, the Americas and Europe/Middle East/Africa). Since the implementation of the regional training concept several years ago, a strong correlation between training forums and increased case referrals and statistics has been demonstrated. Foreign subject matter experts are invited to participate in the regional training events. The inclusion of foreign subject matter experts has fostered better collaboration, opened and sustained investigative dialogues, and facilitated proactive working relationships with foreign counterparts. The goals of the events are to increase awareness within ICE and ICE's foreign law enforcement counterparts and enhance communication and cooperation between Attaché offices and representatives of other U.S. agencies and NGOs. Presentations at the events are provided by ICE subject matter experts and representatives of other U.S. Government agencies including Department of Labor, DOS, and the DOJ as well as a number of NGOs and international organizations. In addition to the three major events, ICE Attachés conduct regional trainings in various international locations.

c. Department of State's International Efforts

The President's Interagency Task Force to Combat Trafficking in Persons (PITF) is a Cabinet-level entity mandated by the Trafficking Victims Protection Act whose purpose is to coordinate government-wide efforts to combat human trafficking. It is chaired by the Secretary of State. The Senior Policy Operating Group (SPOG) coordinates activities of Federal departments and agencies regarding policies, including grants and grant policies, involving trafficking in persons and the implementation of the TVPA. The SPOG consists of senior officials designated as representatives by the PITF members and is chaired by the Director of the Office to Monitor and Combat Trafficking at the Department of State. Three standing committees include Research & Data, Grantmaking, and Public Affairs.

Through the Office to Monitor and Combat Trafficking in Persons (G/TIP), the Department of State helps to lead the international efforts in the global movement to abolish modern-day slavery. It engages with foreign governments, civil society, and multilateral organizations, to fight human trafficking around the world. G/TIP has built global awareness of modern-day slavery through nine annual Trafficking in Persons (TIP) Reports, covering 176 countries in 2009(compared to 82 in 2001). The Report is the U.S. Government's principal diplomatic tool used to engage foreign governments on the subject as well as an important reference for targeting U.S. foreign assistance funding. It is also the world's most comprehensive compendium of antihuman trafficking efforts and reflects the USG's global leadership on this key human rights issue. In preparation for the 2010 Report due to be released in June, the Ambassador-at-Large and/or G/TIP Reports and Political Affairs staff traveled to 50 countries to meet with foreign government officials, international organizations and NGO representatives.

Pursuant to the TVPRA of 2005, the TIP Report now includes assessments of foreign governments' efforts to combat demand, including punishment of its citizens for engaging in child sexual exploitation overseas. G/TIP has widely disseminated anti-TIP information through electronic and print media, the Internet, and digital video conferences – reaching over 1 billion people in 2009. In FY 2009, G/TIP obligated more than $26 million for anti-human trafficking programs: 80 projects in 50 countries totaling approximately $21.85 million, five regional projects totaling $2.25 million, and eight global projects totaling roughly $1.9 million. Nearly all of these awards were funded through the office's annual competitive grant process. A complete list of G/TIP awarded projects and descriptions are available at http://www.state.

G/TIP's programmatic work is part of a larger effort of United States agencies which has spent over $688 million on international anti-human trafficking programs since FY 2001 – efforts G/TIP helps coordinate by chairing the SPOG. G/TIP has also raised awareness on child sex tourism (CST) through funding public awareness and deterrence campaigns, supporting research on CST, engaging the travel, tourism, and hospitality community, compiling informational resources, and facilitating educational film releases on the topic.

Finally, G/TIP has worked extensively with the relevant State Department bureaus in engaging with multilateral organizations such as the UN, the Organization of American States, the Organization for Security and Cooperation in Europe and the Group of Eight to promote a victim-centered and multidisciplinary approach based on the U.S. experience, and to promote ratification and implementation of the Protocol to Prevent, Suppress and Punish Trafficking in Persons, Especially Women and Children, Supplementing the United Nations Convention against Transnational Organized Crime.

d. U.S. Agency for International Development's International Efforts

The U.S. Agency for International Development (USAID) has played a leading role in addressing the sexual exploitation of children and adolescents abroad through a number of activities or interrelated initiatives. The majority of USAID's programs are bilateral, multilateral, or regional arrangements that complement and support in-country enforcement actions directly or in-directly. Specifically, since 2001 USAID has provided more than $100 million for programs directed at the elimination of human trafficking, a major factor behind the sexual exploitation of children and adolescents worldwide, through a wide range of activities in more than 70 countries. To complement anti-trafficking activities, USAID has also instituted a number of parallel development efforts to include girls' education, administration of justice, and refugee assistance.

For example, since 2005, USAID has worked to prevent the trafficking of girls in the Mekong Delta through scholarships, vocational training and job placement to at-risk girls. In Mozambique, USAID partnered with the government and an NGO network to draft anti-trafficking legislation that passed unanimously in the National Assembly in 2008. Simultaneously, in Benin USAID helped promote awareness of the Family Code, which established a legal marriage age of 18. In Ecuador USAID continues to provide technical assistance and training towards the implementation of a national anti-trafficking plan, which aims to increase protections for vulnerable children. To create awareness of trafficking in Asia, USAID and MTV collaborated to target a young media-savvy audience through a television special featuring well-known models, actors and musicians. This public-private partnership spearheaded a collaborative partnership with Radiohead, a popular rock band that reached out to as many as 560 million households. In Moldova, USAID set up regional centers for job skills, job search, technical training, legal assistance and counselling for trafficking victims. More than 25,000 women received services and nearly 10,000 rural women were assisted through established mobile units.

The totality of USAID's efforts has been instrumental in mitigating and resolving the negative affects attributed to the sexual exploitation of children and adolescents, and USAID will continue to place a high priority on this and other associated issues.

e. Department of Labor's International Efforts

The United States contributes to a wide array of programs that support the elimination of the worst forms of child labor worldwide, including programs to address the sexual exploitation of children. Since 1995, the Department of Labor has provided approximately $720 million for technical assistance projects aimed at eliminating exploitative child labor internationally. Of this amount, over $330 million has gone to organizations to carry out projects to combat commercial sexual exploitation of children and child trafficking for the purpose of labor and commercial sexual exploitation. The projects supported by the Department of Labor aim to remove or prevent children from exploitive labor through the provision of educational and training opportunities. In addition, projects provide alternative income generation and skills training for families; workplace and community-based monitoring systems to ensure that children do not return to exploitive work; capacity building of national and local organizations to ensure sustainability; awareness raising on the hazards associated with exploitive child labor and the benefits of education and data collection and research to inform policymakers on child labor, forced labor and human trafficking. For projects focused on commercial sexual exploitation and trafficking, additional activities include provision of medical care and psychosocial services to survivors, as well as legislative and policy reform to incorporate anti-trafficking efforts at the local, national, and regional levels.

f. Interdepartmental Government Efforts

The Human Smuggling and Trafficking Center (HSTC) was formally established under Section 7202 of the *Intelligence Reform Act and Terrorism Prevention Act of 2004*. The Secretary of State, Secretary of Homeland Security, Attorney General, and members of the national Intelligence Community jointly oversee the HSTC through a high-level interagency steering group. The HSTC serves as a fusion center for information on human smuggling and trafficking, bringing together analysts, officers, and investigators from such agencies as the CIA, the Department of Justice, the Department of State, and the Department of Homeland Security. The HSTC coordinates activities with foreign governments to ensure that efforts are addressed globally, and brings together subject matter experts from the policy, law enforcement, intelligence and diplomatic arenas to leverage participating agencies' knowledge, expertise and authorities to address the global threat. HSTC regularly shares information on human trafficking, including child sex trafficking.

F. Review of Internet Safety Programs

The Act also required the Department review all its work related to programs educating the public on Internet Safety.[92] The search for federally funded programs was conducted both online and through document review. In all, 18 programs were identified, 16 of which are educational programs for children, youth, or adults. Two are federally funded research projects that include recommendations to prevent the online victimization of children.

The federally funded programs included in this inventory address a number of Internet safety issues including:

- Safety in online relationships.
- Avoiding pornography and other offensive materials.
- Copyright, plagiarism, and intellectual property theft.
- Internet citizenship.
- Cyberbullying.
- Identity theft and privacy concerns.
- Hacking and malicious programming.

The programs are designed for a variety of audiences, including children and youth, parents, teachers and other school personnel, and law enforcement. Many of the programs deliver their content through a Web site. Others make printed materials available, including lesson plans and classroom activities, books, or reports.

This inventory of federally funded Internet safety programs reveals much overlap in programs funded and much potential for collaboration among programs to ensure that they reach the widest possible audience.

Programs were deemed to be federally funded if they were entirely or largely funded with federal funds or, when funding information was not available, if the program identified itself as being the product of a federal initiative. The target audiences for programs included in the inventory are youths ages 21 and younger and parents, teachers, and leaders of youth groups (e.g., boy scouts, girl scouts, boys and girls clubs). "Internet safety" was defined broadly to include not only programs to teach children how to avoid online contact with adults who might harm them, but also programs that educate youth about online issues such as avoiding unwanted exposure to pornography, copyright and intellectual property theft, good Internet citizenship, cyberbullying, identity theft, and hacking. The term "programs" also was construed broadly to mean interactive Web sites with a didactic purpose (but not Web sites that only listed safety rules), curriculums, online games and activities, and scholarly articles or other materials with an educational focus. Major federally funded research programs on the topic of Internet safety were included because the recommendations they yield contribute to public awareness about the topic.

Web pages with lists of Internet safety rules with no other interactive content did not meet the criteria for inclusion in this inventory. Software packages marketed to parents, schools, and libraries for blocking, recording, or monitoring Internet usage by youth were also outside the scope of this inventory because they are products of private commercial enterprises.

1. Methodology of Review

The search for English-language materials was conducted both online and through document review. The search engines Google and Yahoo were used to scan for the term "Internet safety," and a list of hits was compiled for review. Programs that were linked to these sites as additional resources[93] The home pages of federal agencies and departments were included, and the page search function, if available, was used to search for the term "Internet safety." In addition, persons working in federal agencies were asked to describe their own departments' efforts in this area. In all, 18 federally funded programs were identified, 16 of which are educational programs for children, youth, or adults. Two are federally funded research projects that include recommendations to prevent the online victimization of children. (See appendix 1 for a description of all 18 federally funded programs.) Appendix 2 lists a representative (but not exhaustive) set of nonfederally funded Internet safety programs. It is not within the scope of this inventory to discuss these programs in detail or to evaluate the programs identified.

Pursuant to Pub. L. No. 108–447, this inventory was prepared in coordination with the Coordinating Council on Juvenile Justice and Delinquency Prevention. On January 7, 2005, J. Robert Flores, OJJDP Administrator and Vice Chair of the Coordinating Council, sent a letter to Coordinating Council members requesting, among other things, their cooperation in preparing this chapter. Mr. Flores also discussed the preparation of the inventory at the meeting of the Coordinating Council on March 4, 2005. OJJDP appreciates the cooperation of Council member agencies in providing and reviewing information incorporated in this chapter.

a. History of Federal Involvement in Internet Safety Programs for Youth

The federal government's first broad foray into the field of Internet safety for children was marked by the passage of the Child Online Protection Act of 1998 (COPA). COPA created a commission to "identify technological or other methods that will help reduce access by minors that is harmful to minors on the Internet." The COPA Commission was charged with evaluating the accessibility, cost, and effectiveness of technology designed to prevent children from accessing sexually explicit material over the Internet and also with assessing the possible effects on privacy of that technology. The commission released its final report in 2000, reporting on the viability of filtering and blocking services, labeling and rating services, age verification strategies, "green spaces" containing only material appropriate to children, monitoring and time-limiting technologies, acceptable-use policies and family Internet- use contracts, and options for more vigorous prosecution of persons who distribute illegal online material.

b. Programs Identified for This Inventory

The 18 programs identified through the search methodology are described below. They are primarily organized according to funder and secondarily organized by function (educational programs first, research programs second). The narrative descriptions are based on information provided in the referenced Web sites. Note that inclusion in the inventory does not constitute an endorsement. In producing this inventory, no attempt has been made to evaluate the content or effectiveness of any program.

2. U.S. Department of Justice Funded Programs

a. i-SAFE America

Program name: Contact information:	• i-SAFE America, Inc. • www.isafe.org
Funder:	• U.S. Department of Justice, Office of Juvenile Justice and • Delinquency Prevention
Audience:	• Children and youth grades K–12
Focus/scope:	• Safety in online relationships; avoiding pornography and other offensive materials; copyright, plagiarism, and intellectual property theft; Internet citizenship; cyberbullying; identity theft and privacy concerns; hacking and malicious programming
Media:	• Workbooks and Web-cast videos for students; instructor materials
Delivery:	• Classroom

i-SAFE America, Inc., a nonprofit foundation founded in 1998, is dedicated to educating and empowering youth to safely and responsibly take control of their Internet experiences. i-SAFE produces and distributes a curriculum for classroom use in grades K–12. The i-SAFE program is designed to teach students to recognize and avoid dangerous, destructive, or unlawful behavior online and to respond appropriately. The i-SAFE curriculum includes online exercises and activities, pen-and-paper activities, and class projects. Training and technical assistance for teachers are provided free of charge.

b. NetSmartz Workshop

Program name:	• NetSmartz Workshop
Contact information:	• www.netsmartz.org
Funder:	• U.S. Department of Justice, Office of Juvenile Justice and Delinquency Prevention; National Center for Missing & Exploited Children; Boys & Girls Clubs of America
Audience:	• Children and youth grades K–12
Focus/scope:	• Safety in online relationships; avoiding pornography and other offensive materials; Internet citizenship; cyberbullying; identity theft and privacy concerns; Internet "addiction"
Media:	• Internet; activity cards for group or class projects
Delivery:	• Classroom; afterschool programs; community education programs delivered by law enforcement or others; independent exploration

The NetSmartz Workshop® is an online interactive, educational safety resource from the National Center for Missing & Exploited Children® (NCMEC) and Boys & Girls Clubs of America (BGCA) for children ages 5 to 17, parents, guardians, educators, and law enforcement. The goal of the NetSmartz Workshop is to extend the safety awareness of children to prevent their victimization and increase their self-confidence whenever they go online.

c. Internet Crimes Against Children Task Forces

Program name:	• Internet Crimes Against Children Task Forces
Contact information:	• ojjdp.ncjrs.org/programs/ProgSummary.asp?pi=3
Funder:	• U.S. Department of Justice, Office of Juvenile Justice and Delinquency Prevention
Audience:	• Varies by state/regional task force; typically adults, children, and youth
Focus/scope:	• Varies by state/regional task force; may include safety in online relationships; avoiding pornography and other offensive materials; and other topics
Media:	• Varies by state/regional task force; many task forces have developed educational materials and presentations
Delivery:	• Varies by state/regional task force; typically classroom or community education programs; public service announcements

The Internet Crimes Against Children (ICAC) Task Force Program helps state and local law enforcement agencies develop an effective response to cyberenticement and child pornography cases. This help encompasses forensic and investigative components, training and technical assistance, victim services, and community education. Forty-five state and regional task forces have been established throughout the United States.

The ICAC Program was developed in response to the increasing number of children and teenagers using the Internet, the proliferation of child pornography, and the heightened online activity by predators searching for unsupervised contact with underage victims. The fiscal year 1998 Justice Appropriations Act (Pub. L. No. 105–119) directed OJJDP to create a national network of state and local law enforcement cyberunits to investigate cases of child sexual exploitation (i.e., ICAC Program). In addition to assisting law enforcement with investigations, many ICAC Task Forces also sponsor community outreach to help families understand rules for safe Internet use. Some of the ICAC Task Forces have developed their own educational materials.

d. A Parent's Guide to Internet Safety

Program name:	• A Parent's
Contact information:	• www.fbi.gov/publications/pguide/pguidee.htm • Corresponding list of safety rules for children posted at www.fbi.gov/kids/k5th/safety2.htm
Funder:	• U.S. Department of Justice, Federal Bureau of Investigation, Crimes Against Children Program
Audience:	• Parents
Focus/scope:	• Safety in online relationships; avoiding pornography and other offensive materials
Media:	• Online guide
Delivery:	• Individual use by parents

The Federal Bureau of Investigation's Crimes Against Children Program produced *A Parent's Guide to Internet Safety* to inform parents of the risks children face online of encountering adults who might sexually exploit them and how to recognize child behaviors that might indicate the child is at risk for being exploited. The guide is available in hard copy and online at www.fbi.gov/publications/pguide/pguidee.htm . The FBI also posts a list of safety rules for children using the Internet at www.fbi.gov/kids/k5th/safety2.htm.

e. Cybercitizen Awareness Program

Program name:	• Cybercitizen Awareness Program
Contact information:	• www.cybercitizenship.org/aboutus/aboutus.html
Funder:	• U.S. Department of Justice with the Information Technology Association of America
Audience:	• Children and youth; parents
Focus/scope:	• Cyberethics; Internet citizenship/"netiquette"; cybercrime; identity theft and privacy concerns; copyright, plagiarism, and intellectual property theft; hacking and malicious programming
Media:	• Online
Delivery:	• Self-exploration

The Cybercitizen Awareness Program is intended to educate children and young adults about the dangers and consequences of cybercrime. By reaching out to parents and teachers, the program is designed to establish a broad sense of responsibility and community in an effort to develop in young people smart, ethical, and socially conscious online behavior. The Cybercitizen Partnership was created with a grant from the U.S. Department of Justice and is managed by the Information Technology Association Foundation.

f. Cyberethics for Kids/Cyberethics for Teachers

Program name:	• Cyberethics for Kids/Cyberethics for Teachers
Contact information:	• www.cybercrime.gov/rules/kidinternet.htm and www.cybercrime.gov/rules/lessonplan1.htm
Funder:	• U.S. Department of Justice, Criminal Division
Audience:	• Children and youth; separate component for teachers
Focus/scope:	• Identity theft and privacy concerns; copyright, plagiarism, and intellectual property theft; hacking and malicious programming; safety in online relationships; avoiding pornography and other offensive materials; cyberethics; Internet citizenship/"netiquette"
Media:	• Online
Delivery:	• Self-exploration for children and youth; lesson plans for classroom presentation

The Cyberethics for Kids site presents information for youth about good "net citizenship" and addresses hacking, intellectual property theft through illegal file trading and copyright violations, plagiarism, using others' passwords and accounts without their permission, and malicious programming (worms and viruses). A related site, Cyberethics for Teachers, offers an elementary or middle school lesson plan on the same topics. Both sites discuss safe "chatting" online and appropriate responses to encountering material or people online that make a child uncomfortable.

g. ChildSafeNet

Program name:	• ChildSafeNet
Contact information:	• www.childsafenet.org
Funder:	• U.S. Department of Justice, Office of Juvenile Justice and Delinquency Prevention
Audience:	• Law enforcement; parents
Focus/scope:	• Preventing sexual abuse of children via Internet exploitation
Media:	• Online; community programs
Delivery:	• Self-exploration for parents; community programs by law enforcement

The mission of ChildSafeNet is to proactively combat the sexual abuse and exploitation of children and to educate local communities about risks to children, both on the Internet and in the community. ChildSafeNet's signature program, Protecting Children Against Sex

Offenders (P'CASO), represents a collaborative public/private partnership between ChildSafeNet, Inc., a 501(c) (3) nonprofit organization, and its first law enforcement partner, the Fairfax County [Virginia] Police Department, with funds from the Office of Juvenile Justice and Delinquency Prevention.

3. Federal Trade Commission and Department of Commerce Funded Programs

a. Kidz Privacy

Program name:	• Kidz Privacy
Contact information:	• www.ftc.gov/bcp/conline/edcams/kidzprivacy • The FTC also posts a list of suggested rules for family Internet use at www.ftc.gov/bcp/conline/pubs/online/sitesee.htm.
Funder:	• Federal Trade Commission
Audience:	• Parents, children, and youth
Focus/scope:	• Identity theft and privacy concerns; plagiarism and intellectual property theft
Media:	• Online
Delivery:	• Self-exploration

The Kidz Privacy site offers information tailored to youth and parents about the Children's Online Privacy Protection Act of 1998. As described by the Kidz Privacy Web site, the Act prohibits the release of personal information collected from a child in identifiable form by an operator for any purpose. An exception is made when this information is provided to a person other than the operator who provides support for the internal operations of the Web site and does not disclose or use that information for any other purpose. In addition, the Act makes it a violation to make personal information public if that information was collected from a child by a Web site or service directed toward children. The site offers rules for youth and families to follow to avoid disclosing private information online that might put them at risk.

B. Kids.Us

Program name:	• kids.us
Contact information:	• www.kids.us
Funder:	• U.S. Department of Commerce, National Telecommunications and Information Administration
Audience:	• Children and youth
Focus/scope:	• Safety in online relationships; avoiding pornography and other offensive materials
Media:	• Online
Delivery:	• Self-exploration

The kids.us domain went live in fall 2003 to provide a moderated online forum for children ages 13 and younger. Created by the Dot Kids Implementation and Efficiency Act of 2002 (Pub. L. No. 107–317), it is designed to be a youth-friendly Web space. A private firm, NeuStar, developed the kids.us content policy, monitors domain content, and enforces the content policy on behalf of the federal government.

4. U.S. Department of Education Funded Programs

Program name:	• List of Internet safety resources
Contact information:	• www.ed.gov/about/offices/list/os/technology/safety.html
Funder:	• U.S. Department of Education, Office of Educational Research and • Improvement, • Office of Educational Technology
Audience:	• Parents, teachers, youth, children
Focus/scope:	• Safety in online relationships; avoiding pornography and other offensive materials; privacy concerns
Media:	• Online
Delivery:	• Self-exploration

5. Federal Communications Commission Funded Program: E-rate

Program name:	• E-rate
Contact information:	• www.sl.universalservice.org
Funder: Audience:	• Federal Communications Commission • Schools and libraries
Focus/scope:	• Discount Internet access available to schools and libraries that certify that safety measures are in place to protect children from harmful Internet content
Media:	• n/a
Delivery:	• Makes discount Internet access available to schools and libraries

Under the E-rate program, schools and libraries are afforded Internet access at discounted fees for students and patrons. According to the E-rate Web site, the Children's Internet Protection Act (CIPA), enacted by Congress in December 2000, governs access to E-rate funds. E-rate recipients must certify that they have certain Internet safety measures in place. These include measures to block or filter pictures that (a) are obscene, (b) contain child pornography, or (c) are otherwise harmful to minors.

6. U.S. Department of Agriculture Funded Program: Technology 4-H

Program name:	• Technology in 4-H
Contact information:	• www.4-h.org • Lists Internet safety rules at its Web site, 4-h.org/index.php?option=com_content&task=view&id=97&Itemid=27 •

(Continued)

	• Discusses home security for your identity and your computer at 4-h.org/index.php?option=com_content&task=view&id=40&Itemid=53
Funder:	• U.S. Department of Agriculture, 4-H
Audience:	• Children and youth
Focus/scope:	• Safety in online relationships; avoiding pornography and other offensive materials; cyberbullying; privacy concerns
Media:	• Online
Delivery:	• Self-exploration; organized 4-H activities

The 4-H program disseminates information about Internet education and safety through its technology programming. The Department of Agriculture's Rural Utility Service also posts Internet safety tips at www.usda.gov/rus/educate/tel_safe.htm.

7. U.S. Department of Health and Human Services Funded Program: 4Girls Health: How To Be Safety Savvy

Program name:	• 4Girls Health: How To Be Safety Savvy
Contact information:	• www.4girls.gov/safety/internet.htm
Funder:	• U.S. Department of Health and Human Services, Office on • Women's Health
Audience:	• Girls ages 10–16
Focus/scope:	• Safety in online relationships; avoiding pornography and other offensive materials; cyberethics; privacy and personal information on the Internet; cyberbullying
Media:	• Online
Delivery:	• Self-exploration

This Web site for adolescent girls includes a list of Internet rules, a quiz about Internet safety, and an FAQ-style document about Internet issues.

In addition, the Substance Abuse and Mental Health Services Administration, a unit within the U.S. Department of Health and Human Services, has Internet safety tips listed at www.mentalhealth.org/kidsarea/internettips.asp.

8. U.S. Department of Homeland Security

A search for Internet safety programs funded by the Department of Homeland Security (DHS) revealed no such programs. However, the Department's Federal Emergency Management Agency (FEMA) lists tips for children and parents on Internet safety on its FEMA for Kids Web site: www.fema.gov/kids/on_safety.htm.

9. U.S. Department of Defense Funded Program: Safekids

Program name:	• Safekids
Contact information:	• www.ncis.navy.mil/info/safekids.cfm
Funder:	• U.S. Department of Defense, U.S. Naval Criminal Investigative Service
Audience:	• Parents
Focus/scope:	• Safety in online relationships; avoiding pornography and other offensive materials
Media:	• Online
Delivery:	• PowerPoint briefing for parents

The Safekids Web site includes lists of Internet rules and a downloadable PowerPoint presentation for parents, which can be used in a community education setting. Resources for military families who encounter Internet predators also are listed.

The Navy Morale, Welfare and Recreation unit also posts an Internet Safety Kit with resources for children and parents at www.mwr.navy.mil/mwrprgms/y2tinternet.htm.

10. National Aeronautics and Space Administration (NASA) Funded Program: NASA explores Cybersafety

Program name:	• NASAexplores Cybersafety
Contact information:	• www.nasaexplores.nasa.gov/show_k4_teacher_st.php?id=030221120608
Funder:	• National Aeronautics and Space Administration
Audience:	• K–4 students and their teachers
Focus/scope:	• Safety in online relationships; avoiding pornography and other offensive materials
Media:	• Online
Delivery:	• Teacher lesson plans; student worksheets

This lesson on cybersafety is posted in the NASA Explores section of NASA's education Web pages.

11. Interagency/Federal–State Collaboration Funded Program

"I Keep Safe"—Faux Pas, the Techno Cat

Program name:	• "I Keep Safe"—Faux Pas, the Techno Cat
Contact information:	• www.ikeepsafe.org
Funder:	• "I Keep Safe" is state funded and managed by a nonprofit organization. The organization sought the input of, and continues to collaborate with, federal agencies and the National Crime Prevention Council, including the and the U.S. Department of Justice.
Audience:	• Parents and children (grades 2–4)

(Continued)

Focus/scope:	• Safety in online relationships; privacy concerns
Media:	• Online; hard-cover storybook available
Delivery:	• Online games; printable workbooks and puzzles; hard-cover storybook. Future plans include school programs with costumed characters.

Launched February 28, 2005, "I Keep Safe" is the creation of a coalition of the spouses of 47 state governors and federal and private agencies. The program will expand from online delivery to a traveling cast of characters who visit schools to deliver the Internet safety message.

12. Congressionally Mandated - Federally Funded Research

National Academy of Sciences Study: Youth, Pornography, and the Internet

Program name:	• *Youth, Pornography, and the Internet*
Contact information:	• books.nap.edu/html/youth_internet
Funder:	• Federally funded study conducted by the National Academy of Sciences
Audience:	• Adults, researchers, practitioners
Focus/scope:	• Safety in online relationships; avoiding pornography and other offensive materials
Media:	• Book in print; also available online
Delivery:	• N/A

This federally funded study was conducted by the Committee on Tools and Strategies for Protecting Kids from Pornography and Their Applicability to Other Inappropriate Internet Content, part of the Computer Science and Telecommunications Board, National Academy of Sciences. The committee report, published in 2002, examines options for protecting children from inappropriate sexually explicit material on the Internet and discusses social and educational strategies, technological tools, and policy options for how to teach children to make safe and appropriate decisions about what they see and experience on the Internet.

13. U.S. Department of Justice-Funded Research

Crimes against Children Research Center Juvenile Online Victimization Study

Program name:	• Crimes against Children Research Center Juvenile Online Victimization Study
Contact information:	• www.unh.edu/ccrc/NJOV_info_page.htm
Funder:	• U.S. Department of Justice, Office of Juvenile Justice and Delinquency Prevention
Audience:	• Adults, researchers, practitioners

(Continued)

Focus/scope:	• Safety in online relationships; avoiding pornography and other offensive materials; cyberethics; identity theft and privacy concerns; Internet "addiction"; cyberbullying
Media:	• Report in print; also available online
Delivery:	• N/A

The Office of Juvenile Justice and Delinquency Prevention and the National Center for Missing & Exploited Children fund the University of New Hampshire's Crimes Against Children Research Center Juvenile Online Victimization (N–JOV) Study. The N–JOV study collected information from a national sample of law enforcement agencies about the characteristics of Internet sex crimes committed against minors and the numbers of arrests for these crimes during a 1-year period. The resulting N–JOV statistics about online victimization of children were published in 2004 and are the most widely cited statistics in this area.

Table 1.F. Ederally Funded Internet Safety Programs[94]

Program/ Product Name and Contact Information	For Kids	For Parents	For Schools and Teachers	For Others	Safety in Online Relationships	Avoiding Pornography and Other Offensive Materials	Copyright, Plagiarism, and Intellectual Property Theft	Cyberethics/InternetCitizenship	Cyberbullying	Identity Theft and Privacy Concerns	Hacking and Malicious Programming	Internet "Addiction"
i-SAFE America, Inc. www.isafe.org	√		√	Law enforce-ment	√	√	√	√	√	√	√	
NetSmartz Workshop www.netsmartz.org	√	√	√	Boys & Girls Clubs of America	√	√		√	√	√		√
Internet Crimes Against Children Task Forces www.ojjdp.ncjrs.org/programs/ProgSummary.asp?pi=3	√	√	√	General comm-unity education and outreach	Varies by local task force							
A Parent's Guide to Internet Safety www.fbi.gov/publications/pguide/pguidee.htm	√				√	√						
FBI Safety Tips for Kids www.fbi.gov/kids/k5th/safety1.htm	√			√	√							

(Continued)

Program/ Product Name and Contact Information	For Kids	For Parents	For Schools and Teachers	For Others	Safety in Online Relationships	Avoiding Pornography and Other Offensive Materials	Copyright, Plagiarism, and Intellectual Property Theft	Cyberethics/InternetCitizenship	Cyberbullying	Identity Theft and Privacy Concerns	Hacking and Malicious Programming	Internet "Addiction"
Cybercitizen Awareness Program www.cybercitizenship.org/aboutus/aboutus.html	√	√					√	√		√	√	
Cyberethics for Kids www.cybercrime.gov/rules/kidinternet.htm	√				√	√	√	√		√	√	
Cyberethics for Teachers www.cybercrime.gov/rules/lessonplan1.htm			√	√	√	√	√	√	√			
Childsafenet www.childsafenet.org	√		Law enfor-ceement	√								
Kidz Privacy www.ftc.gov/bcp/conline/edcams/kidzprivacy	√	√	√				√			√		
kids.us www.kids.us	√				√	√						
Parents Guide to the Internet www.ed.gov/pubs/parents/internet/index.html		√			√	√				√		
E-rate www.sl.universalservice.org	√		√	Library		√						
Technology in 4-H www.4-h.org	√			4-H	√	√			√	√		
4Girls Health: How to be Safety Savvy www.4girls.gov/safety/internet.htm	√				√	√		√	√	√		
Safekids www.ncis.navy.mil/info/safekids.cfm		√			√	√						
NASAexplores Cybersafety www.nasaexplores.nasa.gov/show_k4	√		√		√	√						

Table 1. (Continued)

Program/ Product Name and Contact Information	For Kids	For Parents	For Schools and Teachers	For Others	Safety in Online Relationships	Avoiding Pornography and Other Offensive	Materials Copyright, Plagiarism, and Intellectual Property Theft	Cyberethics/InternetCitizenship	Cyberbullying	Identity Theft and Privacy Concerns	Hacking and Malicious Programming	Internet "Addiction"
_teacher_st.php?id=030221120608												
I Keep Safe—Faux Pas, the Techno Cat www.ikeepsafe.org	√	√	√		√					√		
Youth, Pornography, and the Internet books.nap.edu/html/youth_internet				Researc-hers, Practitio-ners, interest-ed adults	√	√						
Crimes Against Children Research Center Juvenile Online Victimization Study www.unh.edu/ccrc/NJOV_info_page.htm				Researc-hers, Practitio-nerrs, interested adults	√	√		√	√	√		√

Table 2. Sample of Private Nonprofit, Commercial, and State and Local Resources Focused on Internet Safety[95]

Program/ Product Name	Producer	For Kids	For Parents	For Schools	For Others	Web Site
Chatdanger	Childnet International	√				www.chatdanger.com
Copyright Kids	Copyright Society of the U.S.A.	√	√	√		www.copyrightkids.org
CyberAngels	Guardian Angels, Inc.	√	√	√		www.cyberangels.org
CyberNetiquette Comix	Disney Online	√	√			disney.go.com/cybersafety

Table 2. (Continued)

Program/ Product Name	Producer	For Kids	For Parents	For Schools	For Others	Web Site
CyberSafety	CyberSafety.us	√	√			www.cybersafety.us/step1.html
CyberSmart! Curriculum	CyberSmart!® Education Company	√		√		www.cybersmart.org
GetNetWise Online Safety Guide	GetNetWise	√	√			kids.getnetwise.org/safetyguide
GoCyberCamp	University of Minnesota, University of Nebraska—Lincoln, North Carolina State University, Zope Corporation, Ohio State University, New Mexico State University	√			4-H	www.gocybercamp.org
ProtectKids.com	Enough Is Enough	√	√			www.protectkids.com
responsiblenetizen.org	Center for Safe and Responsible Internet Use	√		√	Technology planning organizations	www.responsiblenetizen.org
Internet Safety and Safe Surfing for Kids	ProtectYourKids .info		√			www.safesurfing.itgo.com
Internet Safety Awareness	Illinois State Library, a Division of the Office of the Secretary of State, using federal LSTA funding	√	√			www.internet-safety.org/scripts/content.cgi?template=default&args=guides,introduction
Internet Safety for Teachers and Students	Center for Innovation in Engineering and Science Education, Stevens Institute of Technology	√	√	√	Librarians	www.k12science.org/internetsafety.html
Kidscomjr. Internet Safety Game	Circle 1 Network	√	√			www.kidscomjr.com/games/safety/safety.html
Netforce		√				www.geocities.com/net_enforce

Table 2. (Continued)

Program/ Product Name	Producer	For Kids	For Parents	For Schools	For Others	Web Site
NetSafeKids	National Academy of Sciences		√			www.nap.edu/netsafekids/res_helpful.html
Online Guardians™	OnlineGuardians.org		√			www.onlineguardians.org/parents.htm
P2P PATROL: Peer-to-Peer Parents and Teens React On Line	Distributed Computing Industry Association (DCIA)		√		Distributed computing companies	www.p2ppatrol.com
PBSKids.org Get Your Web License	Public Broadcasting Service (PBS)	√				www.pbskids.org/license
Planet CRuSH/Project CRuSH	TOUCH Community Services	√				www.planetcrush.org
Play It Cyber Safe	Business Software Alliance	√	√	√		www.playitcybersafe.com
Safe Surfing Tips for Teens	Nemours Foundation	√				www.kidshealth.org/teen/safety/ safebasics/internet_safety.html
SafeKids.com SafeTeens.com	NetFamilyNews.org	√	√			www.safekids.com
staysafeonline.info	National Cyber Security Alliance, a public-private partnership	√	√		Small businesses	www.staysafeonline.info
WebMonkey for Kids	Lycos, Inc./ Carnegie Mellon University	√	√			webmonkey.wired.com/webmonkey/ kids/planning/safety.html
Web Wise Kids	Web Wise Kids	√	√			www.webwisekids.org
What Can I Do To Be Net Safe?	University of Oklahoma Campus Police	√				www.ou.edu/oupd/kidsafe/inet.htm
Wired Kidz	Wired Safety	√				www.wiredkidz.org/kids.html
Wired Teens	Wired Safety	√	√			www.wiredteens.org
WiredSafety	WiredSafety	√	√	√	Law enforcement	www.wiredsafety.org
Yahooligans! Parents' Guide	Yahoo! Inc.		√			www.yahooligans.yahoo.com/docs/safety

G. Results of the 2008 Project Safe Childhood Conference

The 2008 National Project Safe Childhood Conference was held September 23-26 2008 in Columbus, OH. Over 1,400 attendees participated in the PSC Conference, including 455 attendees from federal agencies. The conference agenda included 119 separate lecture and 59 hands-on computer lab workshops for prosecutors, law enforcement, community educators, advocates, and child welfare professionals. Over 120 national and international instructors presented the conference on topics including best practices for working with child victims, new community awareness campaigns, emerging technology to improve child exploitation investigations, winning prosecutorial strategies, and offender characteristics and modus operandi.

The conference was very well received by participants. Table 1 below shows some of the 2008 Project Safe Childhood National Conference evaluation results. The conference program is attached to this chapter in Appendix 2.[96]

This program, which has been funded by the Department for many years, is critical to the continued success of the Department's efforts to prevent and interdict child exploitation.

H. Child Exploitation Computer Forensics

As noted in the Threat Assessment, some of the most egregious and threatening child exploitation crimes are facilitated by the Internet and the use of computers and other digital media. The forensic analysis of the computers is the most important aspect of the investigation. Computer forensic examinations that provide investigators and prosecutors the information they need – a when they need it – are absolutely critical to the investigation and prosecution of these serious crimes. Investigation of these crimes is not simple, however, due to the challenges that ever-advancing technology presents to law enforcement.

Ensuring that timely and adequate computer forensics analysis is provided in child exploitation investigations and prosecutions has become increasingly difficult. The sheer volume of the increase of persons using computers and the Internet is one reason. The number of U.S. households having at least one computer rose from 22.9% in 1993 to 61.8% in 2003. It is estimated that today more than 80% of U.S. households have a computer. In 1997, the percentage of households with Internet access was 18%. By 2009, that percentage had increased to 68.7%. Additionally, it is increasingly easy and inexpensive for individuals to acquire and store large amounts of data. Digital media storage capacity has soared while the cost of storing the data has plummeted. For example, the cost of storing one gigabyte of data in 1995 was approximately $1,000. By 2009, terabyte (1,000 gigabyte) hard drives for home use were available and the cost to store one gigabyte of data approximately 10¢. Further, as described in the Threat Assessment, the wide variety of ever-changing/evolving technologies being used by offenders seriously challenge law enforcement's ability to keep pace.

Table 1. Participant Evaluations of 2008 Project Safe Childhood Conference (N=939)

	Percent of Favorable Responses from participants
"The conference program was relevant to my needs."	100%
"I would attend the conference next year."	97%
I would recommend the conference to others in my field."	97%

Source: Fox Valley Technical College

1. State and Local Agencies

The majority of computer forensic examinations conducted in child exploitation investigations are performed by State and local law enforcement agencies. Of the more than 17,000 State, local, and tribal law enforcement agencies in the U.S., more than 2,500 are members or affiliates of one of the 61 Internet Crimes Against Children Task Forces. The ICAC Task Forces have demonstrated a dramatic increase in the number of computer forensic examinations they have conducted. In 2007, they reported nearly 10,500 computer forensic examinations. ICAC computer forensic capacity was increased in 2007 through targeted grants to 13 of the then-59 ICAC Task Forces, totaling $2.6 million, for that purpose. These grants, which expanded capacity at roughly one fourth of the ICAC Task Forces, had a direct impact – in 2008, ICAC Task Forces reported 14,339 computer forensic examinations in 2008 and 19,269 in 2009. In short, following the issuance of capacity-increasing grants, the ICAC Task Forces performed about twice as many forensic examinations in 2009.

2. FBI Computer Analysis Response Team and Regional Computer Forensic Laboratory Programs

Child exploitation investigators, as well as other federal, state and local law enforcement agencies rely upon the FBI's Computer Analysis Response Team (CART) and Regional Computer Forensic Laboratory (RCFL) programs to provide digital forensic search and examination support, in support of their investigations. Nominally, the Computer Analysis Response Team (CART) is an organizational component of the FBI's Digital Evidence Section (DES) that began in 1988 under the FBI Laboratory Division as one of the earliest computer forensic examiner groups in the country. Today, the term CART generically refers to three groups: 1) the CART Forensic Analysis Unit (CART-FAU) that staffs and manages the FBI's Digital Evidence Laboratory (DEL) which is fully accredited by American Society of Crime Laboratory Director's Laboratory Accreditation Board (ASCLD-LAB) and assists in setting written, tested, verified, vetted, defensible forensic procedures and protocols for all CART-certified personnel that are designed to meet and exceed the expert witness technical/scientific admissibility requirements of *Daubert v. Merrill Dow Pharmaceuticals, Inc.*, 509 U.S. 579 (1993) and its progeny; 2) The CART Operational Support Unit (CART-OSU) which supports and equips but does not manage CART-certified digital evidence forensic examiners but who are annually proficiency tested, monitored and periodically trained by the DES, and; 3) The CART Field Examiners, themselves, who are trained, certified, tested and monitored by CART-OSU and other DES units but are exclusively supervised and controlled by the management staff of each individual FBI Field Division in which they are located.

In the FBI, there are approximately 225 CART-certified digital evidence forensic examiners dispersed at nearly 98 FBI locations, approximately 45% of which are sworn FBI Agents while the remainder are professional support staff. An additional 200 or so state and local task force officers and professional support from approximately 130 police agencies are also "CARTcertified" and are located at 16 Regional Computer Forensic Laboratories (RCFLs) geographically dispersed around the country.

The RCFL Program is built on partnerships between the FBI and other law enforcement agencies at the federal, state and local levels operating within a geographic area. An RCFL is a computer forensics laboratory and training center devoted to the forensic examination of digital evidence in support of criminal investigations. The RCFL Program currently manages a network of 14 existing laboratories in major cities across the United States with two more labs due to open by FY 2011. The primary forensics responsibilities of an RCFL are to conduct a comprehensive examination of digital evidence, provide a complete and timely report to the contributor, provide testimony as needed, and to generally act as a regional focal point for digital evidence issues. RCFL Examiners can extract information from a computer system and/or digital media, and can recover deleted, encrypted, or damaged files. Any or all of this information may be useful during discovery, depositions, or litigation. Over 130 different state and local agencies participate in and have personnel assigned to a RCFL.

The RCFL Program has supported a substantial number of investigations over the last several years. For example, from FY 2007 to FY 2009 the RCFL Program achieved a 60% increase in the total number of examinations completed for investigations relating to crimes against children – increasing from 1,386 to 2,194. The RCFL Program is also far reaching in that it has conducted examinations for over 650 separate state and local law enforcement agencies.

Resources from the Department of Justice's Asset Forfeiture Fund (AFF) have enabled the RCFL Program to fight the backlog of forensic service requests at the RCFLs by providing overtime reimbursement to sworn law enforcement staff detailed to RCFLs. In the National Academy of Sciences (NAS) report, "Strengthening Forensic Science in the United States: A Path Forward" (page 1-4), backlog statistics from the 2005 Bureau of Justice Statistics (BJS) census report are cited. Specifically, the NAS report states that:

> *"... in a typical publicly funded crime laboratory ended the year with a backlog of about 401 requests for services, received another 4,328 such requests, and completed 3,980 of them. The average backlog has risen since the 2002 census, with nearly 20 percent of all requests backlogged by year end."*

In comparison to the trend at general (*i.e.*, non-computer-forensic) crime laboratories, the RCFL Program has steadily reduced the overall backlog in digital forensic exams at RCFLs over the last 3 years. As a result, RCFL statistics show a drop of 36% from FY 2007 – FY 2009. In FY 2009 the total number of service requests for FY 2009 was 5,616. The total number of backlogged cases at the end of that year was 506 - resulting in a backlog of just 9% of all cases received.

Despite the sustained efforts from both the CART and RCFL Programs, FBI studies indicate that there have not been enough trained, certified, annually proficiency tested, peer-reviewed, monitored digital evidence forensic examiners or laboratories to meet the growing demand for forensic analysis. With more than five thousand independent state/ local law enforcement agencies in the United States, 16 RCFLs and dozens of ICAC task forces with non-laboratory "forensic capacity" to help address the growing volume of data and requests associated with child exploitation investigations, there is still a need for additional resources to handle the forensic processing and analysis of digital evidence. To this end, the FBI has been exploring and utilizing a number of strategies to increase the number of trained, digital evidence forensic examiners both for its own investigations and for the RCFLs.

The FBI believes that providing training to the law enforcement community both builds the digital forensics capacity and also reduces the burden on CART/RCFL examiners. ImageScan is a user-friendly software tool developed by the FBI CART Program and deployed in conjunction with the RCFLs at CART offices and RCFLs across the country. It is specifically designed to locate graphic image files such as child pornography–without altering any data on the electronic device. Through the CART/RCFL Training Program, which provides training to Law Enforcement Personnel free of charge, ImageScan software and training have been provided to over 10,000 Law Enforcement Personnel throughout the United States in the past 6 years.

There are numerous free training initiatives the RCFL Program uses to educate the law enforcement community on a variety of topics ranging from the use of the freely distributed ImageScan software, to distributing free field guides on handling digital evidence to providing free web-based world-wide training events in handling mobile devices properly. The use of free preview tools such as ImageScan and DriveQuest provides investigators and prosecutors with more actionable information early on in the investigation. The strategy of providing free, continuing education, over time, will minimize the need later in the investigation to absorb additional forensic resources for "full" forensic examination and thus reduce the overall backlog.

Other initiatives from the CART and RCFL programs that have enhanced service offerings while increasing efficiency with very limited resources include a network of self service kiosks at FBI field offices and RCFLs around the country. Cell Phone Investigative Kiosks (CPIK) are available to all law enforcement officers wishing to merely extract readily retrievable data from cell phones, such as contacts, calendars and recent calls. The cell phone kiosk allows users to extract data from a cell phone, insert that data into a report, and burn the report to a CD or DVD in as little as 30 minutes. In FY 2009, the Heart of America RCFL (HARCFL) was able to reduce its backlog by 60 percent in part by making extensive use of their Cell Phone Kiosk for cell phones and videos. Currently 13 of the 14 operational RCFLs have these kiosks. The CART and RCFL programs are also prototyping Loose Media Kiosks (LMK) in testing at WFO and San Diego RCFL (SDRCFL). This tool enables investigators to quickly review removable media in a forensically sound manner and analyze evidence related to child exploitation investigations to determine its value in an investigation without waiting for the availability of a forensic examiner.

The FBI is also developing new tools, including, DriveQuest, which is now nearing completion of it development phase and should begin BETA field testing soon. DriveQuest is a program that has been designed to provide investigators with new, configurable, capabilities while conducting consent or triage searches on-scene including; text string search on user defined dictionaries to user defined areas of a computer system, view and search through Internet History Files, view Windows Registry Information, and search and Identify Encryption, Data Hiding, and Data Destruction Utilities.

3. U.S. Postal Inspection Service Digital Evidence Unit

The Digital Evidence Unit (DEU) has offices throughout the country. The unit is led by an Assistant Inspector in Charge located at Dulles, Virginia and is comprised of Inspector Program Managers, Forensic Computer Analysts and Ad Hoc analysts domiciled in each of the eighteen Inspection Service Field Divisions. In addition, there are Audio/Video Forensic Analysts located at the USPIS National Forensic Laboratory.

The DEU is the principal group responsible for the collection, preservation, and examination of computer digital evidence in support of all Inspection Service investigations. Digital evidence analysts are tasked with examining computer evidence and any digital media for information or data pertinent to Postal Inspection Service investigations. Examples of cases that may incorporate this type of evidence are: child pornography/exploitation, homicide, rape, suicide, mail theft, fraud, identity theft, or other related crimes against the Postal Service. Approximately 26% of the digital forensic work conducted by the DEU involves child exploitation cases. In FY 2008, the DEU conducted 269 child exploitation forensic examinations; in FY 2009, it conducted 260; and in the first six months of FY 2010, it has conducted 105. In addition to processing cases, the Digital Evidence Unit is available for technical advice and assistance in seizing and preserving evidence at the crime scene.

4. ICE Computer Forensics Program

The ICE Computer Forensics Program (CFP) was formalized under the legacy U.S. Customs Service in 1997 under the Office of Investigations. The ICE CFP continues to operate under the ICE Office of Investigations as a Section within the ICE Cyber Crimes Center (C3).

The Computer Forensics Section (CFS) provides programmatic oversight, equipment, technical support, guidance and training to the entire ICE Computer Forensics Program (CFP). The ICE CFP is comprised of ICE Special Agents and Criminal Research Officers, trained and equipped to conduct analysis of digital evidence in furtherance of criminal investigations. The successful investigation and prosecution of criminal violations by ICE is largely dependent on the ability to quickly seize, process, and analyze evidentiary digital data obtained from seized electronic devices and digital media. To meet the goals and objectives of the overall ICE mission, the ICE CFS draws upon a long-standing, comprehensive training curriculum that provides Computer Forensics Agents/Analysts (CFA) with basic and advanced computer forensics training skills. To support the CFP, the CFS also conducts research and development and initiates projects in new and challenging technologies. The CFS continually procures software, equipment, supplies, upgrades, storage media, and new digital forensic equipment to support the CFP in meeting the demands posed by these ever-changing technologies. The CFS also monitors and tracks the efficiency and production of the CFP and responds to requests for assistance and operational support. The CFS promotes continuing education, such as professional and industry-standard certification initiatives, in an effort to ensure that CFAs in the field are trained and certified in the most current computer forensics techniques. There are currently 240 trained Computer Forensics Agents in 105 field offices worldwide.

The Treasury Computer Forensics Training Program (TCFTP) is at the core of the ICE CFP and is a joint training initiative funded by the Treasury Executive Office of Asset Forfeiture (TEOAF). The TCFTP is comprised of the respective computer forensics and training programs of ICE, the U.S. Secret Service, and Internal Revenue Service. Since the inception of the TCFTP in 1997, approximately 325 ICE Special Agents have been trained.

In FY 2005, ICE initiated a Regional Computer Forensic Storage Program with funding from a Congressional earmark. During the past four years, ICE has provided funding for the project, which has allowed for its continued expansion. There are currently 13 operational and interconnected storage locations nationwide: C3, Newark, Tampa, Detroit, Chicago, Houston, Denver, Los Angeles, Seattle, San Diego, Boston, Miami and San Juan.

In 2007 there were over 3 billion mobile phone subscribers in the world. With the popularity of smartphones, iPhones and wireless internet communication, that number has grown and the amount of data contained within a mobile device has also grown. To keep up with this evolving technology the CFP has created a two tier system of analyzing mobile devices. In FY 2008, equipment was issued to every ICE office with at least one CFA. The agents that have this equipment are to be utilized to perform the analysis of mobile devices in their Area of Responsibility (AOR). If the agent cannot acquire the necessary data or the device is not supported by the tools they have, then the device should be sent to the CFA that has advanced training within their SAC AOR. Every SAC office has at least one CFA with advanced mobile device training and tools, within their AOR. In FY 2009, the CFP trained and equipped over 40 CFA's in mobile device forensics. The goal of the mobile devices program is to continue to train as many CFA's as possible in advanced mobile devices data extraction and analysis techniques.

Digital data analysis efforts continue to be a critical project under the CFS. The Pathfinder program has effectively supported numerous field investigations that have required the ability to search vast amounts of digital data for evidentiary content. It is used to organize and then search through seized evidence data, primarily on cases with large amounts of data. This data is typically electronic evidence files contained on hard drives, CDs, or other storage mediums. This project has recently supported national child pornography investigations, major corruption investigations, Counter Proliferation Investigations (CPI), and numerous worksite enforcement operations.

The CFS is responsible for the development of the policies and procedures associated with the Computer Forensics Program. The CFS also provides guidance to the field on legal, technical, procedural and other issues related to the CFP. The CFS is also responsible for the development of the Computer Forensics Handbook.

As password and encryption technology becomes more available and easier for the average user to implement, it has become necessary for the CFS to development a program to assist the field in investigations where passwords and encryption are encountered. The CFS currently utilizes a powerful array of computers, mathematical accelerators and PlayStation 3s, capable of generating nearly four million passwords per second for data decryption.

The CFS can assist field offices with reducing backlogs by coordinating assistance among CFA's located throughout various SAC Offices. The CFS can also conduct computer forensics examinations at C3 for offices without a CFA, to help reduce backlog or provide additional technical assistance in support of field investigations. The CFS manages the hard drive repair program for active investigations. In situations where a CFA encounters a hard drive or other type of media that has been damaged beyond their ability to fix, the CFS will assist in having the drive repaired when possible, and returning the recovered information back to the field for analysis. The CFS also utilizes equipment that can repair scratched or otherwise damaged CD/DVDs. The CFS has the capability to assist in processing large volumes of CD/DVDs and preparing them for analysis by the field.

The ICE Computer Forensics Program has seen a significant increase in the amount of data presented for examination. In 2004, the ICE CFP processed over 22,000 pieces of digital media, totally 73TB (Terabytes) of data. Compare that to 2009, in which the ICE CFP processed nearly 30,000 pieces of media and 824TB (Terabytes) of data. While this is a 36% increase in the number of pieces of media processed, it is a 1029% increase in the amount of data processed over the same time period. It is anticipated that the ICE CFP will process over 1,100TB (Terabytes) in FY2010.

IV. Fighting the Threat Going Forward

While the Department has vigorously fought all aspects of child exploitation, much more work remains to be done. This work includes better coordination among all the nation's investigators, better training for investigators and prosecutors, advancing law enforcement's technological capabilities to stay one step ahead of the exploiters, and better research to help us understand the abusers of our children in order to make more informed decisions on deterrence, incarceration, and sex offender monitoring. It also includes an expanded commitment to public awareness and community outreach.

Ever-changing technologies and tactics by offenders demand nimble and innovative training for law enforcement. The Threat Assessment revealed a growing problem that will require more investment in investigators, prosecutors, technology, tools, and research to search out and find offenders. The market that demands younger victims, violent images, and on-demand sexual assaults must be diminished. The Threat Assessment revealed troubling links between those who traffic in child pornography and those who participate in the production of the images or molest children offline. Well-trained investigators are critical to finding and arresting those who profit, in money or otherwise, from the pain of our children.

The Department's goals and priorities include: (1) broad goals to direct the National Strategy; (2) more specific goals to address the dangers identified by the Threat Assessment; (3) programmatic goals that can provide some measurable information and results to help guide the Strategy going forward; and (4) individualized goals by each of the relevant Department components that are designed to support both the broad goals of the Strategy and the programmatic goals of the Department.

At its core, the goal of this National Strategy is to reduce the incidence of the sexual exploitation of children. This goal is the guiding principle for all the Department's current and future efforts. The sexual abuse and exploitation of children rob the victims of their childhood, irrevocably interfering with their emotional and psychological development. The cost to society is profound. Working toward reducing this blight on society will include a coordinated effort to achieve the broad Strategy goals, specific goals to address the current threats identified, the programmatic goals of the Department, and the goals of each of the components.

A. The National Strategy's Broad Goals

As noted above, the guiding principle of all of the Department's work must be to reduce the incidence of the sexual exploitation of children. This Strategy recognizes that investigation and prosecution will not alone defeat the threat our children face. A multi-disciplinary approach to the problem is required because of the complexity of the threats involved. Solving this problem must include not only investigators and prosecutors, but social service providers, educators, medical professionals, academics, non-governmental organizations, and members of industry, as well as parents and families.

First, the Department will continue to partner closely with state, local, tribal, and non-governmental entities, as well as other federal agencies and the private sector to implement the National Strategy in a coordinated fashion.

Second, the Department will build on the success of the Project Safe Childhood initiative.

Third, the Department will increase its commitment to a leadership role in finding a global solution to the transnational problem of the sexual exploitation of children.

Fourth, the Department will work toward improving the quality, effectiveness, and timeliness of computer forensic investigations and analysis.

Fifth, the Department will increase its commitment to effective and sophisticated training for prosecutors and investigators.

Sixth, the Department will continue to partner with Industry to develop objectives to reduce the exchange of child pornography.

Seventh, the Department will explore opportunities to increase the education and awareness of federal, state, local and tribal judges of the difficult issues involved in child sexual exploitation.

In support of the goals above, the Department has set priorities for accomplishing the goals of this National Strategy. The following is a summary of those priorities.

B. Goals to Address Dangers Identified by the Threat Assessment

To address the specific dangers identified by the Threat Assessment, the Department will emphasize certain areas of priority, including: (1) child pornography and online enticement of children for sexual purposes; (2) commercial sexual exploitation of children (domestic prostitution), (3) child sex tourism; and (4) child exploitation in Indian Country.

1. Child Pornography and Online Exploitation

The Threat Assessment revealed that the expansion of the Internet has lead to an explosion in the market for child pornography, leading, in turn, to increased access, creation, and distribution of these abusive images.

As noted above, Project Safe Childhood was designed to develop district-specific strategies between U.S. Attorney's offices, ICAC task forces, and other federal, state, and local partners, to combat Internet-facilitated child exploitation. PSC has lead to a dramatic increase in the federal prosecution of these cases, and to the rescue and identification of many victims.

Priorities

Utilizing enhanced investigative and technological resources, the Department will focus its efforts on the most dangerous, most prolific offenders. Sophisticated training for investigators and prosecutors, as well as enhancing forensic and technology available to both, will increase the impact the Department can make on this problem. Through partnerships with Industry, the Department will explore strategies to reduce the ability of offenders to use the Internet to traffick in these vile images. The Department will also increase the level of coordination between PSC and the ICAC task forces, leveraging all the nation's child exploitation investigative capabilities together.

The Department will assess its current methods of collecting data on the scope of the problem, and determine whether further, or different, data collection would contribute more fully to eradicating this problem. The Department will also increase training coordination between PSC and the ICAC task forces, so that investigative tactics, techniques, technologies, forensics, and analysis are more fully standardized and continuously updated as information is shared and technology advances. The Department will explore close partnerships with the State Attorneys General and District Attorneys to share best practices, standards, information and strategies to attack this threat. These partnerships should include education, outreach, sex offender monitoring and deterrence.

The Department is also fully committed to its role in the global battle against the sexual exploitation of children, and will foster international cooperation in sharing information, technology, victim identification, forensics, and best practices. We will also participate in transnational enforcement operations and training opportunities. As previously noted, research into various aspects of child sexual exploitation, from offender behavior to victim impact, is critically important so that the Department can adjust to the ever-changing practices of those who prey on our children. The Department will focus substantial research funding into these important areas, and will ensure that this research is informed by all the key partners involved in child exploitation prevention and interdiction.

2. The Domestic Prostitution of Children

The Threat Assessment described that children, often runaways, are recruited and coerced into prostitution by pimps who lure the children with food, clothes, attention, friendship, and love. They then use violence or intimidation to trap these children into a life of prostitution.

Through the Innocence Lost Initiative, a joint effort of the FBI, CEOS, and NCMEC, 38 task forces operate to collect intelligence on pimps, recover child victims, and prosecute the pimps and madams who prey on these vulnerable children. These cases are uniquely difficult to investigate and prosecute, but progress has been made, as noted previously in this chapter.

Priorities

The Department will explore the expansion of the Innocence Lost Initiative into other cities. We will also work to ensure that adequate victim services for this group of child victims are available to assist these victims break free from their offenders and aid law enforcement in investigating and prosecuting those who have abused them. The Department will also explore strategies to reduce the demand for prostituted children through public awareness campaigns and systematic enforcement. The Department will also explore further coordination between ICAC task forces and the Innocence Lost task forces, both of which are staffed by largely local investigators with a wealth of experience in investigating crimes against children. The Department can learn much in this area from the many NGOs operating to assist victims, and will organize "listening sessions" to aid in the development of plans to address this problem.

The Department will work closely with the Departments of Education and Health and Human Services to develop comprehensive strategies to combat the glorification of pimps and prostitution often found in popular culture. The Department will also focus resources on coordinated training to include first responders and medical providers, so that these personnel can better recognize the signs that a child might be a victim of forced prostitution.

3. Child Sex Tourism

The Threat Assessment revealed that some Americans capitalize on their relative wealth and travel to foreign nations to purchase the sexual assault of children for as little as five dollars. Many countries are considered an easy target for these predators, due to a variety of reasons.

CEOS, working with ICE and the FBI to address this problem, has traveled to countries where child sex tourism is high to gain intelligence about these activities to inform the Department's enforcement efforts. CEOS has conducted training for law enforcement in these high-risk countries, and has met with foreign officials to foster a cooperative law enforcement relationship.

Priorities

The Department will continue to increase its capacity to investigate Americans who sexually exploit children abroad. We will explore opportunities to partner with foreign law enforcement and NGOs who can assist in identifying victims and perpetrators. We will also pursue opportunities for international cooperation, information sharing, and training across borders to reduce this crime. The Department of State will be a key partner in these efforts, and the Department will pursue a close working relationship to develop strategies and initiatives to combat child sex tourism. The Department will also explore formulating "jump teams" to travel to foreign hot spots for sustained efforts to coordinate with foreign law enforcement, and in developing proactive enforcement operations. In this area, like in the others in this chapter, research is critical, and will be fully supported by the Department. Offender behavior is an area ripe for research, and will aid law enforcement in identifying those likely to offend in this way.

4. Indian Country

The Threat Assessment noted that there is a lack of data available to measure the threat that sexual exploitation poses to children in Indian Country. There is, however, widespread agreement among child exploitation professionals that the threat is a serious one.

The Department, through the FBI and the U.S. Attorney's Offices in Indian Country, has already committed resources to this problem, and will continue to maintain a strong focus on this unique area of the country. Resources are devoted to training investigators and prosecutors in this area.

Priorities

The Department is dedicated to decreasing child sexual exploitation in Indian Country. Toward that end, the Department will continue its efforts to assess the scope of the problem and build upon resources already being devoted to fighting this threat. A key partnership that must be developed is between the Department and the Department of Education. The two should pursue development of prevention and education measures for schools in Indian Country. The Department will also explore targeted grant funding for education, awareness and the promotion of reporting of child exploitation in Indian Country. The Department will also commit to assisting in the expanded training of first responders, investigators and prosecutors in Indian Country. Further research into the scope of the problem will be necessary, and will be a priority for the Department.

End Notes

[1] Nelson Mandela
[2] The Honorable John Adams, Northern District of Ohio, *U.S. v. Cunningham*, 1:09-CR-00154-JRA.
[3] *See* the Act, Section 101(c)(16-17).
[4] *See* the Act, Section 101(c)(5-13, 15, 20).
[5] *See* the Act, Section 101(c)(1-4, 14).
[6] *See* Appendices E and F.
[7] Findings presented within this Assessment are supported by available data, information, and anecdotes from national law enforcement operations, federal child exploitation prosecutions, and academic research, as well as from governmental and nongovernmental agencies (NGOs) found in the appendices.
[8] Attached to this chapter are several appendices that provide additional details relating to the findings of the Threat Assessment. *See* Appendices A-D.
[9] *See* Appendix D.
[10] *See* Appendix A, Operation Hamlet, and Appendix B, *U.S. v. Witt.*
[11] *See* Appendix B, *U.S. v. Merz*.
[12] *See* the Act at Section 101(c)(16)(a-c).

[13] These files are documented images of known child pornography

[14] Operation Fairplay includes data for FY 2008 and data for the period January through June 2009. The number of unique IP addresses logged by law enforcement for Operation RoundUp includes data for a shorter period, because it is a new application only recently released for use by law enforcement.

[15] One particular network is also used because its configuration supports the efficient investigation of online transactions and because this network was specifically noted in a GAO report as a major source of pornography trading. U.S. General Accounting Office (2003). Statement of Linda D. Koontz Director, Information Management Issues. "File-Sharing Programs. Child Pornography Is Readily Accessible over Peer-to-Peer Networks." GAO-03-537T.

[16] GUID is a unique computer identifier.

[17] United Nations. (2000). Report of the Special Rapporteur on the sale of children, child prostitution and child pornography, Najat M'jid Maalla. A/HRC/12/23. 13 July 2009.

[18] *Ibid.*

[19] A complaint is defined as any information requiring review by law enforcement in order to determine further investigative merit. A complaint may come from a variety of sources, including: citizen call ins, CyberTipline reports, referrals from other law enforcement agencies, or undercover activity and may not lead to an actual investigation.

[20] *See* Appendix B, Operation Lost Innocence: *U.S. v. Mariscal.*

[21] *See* Appendix A, Operation Joint Hammer.

[22] *See* Appendix A, Operation Hamlet.

[23] *See* Appendix C, *Quayle et al.*

[24] *See* Appendix C, *Quayle* (Fathers Victimizing Their Children.)

[25] See Appendix B, *U.S. v Curry.*

[26] *See* Appendix C, *U.S. v. Wolak, et al.*

[27] This IIOU Initiative is an FBI online undercover operation targeting subjects who are actively distributing mass quantities of child pornography.

[28] *See* Appendix B, Executive Office of U.S. Attorneys (EOUSA).

[29] *See* Appendix D, EOUSA.

[30] *See* Appendix D, USPIS.

[31] *See* Appendix A, Operations Achilles, Avalanche, Insider, Falcon, Joint Hammer.

[32] *See* Appendix C, *Quayle.*

[33] Although some offenders interviewed for research studies have made the claim that viewing child pornography prevents them from engaging in contact offending, *see* Appendix C, *Quayle,* no empirical studies have been identified supporting those claims.

[34] *See* Appendix D, NCMEC Child Victim Identification Program.

[35] *See* Appendix D, NDIC.

[36] *See* Appendix D, U.S. Sentencing Commission.

[37] *See* Appendix C, Finkelhor, and Appendix D, IWF.

[38] An IP address is a numeric address that is assigned to devices participating in a computer network utilizing the Internet. Most DSL and cable Internet subscribers have "sticky dynamic" IP addresses which are changeable but do not change often. When an ISP provides dynamic IP address service, the user's identification is reassigned at login to a new node *(*computer*)* in the IP network and is always different. The ISP assigns the user an IP address which is traceable only to the ISP and does not reveal information on the user except through the ISP.

[39] A proxy server is a computer system or an application program that acts as a go-between for requests from clients *see*king resources from other servers.

[40] In the United States, there is no federal statute or regulation requiring providers to keep user IP information for any length of time, or at all. Some U.S. providers only keep the information for a few days. In a 2009 survey of 100 U.S. Internet crimes investigators, 61 percent of the investigators reported that they had had investigations detrimentally affected because data was not retained; and 47 percent reported that they had had to end an investigation because data was not retained. (Source: Internet Crime Investigators Survey: Internet Service Provider Interactions, Dr. Frank Kardasz, Sgt./Project Mgr. Phoenix PD / AZ ICAC Task Force.) In Europe, a current EU directive requires member countries to draft laws requiring their providers to keep user IP records for at least 6 months and up to 2 years." In March 2010, the German Constitutional Court struck down such a law. See http://www.thelocal.de/national/20100302-25603.html

[41] *See* Appendix A, Operation Achilles and Operation Joint Hammer.

[42] Standard routers are networking devices that forward traffic on the Internet onto an effective path for finding a particular server; however, Onion Routers (anonymity networks) direct that Internet activity along complex circuitous routes in a network designed to completely obscure its origins.

[43] *See* Appendix D, Governmental and NGO Reports and Data.

[44] A URL is the address of a resource *(*as a document or Web site*)* on the Internet that consists of a communications protocol followed by the name or address of a computer on the network and that often includes additional

locating information (as directory and file names)—called also uniform resource locator, universal resource locator. A Web site is a group of World Wide Web pages usually containing hyperlinks to each other and made available online by an individual, company, educational institution, government, or organization. *See* Appendix D, Governmental and NGO Reports and Data.

[45] *See* Appendix A, Operation Falcon, Operation Avalanche, and Operation Joint Hammer.

[46] *See* Appendix A, Operation Insider.

[47] *See* Appendix A, Operation Achilles.

[48] *See* Appendix A, Law Enforcement Operations.

[49] *See* Appendix A, Operation Joint Hammer.

[50] *See* Appendix A, Operation Achilles.

[51] For Department reporting purposes, a traveler investigation involves the transportation of at least one individual for the purpose of sexual conduct with a minor.

[52] Travelers meet specific children for the purpose of engaging in illegal sexual conduct. Children who make contact with such predators are at great risk of kidnapping, rape, torture, or murder. These predators may travel within a state or region, across the country, or even internationally to meet a potential victim. They also may arrange for a victim to travel to meet them.

[53] *See* Appendix D, NCMEC.

[54] *See* Appendix D, Figure 4.

[55] *See* Appendix D, Figure 7.

[56] Enticement is the unlawful solicitation of a minor by any means for unlawful sexual conduct, according to the Department, Office of Juvenile Justice Programs.

[57] Online predators are defined as sex offenders who use the Internet to seek underage victims. University of New Hampshire Crimes Against Children Research Center.

[58] Criminals who commit the crimes discussed in this section can be referred to as "commercial sex traffickers" or as "pimps." While some believe that the term "pimp" often is used by commercial sex traffickers as a favorable street title for someone who can procure sex for sale and thus should not be used, we use the term as it is commonly known and highlights that these offenders profit by the victimization of children through prostitution.

[59] The pronoun "her or she" is often used in this chapter in discussing prostitution but it represents both male and female victims' involvement in this horrendous crime.

[60] Torture tactics that pimps use include locking children in trunks or closets, burning, and maiming.

[61] According to a study conducted by Richard J. Estes and Neil Alan Weiner, *Commercial Sexual Exploitation of Children in the U.S, Canada and Mexico*, University of Pennsylvania (2001), available at http://caster .ssw.upenn.edu/~restes/CSEC.htm, the average age of entry into prostitution is 12 to 14 years for girls and 11 to 13 years for boys.

[62] Pimps often require girls to meet nightly earning quotas, based on where and when the child is forced to work. For example, average quotas in New York City range from $300 to $500 on a week night and $500 to $1,000 on a weekend night.

[63] The ILNI is a nationwide initiative among the NCMEC, FBI, DEPARTMENT /Child Exploitation and Obscenity Section (CEOS), and their state and local partners to focus on child victims of domestic commercial sexual exploitation in the United States. As part of the initiative, the FBI created task forces in areas where domestic commercial sexual exploitation is prevalent and the NCMEC, FBI, and Department through CEOS developed specialized training courses focused on domestic commercial sexual exploitation prosecution and victim assistance.

[64] The Mann Act prohibits, among other offenses, knowingly transporting an individual across state lines for the purposes of prostitution or criminal sexual activity. The act has been amended several times to provide increased protection for sexually exploited minors and enhanced penalties for child sex traffickers.

[65] The RICO statute provides for enhanced penalties for individuals engaged in organized criminal behavior. Offenders found guilty of racketeering under the RICO statute are subject to extended sentences and fines and must forfeit all interest and property derived from the racketeering activity.

[66] The TVPA is the first federal law specifically enacted to protect victims of human trafficking and to prosecute the individuals who traffic them. The act defines one of the severe forms of trafficking in persons as "sex trafficking in which a commercial sex act is induced by force, fraud, or coercion, or in which the person induced to perform such act has not attained 18 years of age." Subsequent reauthorizations also provide for enhanced services for victims of sex trafficking.

[67] The providers include nongovernmental agencies such as Girls Education & Mentoring Services, Polaris Project, and SAGE.

[68] There are only approximately 50 beds available in the United States in facilities designed specifically for victims of child prostitution. These facilities operate largely on private donations. The TVPA of 2000 allocated funding to establish residential treatment facilities in the United States for juvenile sex trafficking victims; however, this funding was reserved for foreign-born victims. The 2005 TVPA reauthorization included funding for U.S. citizens, but the funding has not yet been appropriated.

[68] Prior to 2009, grants administered by the Department 's Office for Victims of Crime (OVC) related to trafficking in persons were reserved for alien victims trafficked into or within the United States, not domestic victims. However, DOJ has funded three demonstration projects dedicated to serving domestic victims.[68]

[69] American child sex tourists typically are Caucasian males aged 40 or older. Such predators may be either situational or preferential child sex tourists. A situational child sex tourist abuses children by way of experimentation or through the anonymity and impunity afforded by being a tourist. He or she does not have an exclusive sexual inclination for children. Often, the situational offender is an indiscriminate sex tourist who is presented with the opportunity to interact sexually with a person under 18 and takes it. A preferential child sex tourist displays an active sexual preference for children. He or she may still have the capacity to experience sexual attraction for adults but will actively *see*k out minors for sexual contact. The preferential child sex tourist will generally search for pubescent or adolescent children.

[70] Some organizations estimate that U.S. citizens account for 25 percent of child sex tourists worldwide, and as high as 80 percent in Latin America. *See* www.worldvision.org/content.nsf/learn/globalissues-stp-faqs (last visited Apr. 15, 2010).

[71] *See* Appendix D, NCMEC, Figure 7.

[72] Indian Country is the legal term used to describe reservations and other lands set aside for Indian use, such as Indian allotments and lands held in trust for Indians or Indian tribes, according to 18 U.S.C. § 1151.

[73] Federal jurisdiction was ceded under Public Law (Pub. L.) 83-280 (commonly referred to as Public Law 280), 18 U.S.C. § 1162, which required six states to assume jurisdiction over Indian Country crimes and divested the federal government of jurisdiction to prosecute under the Major and Indian Country Crimes Acts in those areas. Public Law 280 also allowed other states the option to assume jurisdiction. Congress also has passed a variety of reservation-specific statutes providing for a similar framework of state jurisdiction over crimes in those locations. The federal government retains jurisdiction to prosecute generally applicable offenses in Public Law 280 areas.

[74] *See* the Act, Sec. 101(c)(5).

[75] *See* the Act, Sec. 101 (c)(8).

[76] *See* the Act, Sec. 101(c)(12).

[77] *See* the Act, Sec. 101(c)(18).

[78] *See* the Act, Sec. 101(c)(6-7).

[79] *See* the Act, Sec. 101(c)(12).

[80] *See* the Act, Sec. 101(c)(19).

[81] *See* the Act, Sec. 101(c)(9-10).

[82] *See* the Act, Sec. 101 (c)(8).

[83] The data elements to be reported for the first time in 2011 include the number of prosecutions and convictions from the criminal referrals to United States Attorneys and the number of local prosecutions and convictions based on ICAC Task Force task force investigations.

[84] Because of the need for continuing education on advanced and emerging topics the count of numbers of persons trained should not be interpreted as an unduplicated total but as units of training delivered.

[85] The New York City Police Department was selected in 2009 as the new ICAC Task Force to serve the New York City metropolitan area.

[86] The Pasadena Independent School District was selected in 2009 as the new ICAC Task Force to serve the Houston metropolitan area.

[87] The New York City and Pasadena Independent School District Task Forces received only one award in FY 2009, as they did not exist when ARRA awards were made in May-June, 2009.

[88] No data are reported for the Pasadena Independent School District and the New York City Police because they were not active Task Forces in the data collection period.

[89] In 2009 OJJDP changed the ICAC Task Force budget cycle from 24 months to 12 months to more efficiently comply with the provision of the PROTECT Act.

[90] 15 January 2010. "Evaluation of DoD Contracts Regarding Combating Trafficking in Persons".

[91] *See* http://www.acf.hhs.gov/programs/orr/
http://www.acf.hhs.gov/trafficking /
http://www.brycs.org /

[92] *Internet safety.* The [congressional] conferees strongly support programs that provide various services and resources to protect children from being vulnerable to online predators. The conferees understand that parents, law enforcement personnel, school personnel, and afterschool program staff can obtain information about Internet safety from a multitude of arenas. The conferees want to better understand what types and how many Internet safety programs are being federally funded. The conferees direct the Administrator of the Office of Juvenile Justice and Delinquency Prevention, in coordination with the Coordinating Council on Juvenile Justice and Delinquency Prevention, to submit a report on federally funded Internet safety programs to the Committees on Appropriations within 180 days of the enactment of this Act. House Report 108–792.

[93] Snowball sampling is an approach where informants are asked to identify other persons knowledgeable about the topic of study. When these persons are interviewed the researcher accumulates more and more information

about the topic. The chain of "recommended informants" initially diverges, but finally converges as a few key persons emerge as the most frequently mentioned names. Patton, Michael Quinn (1990). *Qualitative Research & Evaluation Methods*. Sage: Thousand Oaks, CA, p. 237.

[94] NOTE: Inclusion of a program on this table does not constitute an endorsement of the program. In preparing this inventory, no attempt has been made to evaluate any program.

[95] NOTE: Inclusion of a program on this table does not constitute an endorsement. No attempt has been made to evaluate the content or effectiveness of any program. The sources of the information provided are the referenced Web sites. This list is representative but not exhaustive.

[96] The 4 mb file for the Conference Program of the 2008 Project Safe Childhood national Training Conference is available at: http://www.icactraining.org/agendas/PSC/PSC_Conf_Program_FINAL.pdf

In: National Strategy for Child Exploitation Prevention… ISBN: 978-1-61122-853-3
Editor: Jeremy R. Barnes and Ashley P. Davis

Chapter 2

EFFECTS OF FEDERAL LEGISLATION ON THE COMMERCIAL SEXUAL EXPLOITATION OF CHILDREN

William Adams, Colleen Owens, Kevonne Small and Juvenile Justice Bulletin

In the United States, estimates suggest that as many as 300,000 children may become victims of commercial sexual exploitation each year (Estes and Weiner, 2001). This bulletin describes the findings of a study that the Urban Institute conducted to examine the effects of the passage of the Victims of Trafficking and Violence Protection Act of 2000 (TVPA) on the federal prosecution of commercial sexual exploitation of children (CSEC) cases. It discusses U.S. enforcement of TVPA and succeeding laws enacted to strengthen penalties against CSEC, describes features of successful prosecutions, and examines how the legislation has affected court penalties and service providers. The authors also discuss recommendations for policymakers and practitioners who work with children and youth who have been the victims of commercial sexual exploitation.

BACKGROUND

The 1996 Declaration and Agenda for Action for the First World Congress Against the Commercial Sexual Exploitation of Children provided the first working definition of the commercial sexual exploitation of children and youth:

> [CSEC] comprises sexual abuse by the adult and remuneration in cash or kind to the child or a third person or persons. The child is treated as a sexual object and as a commercial object. The commercial sexual exploitation of children constitutes a form of coercion and violence against children, and amounts to forced labour and a contemporary form of slavery.

TVPA (Public Law 106–386) is considered to be the seminal piece of U.S. legislation in the fight against CSEC. As the first comprehensive law to combat human trafficking, TVPA criminalizes human trafficking on a federal level. Section 112 of TVPA states that sex trafficking of children involves a commercial sex act in which the victim is younger than 18 years old. Traffickers who exploit children younger than age 14 for the purposes of a commercial sex act can be sentenced to up to life in prison (18 U.S.C. § 1591(b)(1)).[1] If the victim is between 14 and 18 years old, the trafficker is eligible for as much as 20 years in prison under TVPA (18 U.S.C. § 159 1(b)(2)); subsequent federal legislation has increased this penalty to life imprisonment (pursuant to the Adam Walsh Act of 2006).[2]

A MESSAGE FROM OJJDP

Each year, as many as 300,000 children become victims of commercial sexual exploitation in the United States. Such victimization can have devastating effects on a child's physical and mental health and well-being.

In an effort to stop the commercial sexual exploitation of children (CSEC), Congress enacted the Victims of Trafficking and Violence Prevention Act (TVPA) in 2000. As the seminal legislation in America's efforts to end CSEC, the Act criminalizes human trafficking on a federal level.

This bulletin describes the results of a study funded by OJJDP to examine TVPA's impact on the prosecution of CSEC cases. The authors draw on CSEC cases processed in federal courts between 1998 and 2005 to take a look at how current laws addressing CSEC are enforced, indicate key features of successful CSEC prosecutions, and describe how legislation has affected sentences imposed on CSEC perpetrators, as well as legislation's effects on the provision of services to victims. The bulletin concludes with a discussion of how the juvenile justice community and policymakers could improve the prosecution of CSEC crimes.

The information provided in these pages should inform our efforts to develop policies and practices to combat CSEC more effectively. To this end, the authors call for comprehensive data collection at the state level, increased training opportunities, and more consistent definitions of this heinous crime.

Several events following TVPA's passage also helped combat CSEC. In 2003, Congress passed the Prosecutorial Remedies and Other Tools to End the Exploitation of Children Today (PROTECT) Act (Public Law 108–21) to help the government fight child sexual exploitation. The PROTECT Act expanded territorial jurisdiction so that Americans abroad who commit CSEC may be prosecuted. It also increased maximum incarceration sentences from 15 to 30 years for U.S. citizens or permanent residents convicted of child sex tourism and for persons convicted of transporting a minor in interstate or foreign commerce with the intent that the minor engage in prostitution or other commercial sex acts (PROTECT Act, Public Law 108–21; Shared Hope International et al., 2006; Fraley, 2005). Additionally, since its launch in 2003, the FBI's Innocence Lost National Initiative has become the largest U.S. government initiative against child sex trafficking. The Innocence Lost Initiative operates task forces and working groups in 28 U.S. cities.[3] As a part of the initiative, the National Center for Missing & Exploited Children (NCMEC) and U.S. Attorneys' offices involved in the task forces or working groups train local and federal law enforcement and social service providers on multidisciplinary approaches to addressing the prostitution of children in the United States.

THE URBAN INSTITUTE'S STUDY

To assess the impact of TVPA on the prosecution of CSEC cases in the United States, the Office of Juvenile Justice and Delinquency Prevention (OJJDP) commissioned the Urban Institute to conduct a study to answer four research questions:

- Is the United States enforcing existing federal laws against CSEC?
- What are key features of successful CSEC prosecutions? What factors predict convictions in cases? What factors predict sentence length?
- Have U.S. courts increased penalties associated with commercial sexual crimes against children?
- What are the effects of CSEC legislation on service providers who work with these victims?

The Urban Institute partnered with the Polaris Project[4] to carry out this research.[5]

RESEARCH METHODS

The Urban Institute researchers used a variety of methods to answer the four research questions and provide guidance for policy and practice. Their methods included a literature review, interviews with four federal prosecutors, a focus group with eight Washington, DC-area CSEC service providers and advocates, and statistical analyses of federal CSEC cases filed by U.S. Attorneys from 1998 through 2005.

Literature review. The researchers examined past publications on CSEC and published definitions of CSEC. In addition, researchers examined:

- Past international actions concerning CSEC.

- United Nations actions concerning CSEC.
- Major conventions and meetings on CSEC.
- U.S. legislation on CSEC.
- Governmental and nongovernmental organization actions related to CSEC.

Interviews with prosecutors. The researchers conducted 1-hour interviews with four federal prosecutors who worked on CSEC cases. Researchers asked about the prosecutors' experience, collaborations, data collection methods, decisionmaking processes, and the definitions of CSEC they used in daily practice.

Practitioner meeting. The Urban Institute hosted a half-day practitioner meeting in June 2007 for eight CSEC service providers and advocates. These experts discussed issues related to the Urban Institute's study and answered the following questions:

- Was information missing in the literature review?
- Did any information in the literature review need clarification?
- How could findings from the statistical analysis inform practice?
- What practical lessons did the data provide?
- How could the data generate future research?

Statistical analysis. The secondary analysis of federal CSEC defendants relied on data obtained from the Federal Justice Statistics Resource Center (FJSRC), a project that the Bureau of Justice Statistics sponsors and the Urban Institute operates. The researchers used the FJSRC database to examine the prevalence and characteristics of CSEC offenses and offenders in the federal criminal justice system. This included criminal suspects investigated by U.S. Attorneys, persons arrested by federal law enforcement, defendants prosecuted and adjudicated in U.S. district courts, and offenders who had been sentenced and imprisoned.

The Urban Institute downloaded the following datasets from the FJSRC Web site (http://fjsrc.urban):

- U.S. Marshals Service (USMS), *Arrests for Federal offenses,* annual file, FY1998–2005.
- Executive Office for U.S. Attorneys (EOUSA), *Suspects in criminal matters opened,* annual file, FY1997–2005.
- EOUSA, *Suspects in criminal matters concluded,* annual file, FY1997–2005.
- Administrative Office of the U.S. Courts (AOUSC), *Defendants in criminal cases filed,* annual file, FY1998–2005.
- AOUSC, *Defendants in criminal cases terminated,* annual file, FY1998–2005.
- U.S. Sentencing Commission (USSC), *Defendants sentenced,* annual file, FY1998–2005.

The Urban Institute examined all stages of case processing for defendants' cases filed in U.S. district courts from 1998 to 2005. To identify CSEC defendants in the FJSRC database, the Institute relied on the appropriate criminal statutes in the United States Code, mainly those from chapter 110 ("Sexual Exploitation and Other Abuses of Children") of Title 18.[6]

The researchers used these data to measure and assess trends in federal prosecution of CSEC offenders. FJSRC data factored prominently in answering the study's key questions.

RESEARCH FINDINGS

Findings from the Literature Review

Analysis of the literature revealed that CSEC remains a major focus of the criminal justice community. Key findings include:

- The Declaration and Agenda for Action for the First World Congress Against the Commercial Sexual Exploitation of Children created a widespread, formal definition of CSEC in 1996.
- Each year in the United States, as many as 300,000 children are at risk for sexual exploitation (Estes and Weiner, 2001).
- The average age a child first falls victim to CSEC is 13 or 14 (Barnitz, 2001; Friedman, 2005).
- Victims are becoming younger, largely because exploiters are concerned about victims having HIV or AIDS (Friedman, 2005; Spangenberg, 2001; Barnitz, 2001).
- Victims cite the presence of existing adult prostitution markets and their or their family members' drug dependency as leading factors contributing to their involvement in CSEC in the United States (Estes and Weiner, 2001).
- Few CSEC studies focus on perpetrators (Barnitz, 2001; Estes and Weiner, 2001; Andrews, 2004; Gragg et al., 2007; Song, 2007).
- The majority of child sexual exploiters are men between the ages of 20 and 65 (Barnitz, 2001; Estes and Weiner, 2001).
- Prior to the passage of TVPA (2000) and the PROTECT Act (2003), prosecutors addressed crimes involving CSEC by using the Mann Act of 1910 (18 U.S.C. § § 2421–2424) and the Violent Crime Control and Law Enforcement Act of 1994 (Katyal, 1993). However, TVPA is considered the seminal piece of U.S. legislation on CSEC.

A HISTORY OF COMMERCIAL SEXUAL EXPLOITATION OF CHILDREN LEGISLATION IN THE UNITED STATES

Before passage of the Victims of Trafficking and Violence Protection Act of 2000 (TVPA), prosecutors primarily used the Mann Act of 1910 (18 U.S.C. § § 2421– 2424) and the Violent Crime Control and Law Enforcement Act of 1994 (also known as the Crime Bill) to address crimes involving the commercial sexual exploitation of children.

The Mann Act, commonly called the White Slave Traffic Act, was enacted in 1910 to fight against forced prostitution as required by the Thirteenth Amendment to the U.S. Constitution (Katyal, 1993). However, the Act did not explicitly protect minors from slavery-like practices until it was amended in 1978 and again in 1986 and 1994. As currently written, the Mann Act makes it a felony to knowingly transport "an individual who has not attained the age of 18 years in interstate or foreign commerce, or in any Territory or Possession of the United States, with intent that such individual engage in prostitution, or in any sexual activity for which any person can be charged with a criminal offense" (18 U.S.C. §§ 2421–2424). Currently, the FBI investigates possible Mann Act violations and refers them directly to U.S. Attorneys. The U.S. Department of Justice's Child Exploitation and Obscenity Section supervises the prosecution of these cases (United States Attorneys Manual, 1997).

The Mann Act was not originally intended to prosecute cases of child sex trafficking or general sex trafficking, but it has been, and still is, used to do so. Rather, TVPA was the fi rst comprehensive law intended to combat human trafficking. It criminalized human trafficking in the United States and focused efforts on prevention, protection, and prosecution. Unlike the Mann Act, TVPA does not require transportation across state lines to prove human trafficking.

In addition to actions prosecuted through TVPA, the 1994 Crime Bill includes a provision, known as the Child Sexual Abuse Prevention Act, which states that traveling outside of the United States with the intent of engaging in sexual activity with a minor is a crime. This provision represented a signifi cant step toward fi ghting child sex tourism, but few cases have been prosecuted using this law (Andrews, 2004). As a result, the Sex Tourism Prohibition Improvement Act of 2002 was passed to address these concerns. Perhaps most signifi cantly, the 2002 Act removed the intent requirement and criminalized the actions of sex tour operators (Fraley, 2005). These acts help provide the basis for CSEC arrests and prosecution.

For more comprehensive information on the federal laws used to prosecute CSEC, see the Urban Institute's full research report: *An Analysis of Federally Prosecuted CSEC Cases since the Passage of the Victims of Trafficking and Violence Protection Act of 2000,* available at www.ncjrs.gov/pdffiles1/ojjdp/grants

- Several major initiatives in 2003—the passage of the PROTECT Act, the reauthorization of TVPA, the start of the Innocence Lost National Initiative, and the "Breaking the Silence" national summit—successfully enhanced CSEC prosecution.

Highlights from Prosecutor Interviews

Interviews with federal prosecutors highlighted several key issues in the field that needed improvement.

Definitions of CSEC. Prosecutors used different definitions of what constitutes CSEC. For example, many felt that CSEC involved U.S. citizen victims, whereas human trafficking involved foreign national victims. These differing definitions affected which legislation they thought pertained to CSEC-related crimes.

Task forces. Task forces need further development, particularly at the local level.

Prosecution. Prosecutors disagreed as to whether certain cases should be processed at the state or federal level. In addition, researchers learned that prosecutors preferred to plea bargain rather than bring cases to court.

Data collection. Prosecutors need to improve their methods of collecting data on CSEC. Currently, their agencies do not prioritize data collection, and they have no automated systems for this purpose.

Prosecutor interviews helped researchers develop advice on policy and practice (see sidebars "Recommendations for Practice" and "Recommendations for Policy").

Findings from the Practitioner Meeting

Researchers convened a focus group meeting attended by CSEC service providers and advocates to elicit feedback on preliminary research findings and to identify issues that had not been addressed previously. Practitioners identified a number of key issues and discussion points and made recommendations for policy and practice (see sidebars "Recommendations for Practice" and "Recommendations for Policy"):[7]

- Current federal CSEC data do not represent the full range of CSEC offenders. Practitioners had concerns about the types of CSEC cases included in federal data sources and suggested that state data might better represent the full spectrum of CSEC cases being investigated nationally. Data collection efforts, particularly at the state level, need improvement (see section 4.1.1 in the full report).

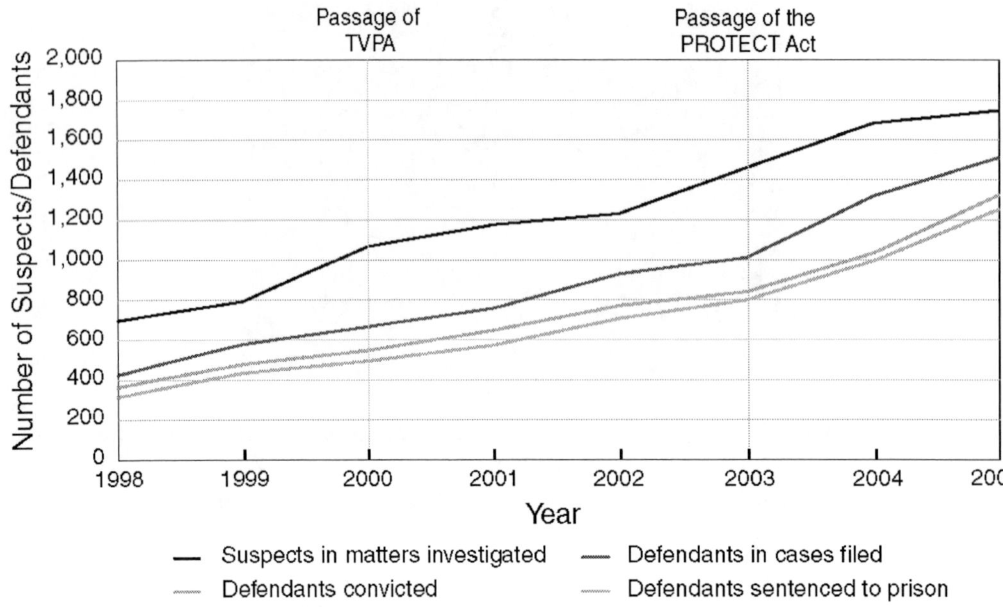

Note: CSEC investigations at the federal level have increased since the Victims of Trafficking and Violence Protection Act of 2000 (TVPA) and the Prosecutorial Remedies and Other Tools to End the Exploitation of Children Today (PROTECT) Act were passed.

Figure 1. Case-Processing Trends for Federal CSEC Cases, 1998–2005

- Children can become overwhelmed as witnesses. The investigation process can make CSEC victims feel criminalized, making them reluctant to testify. Preparing a child to participate in prosecution should be only one of several methods of handling this type of criminal case. Prosecutors should also focus on other types of corroborating evidence that can substantiate a victim's claim (see section 4.1.2 in the full report).
- Language used to discuss CSEC affects how victims are characterized. For example, U.S. child victims may be referred to as "prostitutes" and foreign national child victims may be referred to as "sex trafficking victims." This language difference creates a dichotomy between these two groups of victims. Other considerations include confusion over the terms "pimp," "commercial," and "sex trafficker" (see section 4.1.3 in the full report).
- U.S. citizen and foreign national CSEC victims are treated differently when they are identified, characterized, and offered services (see section 4.1.4 in the full report).

Answers to Key Questions

Researchers analyzed statistical data from the FJSRC Web site to answer the study's key questions (p. 2). These data were placed in context with information gathered from the literature review, prosecutor interviews, and practitioner meeting to provide the following answers.

1. Is The United States Enforcing Existing Federal Laws Against CSEC?

Although legislation existed before 2000 to address criminal acts associated with CSEC, specific federal laws such as TVPA (2000) and the PROTECT Act (2003) were passed to address this crime. At the federal level, the U.S. Department of Justice is using these laws.

The numbers of CSEC investigations, case filings, convictions, and sentences to prison have increased each year since these laws were passed (see figure 1). The average number of case filings increased the most in the following federal judicial districts: the eastern and central districts of California, the Utah district, the northern district of Ohio, the northern district of Georgia, and the southern district of New York (see figure 2).

Although the number of suspects in criminal CSEC matters that the federal government investigated and referred to U.S. Attorneys increased substantially each year between 1998 and 2005, federal prosecutors declined to prosecute more than half of those criminal matters each year in U.S. district courts. Federal prosecution was most frequently denied because the case was referred to other authorities (e.g., the states), there was weak or insufficient evidence for prosecution, or no federal offense was evident.[8] Nonetheless, prosecutors brought a fairly steady proportion of CSEC cases (usually 40 to 45 percent) to federal court, despite a caseload that more than doubled in volume between 1998 and 2005. Therefore, the number of defendants in CSEC cases filed in U.S. district courts more than tripled between 1998 and 2005 (from 412 to 1,512 cases).

CSEC investigations at the federal level have increased since TVPA and the PROTECT Act were passed. From 1998 to 2005, the number of CSEC suspects in criminal cases that U.S. Attorneys investigated and concluded more than doubled (see figure 3). Increases in the number of child pornography suspects accounted for most of this growth. The number of suspects investigated for child prostitution or sex trafficking experienced the greatest proportional growth during this time period, nearly tripling.

These increases in case investigations occurred mostly after 2003, when efforts converged (i.e., legislation, creation of task forces)[9] to bring greater awareness to CSEC and to prosecute its perpetrators by using a collaborative, victim-centered approach (Office of Juvenile Justice and Delinquency Protection, 2002).

To assess the impact of federal legislation (e.g., TVPA) and federal initiatives on the prosecution of CSEC cases over time, the Urban Institute constructed a time series regression model.[10] This model used monthly data on the number of federal CSEC prosecutions from 1998 to 2005 and measured the effect of several occurrences:

- TVPA—enacted in 2000.
- The 9/11 terrorist attacks.
- The PROTECT Act, Trafficking Victims Protection Reauthorization Act, and the FBI's Innocence Lost National Initiative—enacted in 2003.

The model showed a statistically significant effect of the 2003 initiatives on the number of CSEC prosecutions brought to federal court, and the other two occurrences had no statistically significant effect on the number of CSEC prosecutions brought to court (see figure 4). The fact that enacting TVPA in 2000 was not statistically significant does not mean that the Act was ineffective; it took a few years for this legislation to take effect and for federally funded task forces to form and come into operation throughout the United States. These task forces consisted of federal, state, and local law enforcement; victim service providers;

and prosecutors who worked together and shared information that helped identify CSEC victims and prosecute offenders in their communities.

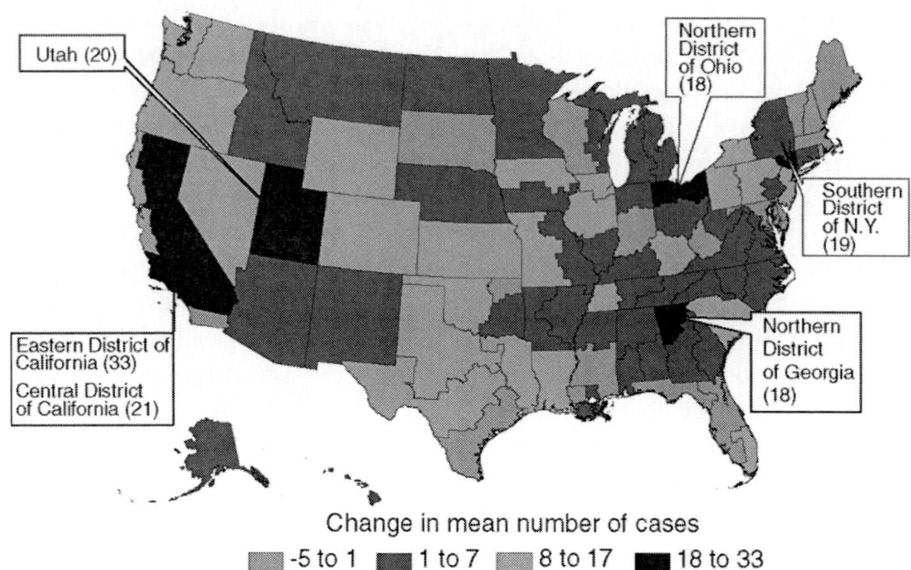

Note: Districts not shown on map include the District of Columbia (5), district of Guam (1), district of the Northern Mariana Islands (0.2), district of Puerto Rico (7), and district of the U.S. Virgin Islands (0.6).

Source: Federal Justice Statistics Resource Center, Administrative Office of the U.S. Courts criminal master files, annual, 1998–2005.

Figure 2. Change in the Number of Defendants in Cases Filed in U.S. District Court Charged With a CSEC Offense, 1998–2005, After Implementation of TVPA

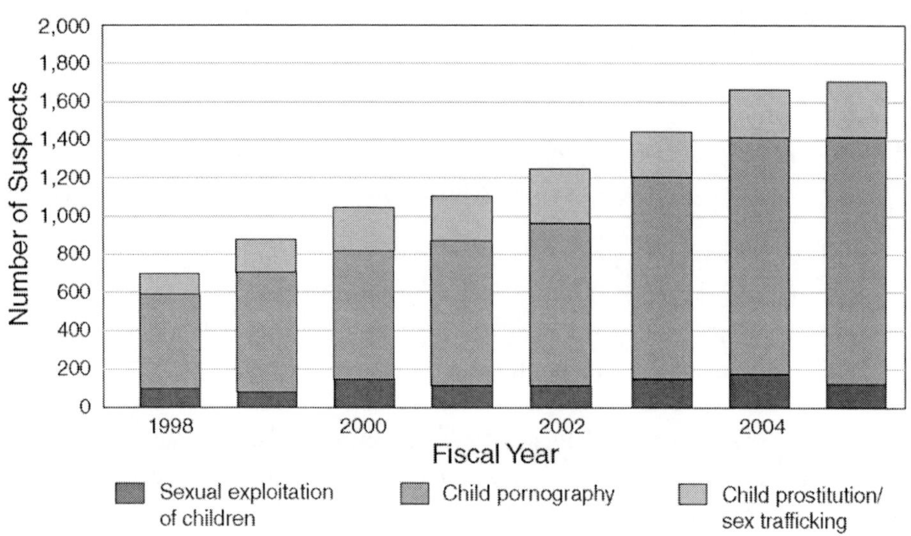

Note: Between 1998 and 2005, the number of suspects investigated in federal criminal matters related to commercial sexual exploitation crimes against children more than doubled.

Figure 3. Suspects Investigated in Federal Criminal Matters

2. What Are Key Features Of Successful CSEC Prosecutions? What Factors Predict Convictions In Cases? What Factors Predict Sentence Length?

Analysis of FJSRC data showed that the following factors are important in predicting conviction in a CSEC case:

- **When the case was filed.** Defendants in cases filed after the passage of TVPA of 2000 had a greater chance of being convicted than defendants in cases filed prior to the enactment of TVPA.
- **Investigative agency.** Cases that the U.S. Customs Service investigated were more likely to result in conviction than cases that the FBI investigated.
- **Case processing time.** Cases with longer processing times were more likely to end in conviction.
- **Presence of codefendants.** Cases with one defendant had greater conviction rates than cases with multiple defendants.
- **Type of CSEC charge.** Offenders charged with possessing or distributing child pornography were more likely to be convicted than those charged with child prostitution or child sexual exploitation.

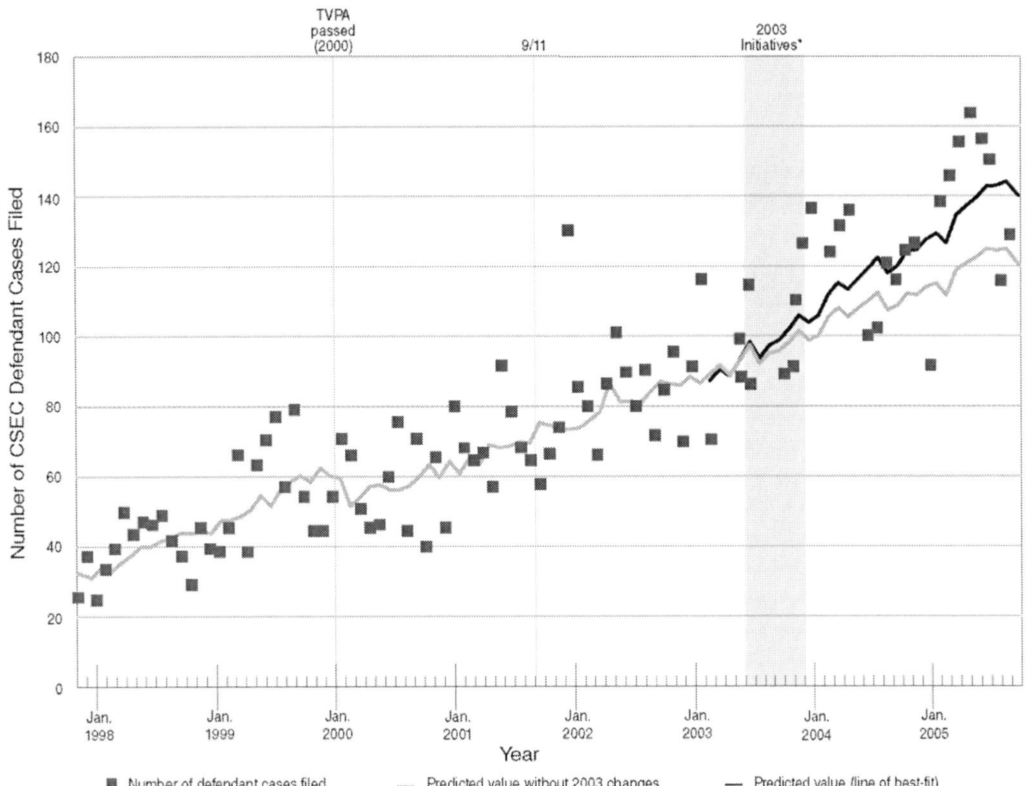

* Federal efforts implemented in early 2003 include the FBI's Innocence Lost National Initiative, the Trafficking Victims Protection Reauthorization Act, and the Prosecutorial Remedies and Other Tools to End the Exploitation of Children Today (PROTECT) Act.

Figure 4. Time Series Regression Model Measuring the Impact of Federal Initiatives on CSEC Prosecutions in U.S. District Courts

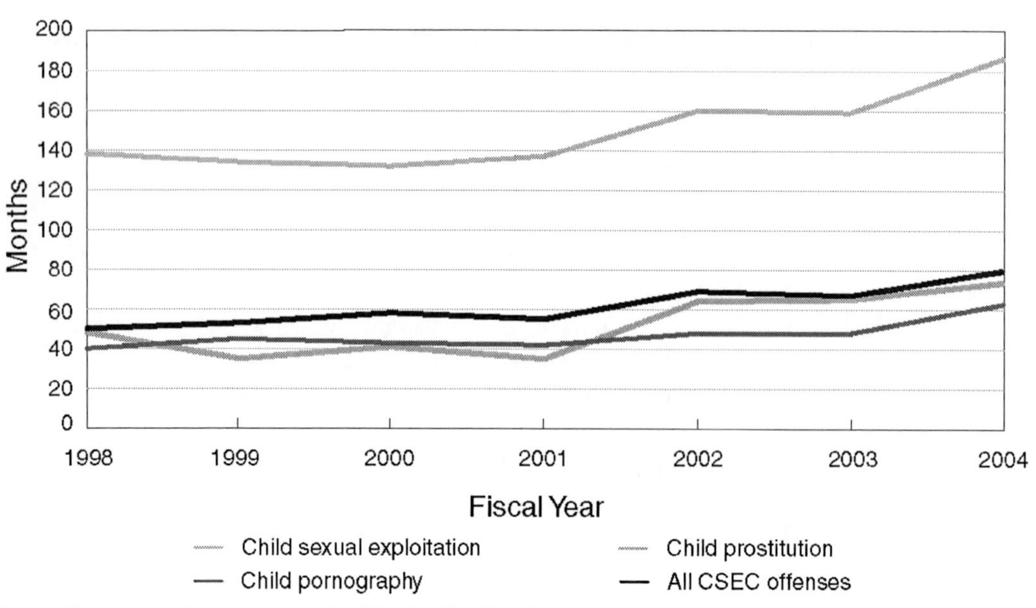

Note: The mean prison sentence for CSEC offenders increased to 80 months in 2004.

Figure 5. Mean Prison Sentence for Commercial Sexual Exploitation of Children (CSEC) Offenses, 1998–2004

The following factors helped predict the prison term imposed on CSEC offenders:

- **Case disposition (plea vs. trial).** Offenders who went to trial received longer sentences (61 months longer, on average) than those who pled guilty.
- **Race.** Nonwhite offenders received longer prison terms (about 16 months longer) than white offenders.
- **Education.** Offenders with lower levels of education (high school diploma or less) received longer sentences than offenders with at least some college education.
- **Type of CSEC charge.** Offenders charged with child sexual exploitation received longer sentences (47 months longer, on average) than those charged with child prostitution or child pornography.
- **Offense seriousness and criminal history.** As an offender's federal guidelines scores[11] on offense seriousness and criminal history increased, so too did the average sentence imposed on the offender.

3. Have U.S. Courts Increased Penalties Associated With Commercial Sexual Crimes Against Children?

Laws associated with CSEC passed since 2000 have increased the penalties associated with CSEC-related offenses. Prosecutors use these laws to secure harsher punishments.

For example, the mean sentence imposed on offenders convicted and sentenced increased from 53 months in 1999 (before TVPA went into effect) to 80 months in 2004 (see figure 5).

4. What Are The Effects Of CSEC Legislation On Service Providers Who Work With These Victims?

Service providers and advocates reported that federal CSEC legislation often focuses on foreign or noncitizen victims, leaving service gaps and questions about the identity of U.S. citizen victims. Providers often have difficulty securing social services for U.S. citizen victims because the legislation focuses on victims from other countries who do not have status in the United States.

The service providers and advocates participating in the practitioner meeting[12] reported that there is an assumption that U.S. citizen CSEC victims have access to specialized services simply because of their citizenship status but suggested that this is not really the case. For example, many juvenile victims do not have access to secured housing.[13] Practitioners also suggested that federal CSEC legislation shapes the identity of victims. Foreign and noncitizen victims may have an easier time identifying themselves as victims because of how the laws are worded and interpreted, but U.S. citizen victims have a more difficult time identifying themselves as victims. U.S. citizen victims may feel "criminalized" by the process of case investigation and prosecution and opt to drop out of prosecutions.

Recommendations for Practice

The authors analyzed the study's findings and provided several recommendations for practice:

- Federal prosecutors should examine the reasons why so many cases are declined for federal prosecution and determine whether some declined cases could be brought forward with different policies or better training and resources.
- Practitioners and prosecutors should support task force participation. If jurisdictions do not have task forces or collaborations, federal and state prosecutors, law enforcement, and service providers should coordinate their efforts to ensure that cases are brought to court.
- Training opportunities for law enforcement, prosecutors, and judges should be uniform nationwide in terms of content but also tailored to local needs. Training topics should include how to define CSEC, how to decide whether a CSEC case should be tried at the federal or state level, and how to conduct an effective CSEC investigation.
- The U.S. government should clearly define CSEC at the federal and state levels. It should develop a universal definition of CSEC so that charging decisions are more uniform.

Conclusion

Key findings from the Urban Institute's study suggest that current federal CSEC-focused legislation is sufficient to address these crimes and that task force efforts are an important component in successful prosecution.

Although considerable progress has been made in CSEC prosecution, more improvements can be made:

- **Maintain consistent definitions of CSEC.** Greater consistency will help identify victims (both U.S. citizens and foreign nationals), inform how the legal and social services communities can help them, and determine how the legal system should handle offenders.
- **Provide better training.** Law enforcement, prosecutors, and judges who handle or encounter CSEC cases should receive more training.
- **Improve data collection.** Researchers should improve efforts to collect and use data to understand what works in preventing and combating CSEC and what helps to identify victims and prosecute cases.

RECOMMENDATIONS FOR POLICY

The authors analyzed the study's findings and provided a number of policy recommendations:

- Prosecutors use current federal laws against commercial sexual exploitation of children (CSEC). Practitioners and prosecutors agree that these laws sufficiently address CSEC at the federal level, and additional legislation is not needed.
- Congress should continue to fund CSEC-specific initiatives such as task forces and the national conference in 2003. Without this coordinated strategy focusing on CSEC legislation, CSEC prosecutions probably would not have increased as much.
- Task force participation is key to success in prosecuting CSEC perpetrators.
- Service providers, advocates, researchers, and policymakers must agree on terms used in the CSEC field. This will help identify victims and cases.
- Everyone involved in working with CSEC should use language that qualifies U.S. citizen CSEC victims as "real" victims (e.g., as sex trafficking victims and not as prostitutes) so that the criminal justice process will not make these victims feel criminalized and so that they will be more willing to participate in prosecutions.
- Victims must have access to specialized services. The U.S. government should conduct a review of services provided to U.S. citizen and foreign national CSEC victims exploited in the United States to ensure that both populations receive the services they need.
- Policymakers and practitioners must support and fund data collection efforts at the state and local levels. Prosecutors and practitioners see the value in collecting and analyzing data but do not make it a current practice for their agencies and organizations. Congress should make reporting data on CSEC incidents, arrests, prosecutions, and sentences a requirement. Data on CSEC crime victims also should be collected and reported.

The findings of this study shed light on some important research questions regarding the handling and outcome of CSEC cases in the federal system, but many questions remain unanswered. Continued research on CSEC is needed to create more effective guidelines for policy and practice.

In particular, studies should be undertaken to collect state-level data and assess the efforts of state and local authorities to prosecute CSEC offenders pursuant to state laws. This study focused solely on the prosecution of CSEC offenders by federal authorities, but these efforts constitute only part of the law enforcement efforts in the United States to apprehend and prosecute CSEC offenders. The efforts of state and local law enforcement should also be examined.

For More Information

To find out more about the study described in this bulletin, read the full report, *An Analysis of Federally Prosecuted CSEC Cases since the Passage of the Victims of Trafficking and Violence Protection Act of 2000,* at www.ncjrs.gov/pdffiles1/ojjdp/ grants/222023.pdf.

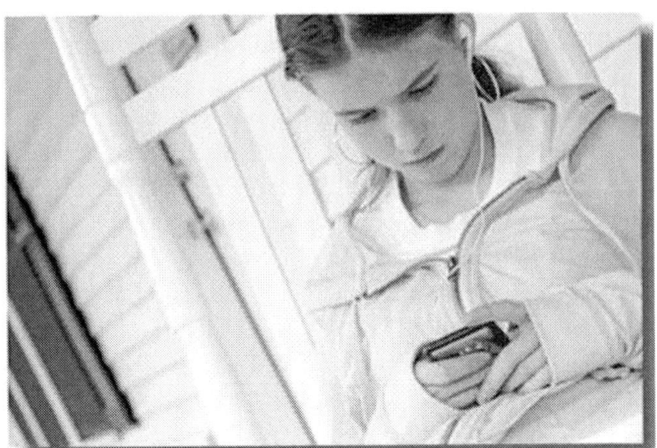

References

Adam Walsh Child Protection and Safety Act of 2006, Public Law 109–248.

Administrative Office of the U.S. Courts. *Defendants in Criminal Cases, 1998–2005.* Available from http://fjsrc.urban.org/ datadictionary.cfm.

Andrews, S. (2004). U.S. domestic prosecution of the American international sex tourist: Efforts to protect children from sexual exploitation. *Journal of Criminal Law and Criminology, 94(2)*, 415–454.

Barnitz, L. (2001). Effectively responding to the commercial sexual exploitation of children: A comprehensive approach to prevention, protection, and reintegration services. *Child Welfare, 80(5)*, 597–610.

Estes, R., and Weiner, N. (2001). *The Commercial Sexual Exploitation of Childrenin the U.S., Canada, and Mexico.* Philadelphia, PA: University of Pennsylvania School of Social Work. Available from www.sp2.upenn.edu/~restes/CSEC.htm.

First World Congress Against Commercial Sexual Exploitation of Children. (1997). (June 5). 1996 Declaration and Agenda for Action. Available from www.hartford-hwp.com/archives/28/024.html.

Fraley, A. (2005). Child sex tourism legislation under the PROTECT Act: Does it really protect? *St. John's Law Review, 79*, 445.

Friedman, S. A. (2005). *Who Is There to Help Us? How the System Fails Sexually Exploited Girls in the United States: Examples From Four American Cities.* Brooklyn, NY: ECPAT–USA.

Gragg, F., Petta, I., Bernstein, H., Eisen, K., and Quinn, L. (2007). *New York Prevalence Study of Commercially Sexually Exploited Children.* Rensselaer, NY: New York State Office of Children and Family Services.

Katyal, N. K. (1993). Men who own women: A Thirteenth Amendment critique of forced prostitution. *Yale Law Journal, 103(3)*, 791– 826.

Office of Juvenile Justice and Delinquency Prevention. (2002). *Protecting Our Children: Working Together To End Child Prostitution.* Proceedings of the National Summit, December 13–14, 2002, Washington, DC. Available from www.ncjrs.gov/pdffiles1/ojjdp/204990.pdf.

Prosecutorial Remedies and Other Tools to End the Exploitation of Children Today (PROTECT) Act of 2003, Public Law 108–21.

Shared Hope International, ECPAT–USA, and The Protection Project of the Foreign Policy Institute, Johns Hopkins University School of Advanced International Studies. 2006. *U.S. Mid-Term Review on the Commercial Sexual Exploitation of Children in America.* Available from www.sharedhope. org/csecmtrusa/index.asp.

Song, S. (2007). *Global Child Sex Tourism: Children as Tourist Attractions.* Washington, DC: Youth Advocate Program International. Available from www.yapi.org/rpchildsextourism.pdf.

Spangenberg, M. (2001). *Prostituted Youth in New York City: An Overview.* Brooklyn, NY: ECPAT–USA.

Trafficking Victims Protection Reauthorization Act of 2003, Public Law 108–193, 117 Stat. 2875–2887. Available from www.glin.gov/view.action?glinID=137996.

United States Attorneys Manual, Title 9, Criminal Resource Manual 2027. 1997. Mann Act. Available from www.usdoj.gov/ usao/eousa/foiajeadingjoom/usam/ title9/crm02027.htm.

United States Code. Title 18. Crimes and Criminal Procedure: Part I Crimes. Chapter 117. Transportation for Illegal Sexual Activity and Related Crimes. Sections 2421–2424 [Mann Act of 1910].

Victims of Trafficking and Violence Protection Act of 2000, 22 U.S.C. § § 7101 *et seq.* Public Law 106–386. Available from www.state organization/10492.pdf.

ACKNOWLEDGMENTS

This bulletin was written by William Adams, M.P.P., Senior Research Associate, Urban Institute; Colleen Owens, Research Associate, Urban Institute; and Kevonne Small, J.D., Ph.D., Trial Attorney, Criminal Section, Civil Rights Division, U.S. Department of Justice (and former Research Associate, Urban Institute).

The authors gratefully acknowledge the contributions of the following individuals: Kevin Roland, Research Associate, Urban Institute, who provided assistance with dataset preparation and analysis; Barbara Parthasarathy, Research Associate, Urban Institute, who prepared maps of U.S. judicial districts displaying the net change in the number of CSEC suspects and defendants; Janine Zweig, Ph.D., Senior Research Associate, Urban Institute, and Senior Advisor on this project; and Terrence Dunworth, Ph.D., Director of the Justice Policy Center at the Urban Institute. Dr. Zweig and Dr. Dunworth both contributed general review and feedback on the content of this bulletin. The authors also acknowledge the contributors of the Polaris Project, our research partners, who provided invaluable expertise and assistance throughout this study, particularly with organizing and conducting our practitioner meeting with CSEC advocates and service providers.

Finally, we would like to acknowledge Jeffrey Gersh, Program Manager at OJJDP, whose input and guidance throughout the course of the research led to improvements in the study's implementation and analyses.

SHARE WITH YOUR COLLEAGUES

Unless otherwise noted, OJJDP publications are not copyright protected. We encourage you to reproduce this document, share it with your colleagues, and reprint it in your newsletter or journal. However, if you reprint, please cite OJJDP and the authors of this bulletin. We are also interested in your feedback, such as how you received a copy, how you intend to use the information, and how OJJDP materials meet your individual or agency needs. Please direct your comments and questions to:

Juvenile Justice Clearinghouse
Publication Reprint/Feedback
P.O. Box 6000
Rockville, MD 20849–6000
800–851–3420
301–519–5600 (fax)
Web: tellncjrs.ncjrs.gov

This bulletin was prepared under cooperative agreement number 2006–JP–FX–K058 from the Office of Juvenile Justice and Delinquency Prevention (OJJDP), U.S. Department of Justice.

Points of view or opinions expressed in this document are those of the authors and do not necessarily represent the official position or policies of OJJDP or the U.S. Department of Justice.

The Office of Juvenile Justice and Delinquency Prevention is a component of the Office of Justice Programs, which also includes the Bureau of Justice Assistance; the Bureau of Justice Statistics; the Community Capacity Development Office; the National Institute of Justice; the Office for Victims of Crime; and the Office of Sex Offender Sentencing, Monitoring, Apprehending, Registering, and Tracking (SMART).

End Notes

[1] 18 U.S.C. § 1591(b)(1) was strengthened under Section 208 of the Adam Walsh Child Protection and Safety Act of 2006. For full text of the legislation, see www.usdoj.gov/olp/pdf/adam_walsh_act.pdf. The William Wilberforce Trafficking Victims Protection Reauthorization Act of 2008 also refined the language of this section. For full text of the legislation, see www.usdoj.gov/olp/pdf/wilberforce-act.pdf.

[2] The Prosecutorial Remedies and Other Tools to End the Exploitation of Children Today (PROTECT) Act of 2003 increased this penalty to 40 years. Subsequently, the Adam Walsh Child Protection and Safety Act of 2006 (Public Law 109–248) strengthened penalties under 18 U.S.C. § 1591(b)(1) to life imprisonment (also see endnote 1).

[3] For more information about the Innocence Lost National Initiative, see www.fbi.gov/innolost/innolost.htm.

[4] The Polaris Project is an international organization, based in the United States and Japan, committed to combating human trafficking and modern-day slavery.

[5] For more detailed and comprehensive background information on CSEC, see the full research report, *An Analysis of Federally Prosecuted CSEC Cases since the Passage of the Victims of Trafficking and Violence Protection Act of 2000*, at www.ncjrs.gov/ pdffiles 1/ojjdp/grants/222023.pdf.

[6] See exhibit 3.1 on p. 14 in the full report for the list of the specific statutes that were included. This list was informed by several interviews conducted with federal prosecutors who routinely prosecute CSEC cases for the U.S. Department of Justice and by advice from the Polaris Project.

[7] The practitioner focus group made suggestions for future research. See pp. 66–68 of the full report for more information.

[8] See figures 3.4 and 3.5; appendix B; and tables 3, 3a, 3b, and 3c in the full report for a more detailed description of reasons why cases were not prosecuted, as listed by CSEC offense.

[9] Legislation addressing CSEC in 2003 included the PROTECT Act and the 2003 reauthorization of TVPA (Trafficking Victims Protection Reauthorization Act, 2003). The FBI, in collaboration with the National Center for Missing & Exploited Children and the Department of Justice's Child Exploitation and Obscenity Section, also launched the Innocence Lost National Initiative in 2003, which created national task forces to address the domestic sex trafficking of children. In addition to legislative efforts, anti-human-trafficking and anti-CSEC organizations from across the country came together in 2003 to host *Breaking the Silence,* the first national youth summit on CSEC (Shared Hope International et al., 2006).

[10] For an indepth description of this time series model and its results, see section 3.4.1 in the full report.

[11] The Federal Sentencing Guidelines, which federal judges were legally required to use for determining all federal sentences during the study period, consist primarily of two factors: offense seriousness and the offender's criminal history score category (a higher category indicates more criminal history). For more information, see the United States Sentencing Commission Web site at www.ussc.gov/ guidelin.htm.

[12] Service providers who participated in the practitioner meeting work primarily with victims of sex trafficking.

[13] Service providers and advocates participating in the practitioner meeting reported that during the prosecution of a CSEC case, service providers have to make sure the children stay in the system to testify. Staying in the system entails being placed in secure housing for the length of the prosecution. For foreign national victims, this housing is often a shelter with staff trained to deal with this special population. However, for domestic victims, this often means being placed in juvenile detention facilities or foster care with limited or no services. If the children leave the criminal justice or welfare system, participants reported that it can bedifficult to find them again and, if found, service providers have to rebuild their trust and willingness to participate in the case process. See chapter 4: Practitioner Meeting in the full report (p. 60) for more details.

In: National Strategy for Child Exploitation Prevention... ISBN: 978-1-61122-853-3
Editor: Jeremy R. Barnes and Ashley P. Davis

Chapter 3

JUVENILES WHO COMMIT SEX OFFENSES AGAINST MINORS

David Finkelhor, Richard Ormrod, Mark Chaffin and Juvenile Justice Bulletin

The Office of Juvenile Justice and Delinquency Prevention (OJJDP) is committed to improving the justice system's response to crimes against children. OJJDP recognizes that children are at increased risk for crime victimization. Not only are children the victims of many of the same crimes that victimize adults, they are subject to other crimes, like child abuse and neglect, that are specific to childhood. The impact of these crimes on young victims can be devastating, and the violent or sexual victimization of children can often lead to an intergenerational cycle of violence and abuse. The purpose of OJJDP's Crimes Against Children Series is to improve and expand the Nation's efforts to better serve child victims by presenting the latest information about child victimization, including analyses of crime victimization statistics, studies of child victims and their special needs, and descriptions of programs and approaches that address these needs.

Although those who commit sex offenses against minors are often described as "pedophiles" or "predators" and thought of as adults, it is important to understand that a substantial portion of these offenses are committed by other minors who do not fit the image of such terms. Interest in youth who commit sexual offenses has grown in recent years, along with specialized treatment and management programs, but relatively little population-based epidemiological information about the characteristics of this group of offenders[1] and their offenses has been available. The National Incident-Based Reporting System (NIBRS) offers perspective on the characteristics of the juvenile sex offender population coming to the attention of law enforcement.

Key findings from this Bulletin include the following:

- Juveniles account for more than one-third (35.6 percent) of those known to police to have committed sex offenses against minors.

- Juveniles who commit sex offenses against other children are more likely than adult sex offenders to offend in groups and at schools and to have more male victims and younger victims.
- The number of youth coming to the attention of police for sex offenses increases sharply at age 12 and plateaus after age 14. Early adolescence is the peak age for offenses against younger children. Offenses against teenagers surge during mid to late adolescence, while offenses against victims under age 12 decline.
- A small number of juvenile offenders— 1 out of 8—are younger than age 12.
- Females constitute 7 percent of juveniles who commit sex offenses.
- Females are found more frequently among younger youth than older youth who commit sex offenses. This group's offenses involve more multiple-victim and multiple-perpetrator episodes, and they are more likely to have victims who are family members or males.
- Jurisdictions vary enormously in their concentration of reported juvenile sex offenders, far more so than they vary in their concentration of adult sex offenders.

A Message from OJJDP

The victimization of youth by adult sex offenders has been an ongoing concern for some time. Although all crimes constitute an assault on civilization, the criminal violation of children is particularly disturbing.

In recent years, there has been increased public interest in the incidence of sexual victimization of youth by other youth. This should not be surprising considering that youth constitute more than one in four sex offenders and that juveniles perpetrate more than one in three sex offenses against other youth.

Research on juvenile sex offenders goes back more than half a century; however, little information about these young offenders and their offenses exists.

This Bulletin draws on data from the Federal Bureau of Investigation's National Incident-Based Reporting System to provide population-based epidemiological information on juvenile sex offending.

It is OJJDP's hope that the findings reported in this Bulletin and their implications will help inform the policy and practice of those committed to addressing the sexual victimization of youth and strengthening its prevention and deterrence—considerations that are critical to success. Their efforts to protect youth from victimization, or from becoming victimizers themselves, have our support and commendation.

Background

Research on juvenile sex offenders goes back more than 50 years, but most of what is known comes from a surge of interest in the subject that began in the mid-1980s (Chaffin, Letourneau, and Silovsky, 2002), culled primarily from populations of youth in sex offender treatment programs. Juvenile sex offender treatment programs saw a 40-fold increase between 1982 and 1992 (Knopp, Freeman-Longo, and Stevenson, 1992). Accordingly, the number of published research articles on juvenile sex offenders increased from a handful prior to the mid-1980s to more than 200 studies currently. Dissemination of information about these offenders has included federally funded efforts from sources such as the Center for Sex Offender Management and the National Center on the Sexual Behavior of Youth. Professional societies such as the Association for the Treatment of Sexual Abusers have also published policy and practice guidelines.

Most of the clinical sample studies on which current knowledge is based have focused on the clinical characteristics of offenders, treatment issues, risk predictors, and recidivism rates (Becker, 1998). The clinical literature has generally considered teenage and preteen offenders as different offender types: teenage sex offenders are predominately male (more than 90 percent), whereas a significant number of preteen offenders are female (Silovsky and Niec, 2002). Most offenses described in the clinical literature involve teenage offenders acting alone with young children as victims. Many specialized intervention systems are designed with this type of behavior in mind.

The National Incident-Based Reporting System (NIBRS)

The U.S. Department of Justice is replacing its long-established Uniform Crime Reports (UCR) system with a more comprehensive National Incident-Based Reporting System (NIBRS). Whereas UCR monitors only a limited number of index crimes and gathers few details on each crime event (except in the case of homicide), NIBRS collects a wide range of information on victims, offenders, and circumstances for a greater variety of offenses. Offenses tracked in NIBRS include violent crimes (e.g., homicide, assault, rape, robbery), property crimes (e.g., theft, arson, vandalism, fraud, and embezzlement), and crimes against society (e.g., drug offenses, gambling, prostitution). Moreover, NIBRS collects information on multiple victims, multiple offenders, and multiple crimes that may be part of the same episode.

Under the new system, as under the old, local law enforcement personnel compile information on crimes coming to their attention and the information is then aggregated at State and national levels. For a crime to count in the system, law enforcement simply needs to report and investigate the crime. The incident does not need to be cleared, nor must an arrest be made, though unfounded reports are deleted.

NIBRS holds great promise, but it is still far from a national system. The Federal Bureau of Investigation (FBI) began implementing the system in 1988, and State and local agency participation is voluntary and incremental. By 1995, jurisdictions in 9 States had agencies contributing data; by 1997, the number was 12; and by 2004, jurisdictions in 29 States submitted reports, providing coverage for 20 percent of the Nation's population and 16 percent of its crime. At the beginning of 2004, only 7 States (Delaware, Idaho, Iowa, South Carolina, Tennessee, Virginia, and West Virginia) had participation from all local jurisdictions, and only 5 cities with a population greater than 500,000 (Columbus, OH; El Paso, TX; Memphis, TN; Nashville, TN; and Milwaukee, WI) were reporting. The crime experiences of large urban areas are thus particularly underrepresented. The system, therefore, is not yet nationally representative, nor do its data represent national trends or national statistics. Nevertheless, the system is assembling large amounts of crime information and providing rich detail about juvenile offending and victimization that was previously unavailable. The patterns and associations these data reveal are real and represent the experiences of a large number of youth. For 2004, the 29 participating States* reported more than 4,037,000 crime incidents, with at least 14,000 involving an identified juvenile sex offender. As more jurisdictions join the system, new patterns may emerge.

More information about NIBRS data collection can be found at these Web sites:

(1) www.fbi.gov/ucr/ucr.htm#cius
(2) www.ojp.usdoj.gov/bjs/nibrs.htm
(3) www.jrsa.org/ibrrc

* In 2004, participating States included Arizona, Arkansas, Colorado, Connecticut, Delaware, Georgia, Idaho, Iowa, Kansas, Kentucky, Louisiana, Maine, Massachusetts, Michigan, Nebraska, New Hampshire, North Dakota, Ohio, Oregon, Rhode Island, South Carolina, South Dakota, Tennessee, Texas, Utah, Vermont, Virginia, West Virginia, and Wisconsin.

Early thinking about juvenile sex offenders was based on what was known about adult child molesters, particularly adult pedophiles, given findings that a significant portion of them began their offending during adolescence. However, current clinical typologies and models emphasize that this retrospective logic has obscured important motivational, behavioral, and prognostic differences between juvenile sex offenders and adult sex offenders and has overestimated the role of deviant sexual preferences in juvenile sex crimes. More recent models emphasize the diversity of juvenile sex offenders, their favorable prognosis suggested by low sex-offense-recidivism rates, and the commonalities between juvenile sex offending and other juvenile delinquency (Letourneau and Miner, 2005).

Clinical studies also underscore a diversity of behaviors, characteristics, and future risk. For example, the sexual behaviors that bring youth into clinical settings can include events as diverse as sharing pornography with younger children, fondling a child over the clothes, grabbing peers in a sexual way at school, date rape, gang rape, or performing oral, vaginal, or anal sex on a much younger child. Offenses can involve a single event, a few isolated events, or a large number of events with multiple victims. Juvenile sex offenders come from a variety of social and family backgrounds and can either be well functioning or have multiple problems. A number have experienced a high accumulated burden of adversity, including maltreatment or exposure to violence; others have not. In some cases, a history of childhood sexual abuse appears to contribute to later juvenile sex offending (Lambie et al., 2002), but most sexual abuse victims do not become sex offenders in adolescence or adulthood (Widom and Ames, 1994). Among preteen children with sexual behavior problems, a history of sexual abuse is particularly prevalent.

In addition to a diversity of backgrounds, diversity in motivation is evident. Some juvenile sex offenders appear primarily motivated by sexual curiosity. Others have longstanding patterns of violating the rights of others. Some offenses occur in conjunction with serious mental health problems. Some of the offending behavior is compulsive, but it more often appears impulsive or reflects poor judgment (Becker, 1998; Center for Sex Offender Management, 1999; Chaffin, 2005; Hunter et al., 2003).

Similarly, clinical data point to variability in risk for future sex offending as an adult. Multiple short- and long-term clinical followup studies of juvenile sex offenders consistently demonstrate that a large majority (about 85–95 percent) of sex-offending youth have no arrests or reports for future sex crimes. When previously sex-offending youth do have future arrests, they are far more likely to be for nonsexual crimes such as property or drug offenses than for sex crimes (Alexander, 1999; Caldwell, 2002; Reitzel and Carbonell, 2007). These empirical findings contrast with popular thought and widely publicized anecdotal cases that disproportionately portray incidences of sex crime recidivism. Nevertheless, a small number of sex-offending youth are at elevated risk to progress to adult sex offenses. To identify those who are more likely to progress to future offending, researchers have developed actuarial risk assessment tools that have demonstrated some predictive validity; efforts to refine these tools are underway (Parks and Bard, 2006; Right-hand et al., 2005; Worling, 2004).

USING NIBRS DATA TO INVESTIGATE JUVENILE SEX OFFENDERS

The information presented in this Bulletin about juvenile sex offenders is based on data collected by the National Incident-Based Reporting System (NIBRS) for 2004 (see discussion of the National Incident-Based Reporting System on page 2). At present, NIBRS is the only available source of geographically diverse and uniformly collected crime data that provides detailed descriptions of juvenile sex offenders, their victims, and the crime incidents they initiate. The offenders and incidents recorded by NIBRS represent only those that come to the attention of police.

The basic unit of data organization in NIBRS is the crime incident. An incident is defined as "one or more offenses committed by the same offender, or group of offenders acting in concert, at the same time and place" (U.S. Department of Justice, Federal Bureau of Investigation, 2004:191). Thus, a single sex offense incident can be characterized by additional offenses beyond a sex offense or even multiple sex offenses, by multiple offenders, and by multiple victims. Most sex offense incidents, however, are not so complex.

For this Bulletin, the basic unit of measure is the individual sex offender, although NIBRS links each offender to broader incident characteristics, such as the number of offenders present, victim age and identity, incident location, and time of day. Although juveniles sometimes commit sex crimes against adults, the majority (96.2 percent) of those known to police target other juveniles. These offenders, juveniles who commit sex offenses against minors, are of particular interest to this analysis. Unless stated otherwise in this Bulletin, "sex offender" (both juvenile and adult) refers to those committing sex offenses against minors.

For purposes of analysis, juvenile victims are defined as persons younger than 18; juvenile offenders are defined as persons of ages 6 through 17. (Although NIBRS records include a small number of children younger than 6 years of age, the notion of very young children committing sex crimes is problematic, so these children were excluded from this analysis.) An adult is defined as a person 18 years of age or older. It is also important to note that the offender ages recorded in NIBRS reflect the ages of the youth at the time the incidents are reported, not the ages at the time the incidents occurred, which are different in 19 percent of cases.

This Bulletin makes some comparisons between an individual offender and an individual victim (e.g., age difference, gender similarity or difference).

For offenders in incidents with multiple victims (12.8 percent of juvenile offenders), this Bulletin uses the youngest victim for these comparisons.

NIBRS data identify a number of specific sex offenses and classify them as either forcible (rape, sodomy, sexual assault with an object, fondling) or nonforcible (incest, statutory rape) sex offenses. It defines a forcible sex offense as "any sexual act directed against another person, forcibly and/or against that person's will; or not forcibly or against the person's will where the victim is incapable of giving consent" (U.S. Department of Justice, Federal Bureau of Investigation, 2004:191). A person may be incapable of giving consent because of temporary or permanent mental or physical incapacity or because of youth. Furthermore, NIBRS guidelines direct that "the ability of the victim to give consent must be a professional determination by the law enforcement agency" (U.S. Department of Justice, Federal Bureau of Investigation, 2004:191). A nonforcible sex offense is defined as "unlawful, nonforcible sexual intercourse" (U.S. Department of Justice, Federal Bureau of Investigation, 2004:192).

Although NIBRS attempts to standardize crime definitions, individual police officers and jurisdictions may categorize similar episodes in very different ways for NIBRS purposes, so the distinctions among various sex offense categories may be less clear than the names might imply. Although statutes do describe illegal sexual behavior that could easily be classified as nonforcible (e.g., showing pornography or making sexual suggestions to a child) and other behaviors that are clearly forcible (e.g., rape), how law enforcement might categorize less straightforward cases (e.g., physically noncoercive fondling between youth of widely disparate ages) may be less reliable. For this Bulletin, "sex offender" refers to a person who has committed either a forcible or nonforcible sex offense, although the majority of juvenile sex offenders (90.5 percent) reported in NIBRS committed a forcible sex offense.

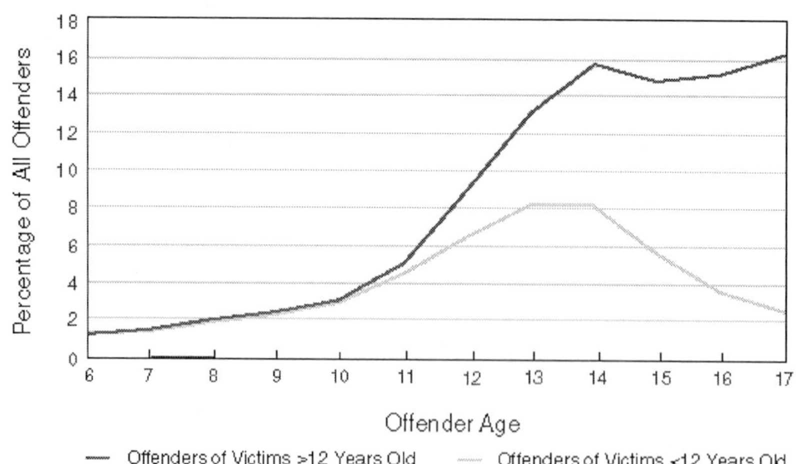

Note: N = 13,471 juvenile offenders.

Source: U.S. Department of Justice, Federal Bureau of Investigation, National Incident-Based Reporting System, 2004.

Figure 1. Age Distribution of Juvenile Sex Offenders, by Victim Age

Unfortunately, research on juvenile sex offenders beyond clinical populations has been more limited. Few studies have surveyed representative youth populations to ascertain population-based rates of juvenile offending (e.g., Elliott, Huizinga, and Menard, 1989).

Juvenile sex offenses reported to authorities yield official crime report data, but these data typically contain limited information about the nature of the incidents involved. As more detailed crime report data become available, and as researchers study these data in conjunction with clinical sample data, the information gained will assist prevention and intervention planning substantially.

JUVENILE AND ADULT SEX OFFENDERS KNOWN TO POLICE

Juvenile sex offenders comprise more than one-quarter (25.8 percent) of all sex offenders and more than one-third (35.6 percent) of sex offenders against juvenile victims (the group that is the focus of this Bulletin). As a percentage of all juvenile offenders, they do not constitute a large group—juvenile sex offenders account for only 3.1 percent of all juvenile offenders and 7.4 percent of all violent juvenile offenders. If other jurisdictions in the country were assumed to be the same as the NIBRS jurisdictions, one would extrapolate approximately 89,000 juvenile sex offenders known to police throughout the United States in 2004.

Known juvenile offenders who commit sex offenses against minors span a variety of ages. Five percent are younger than 9 years, and 16 percent are younger than 12 years (figure 1). The rate rises sharply around age 12 and plateaus after age 14. As a proportion of the total, 38 percent are between ages 12 and 14, and 46 percent are between ages 15 and 17. The vast majority (93 percent) are male.

Juveniles who commit sex offenses against minors are different from adults who commit sex offenses against minors on a number of crucial dimensions captured by NIBRS (table 1, page 5). Juveniles are more likely to offend in groups (24 percent with one or more co-offenders versus 14 percent for adults). They are somewhat more likely to offend against acquaintances (63 percent versus 55 percent). Their most serious offense is less likely to be rape (24 percent versus 31 percent) and more likely to be sodomy (13 percent versus 7 percent) or fondling (49 percent versus 42 percent). They are more likely to have a male victim (25 percent versus 13 percent).

Sex offenses committed by juveniles very often occur in the home, although somewhat less often than their adult counterparts (69 percent versus 80 percent) but are more likely to occur in a school (12 percent versus 2 percent). Their offenses occur somewhat more in the afternoon (43 percent versus 37 percent for adults) than in the evening (25 percent versus 28 percent) or at night (5 percent versus 9 percent).

Juvenile sex offenders are also much more likely than adult sex offenders to target young children as their victims. The proportion of victims younger than the age of 12 is 59 percent for juvenile sex offenders, compared with 39 percent for adult sex offenders. Figure 2 (page 6) shows how adult sex offenders concentrate their offenses against victims age 13 and older. In contrast, the age range of victims of juvenile sex offenders is more dispersed, and 16-and 17-year-old victims actually represent a surprisingly small proportion. Juvenile sex offenders are less likely to target other juveniles who are older than they are. Figure 2 also shows that children younger than age 12 have about an equal likelihood of being victimized by juvenile and adult sex offenders, but adult offenders predominate among those who victimize teens.

Juvenile sex offenders more commonly target other juveniles who are somewhat younger than they are, signaling a clear relationship between the age of juvenile sex offenders and the age of their victims (figure 3, page 6). When juvenile sex offenders are themselves 6 to 9 years old, the mean age of their victims is between 5 and 7. When juvenile sex offenders are age 15 to 17, the mean age of their victims is between 11 and 13. However, when victims are younger than age 12, there is a marked peak for offending by 13- to 14-year-olds, and then a dramatic decline in the targeting of these young victims by youth age 15 and older (figure 1). Youth age 15 and older primarily target postpubescent victims.

Table 1. Characteristics of Juveniles and Adults Who Commit Sex Offenses Against Minors

Characteristic	Sex Offenders (%)	
	Juvenile N (= 13,471)	Adult (N = 24,344)
Multiple offenders in incident	23.9	13.5
Two offenders	14.4	9.1
Three or more offenders	9.5	4.4
Victim identity (youngest victim)		
Family	25.0	31.9
Acquaintance	63.2	54.8
Stranger	2.5	4.4
Victim was also offender	0.8	0.0
Unknown	8.4	9.0
Sex offense (most serious)		
Rape	24.0	30.6
Sodomy	12.5	6.5
Sex assault with object	4.7	4.4
Fondling	49.4	42.1
Nonforcible sex offense	9.5	16.3
Female offender	7.3	5.4
Victim gender		
Any female victim in incident	78.8	88.2
Any male victim in incident	24.7	13.4
Incident location		
Residence/home	68.8	79.6
School/college	11.9	1.6
Store/building	3.8	4.8
Outside	7.1	6.7
Other/unknown	8.3	7.3
Incident time of day		
Morning (6 a.m. to 12 p.m.)	26.7	25.1
Afternoon (12 p.m. to 6 p.m.)	43.0	37.3
Evening (6 p.m. to 12 a.m.)	25.2	28.3
Night (12 a.m. to 6 a.m.)	5.2	9.2
Arrest in incident	30.5	34.1

Source: U.S. Department of Justice, Federal Bureau of Investigation, National Incident-Based Reporting System, 2004.

This relationship between offender age and victim age also varies by victim gender, as shown in figures 4 (page 8) and 5 (page 10). When the victims are boys, a majority are younger than age 12, and there is also a marked peak reflecting 12- to 14-year-old sex offenders targeting 4- to 7-year-old boys. When the victims are girls, by contrast, there is a greater link between the rise in age of the offender and the victim, and the peak is among 15- to 17-year-olds targeting 13- to 15-yearold girls. This suggests that when teen offenders target boys, they tend to focus on much younger and sexually immature boys rather than their peers, whereas when older teen offenders target girls, they tend to focus more on sexually mature females. This finding may stem from the fact that juvenile offenders may find it easier to dominate girls and younger boys than to dominate older boys. However, it could also be that older male victims of teenage offenders are particularly reluctant to report their victimizations to police compared with teenage female victims.

YOUNGER JUVENILE SEX OFFENDERS

Although most juvenile sex offenders are teenagers, about 16 percent of those who come to police attention are younger than age 12. This group has been of particular interest to clinicians, educators, and public safety officials, who have been reluctant to regard them in the same delinquency-oriented framework that has applied to older offenders. Professionals commonly use other terms, such as "children with sexual behavior problems," to describe this group. What proportion of these children come to police attention is unclear because these cases may be handled exclusively within other systems, such as the child protection system or schools. However, the group of younger juvenile offenders who come to police attention does manifest certain characteristics that differentiate them from older offenders (table 2, page 7).

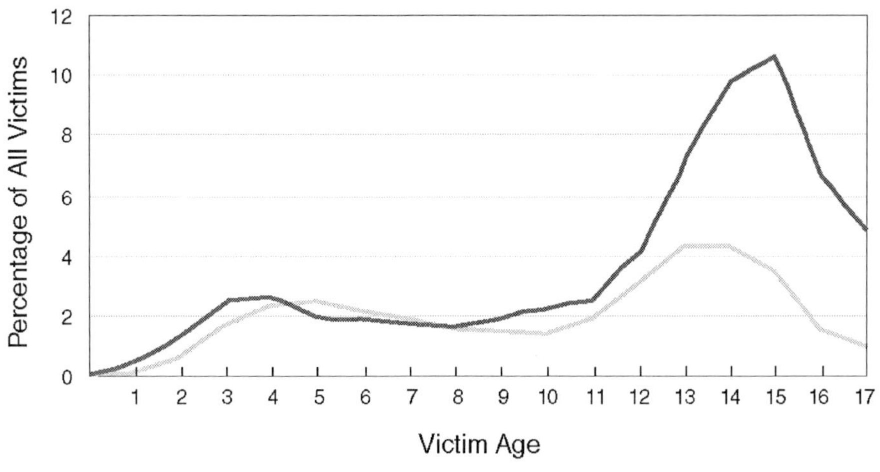

Note: N = 37,815 juvenile victims, 13,471 (36 percent) with juvenile offenders and 24,344 (64 percent) with adult offenders. For offenders with multiple victims, age of youngest victim is shown.

Source: U.S. Department of Justice, Federal Bureau of Investigation, National Incident-Based Reporting System, 2004.

Figure 2. Age Distribution of Juvenile Sex Victims, by Offender Age

Offenders younger than age 12 are somewhat more likely than offenders age 12 or older to be female and to offend in multiple offender and multiple victim episodes. Younger offenders are also somewhat more likely than older offenders to offend against family members and in a residential environment. Younger offenders are more likely than older offenders to target male victims (37 percent versus 20 percent) and younger victims closer to their own age. Their most serious offense is more likely to be fondling and less likely to be rape. Police are considerably less likely to arrest younger offenders than older offenders in the wake of a report (17 percent versus 33 percent).

Female Juvenile Sex Offenders

Female juvenile sex offenders are another group who have attracted a particular interest among clinicians and law enforcement officials. They constitute only a small proportion (7 percent) of all juvenile sex offenders in the NIBRS database, but they have several features that distinguish them from male juvenile sex offenders (table 3, page 9).

Female offenders are younger than their male counterparts. Of the female offenders, 31 percent were younger than 12, compared with only 14 percent of male offenders. Female offenders were considerably more likely than male offenders to offend in conjunction with others (36 percent versus 23 percent) and in conjunction with adults (13 percent versus 5 percent). They were also more likely to be involved in incidents with multiple victims than were male offenders (23 percent versus 12 percent) and to be considered by investigators to be victims at the same time they were offending.

Female offenders are somewhat more likely to offend in a residence or home and less likely to offend at a school. They were more likely than male offenders to have male victims (37 percent versus 21 percent) and victims younger than age 11 (60 percent versus 43 percent).

Reporting Juvenile Sex Offenses

Concern about juvenile sex offenders is a relatively recent phenomenon. Some communities have mobilized quite ener getically in recent years to identify and intervene with such youth, conducting extensive training among law enforcement, child protection staff, and educators and establishing specialized treatment programs. In other communities, however, concern about the problem has been slow to develop. Thus, the spectrum of community activity surrounding juvenile sex offenders ranges from very slight in some jurisdictions to exaggerated or disproportionate in other jurisdictions.

This variability in community response is reflected in the data from NIBRS jurisdictions, which differ considerably in the concentration of juvenile sex offenders in their caseloads. Some jurisdictions may have unusually high concentrations of juvenile sex offenders. In NIBRS jurisdictions with populations greater than 5,000 (classified as "city" type jurisdictions) and that have at least 10 juvenile violent offenders, juvenile sex offenders constitute 6 percent of the total number of juvenile violent offenders overall. However, a considerable number of jurisdictions have particularly high concentrations of juvenile sex offenders. For example, of the identified NIBRS jurisdictions, 8 percent have concentrations of juvenile sex offenders that are three times that of the median jurisdiction (i.e., more than 25 percent of the jurisdiction's juvenile violent offenders are sex offenders). In contrast, just 4 percent of the identified NIBRS jurisdictions have concentrations of adult sex offenders that are triple the rate for the median jurisdiction.

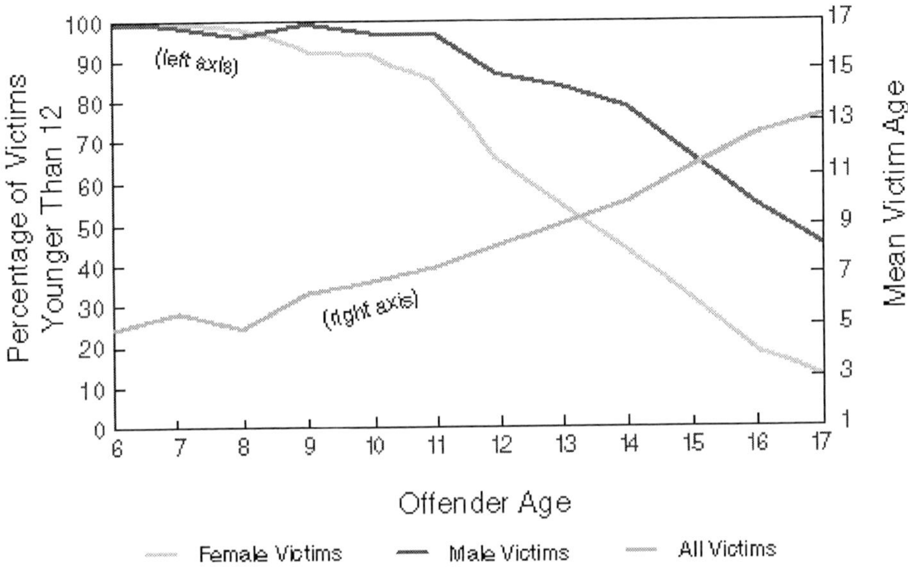

Note: N = 13,471 juvenile offenders. For offenders with multiple victims, age of youngest victim is shown.

Source: U.S. Department of Justice, Federal Bureau of Investigation, National Incident-Based Reporting System, 2004.

Figure 3. Juvenile Sex Victim Age, by Juvenile Offender Age

Table 2. Characteristics of Juvenile Sex Offenders Who Victimize Minors, by Age of Offender

Characteristic	Juvenile Sex Offenders (%)	
	Younger (age < 12 years) (N = 2,104)	Older (age = 12 years) (N = 11,367)
Multiple offenders in incident	29.0	23.0
Adult offender in incident	2.6	5.7
Female offender	14.6	5.9
Multiple victims in incident	16.0	12.1
Victim identity (youngest victim)		
Family	31.6	23.8
Acquaintance	56.0	64.5
Stranger	1.6	2.7
Victim is also offender	1.0	0.8
Unknown	9.7	8.2
Incident location		

Table 2. (Continued)

Characteristic	Juvenile Sex Offenders (%)	
	Younger (age < 12 years) (*N* = 2,104)	Older (age = 12 years) (*N* = 11,367)
Residence/home	73.0	68.1
School/college	10.8	12.1
Store/building	2.9	4.0
Outside	5.0	7.4
Other/unknown	8.2	8.3
Victim gender (youngest victim)		
Male	36.6	19.9
Female	63.4	80.1
Age of youngest victim (years)		
0–6	57.1	21.0
7–10	31.2	15.5
11–14	10.9	43.2
15–17	0.8	20.2
Sex offense (most serious)		
Rape	11.0	26.4
Sodomy	15.4	11.9
Sex assault with object	7.2	4.2
Fondling	61.3	47.2
Nonforcible sex offense	5.1	10.5
Injury in incident		
None	88.8	86.9
Minor	9.6	10.6
Major	1.6	2.5
Incident time of day		
Morning (6 a.m. to 12 p.m.)	28.9	26.3
Afternoon (12 p.m. to 6 p.m.)	45.6	42.5
Evening (6 p.m. to 12 a.m.)	22.7	25.7
Night (12 a.m. to 6 a.m.)	2.8	5.6
Arrest in incident	16.5	32.9

Source: U.S. Department of Justice, Federal Bureau of Investigation, National Incident-Based Reporting System, 2004.

There is also evidence of a tendency in other jurisdictions for juvenile sex offenders to represent a disproportionately small proportion of all juvenile violent offenders. In 29 percent of the identified NIBRS jurisdictions, the concentration of juvenile sex offenders equals half the median concentration (a low proportion) for the group of NIBRS jurisdictions identified above. In contrast, only 19 percent of the identified NIBRS jurisdictions have a similarly low concentration of adult sex offenders. That is, in contrast to the situation with adult sex offender concentrations, more jurisdictions have either a very high concentration of juvenile sex offenders or a concentration that is particularly low, reflecting, perhaps, contrasting levels of interest in this offender group. Table 4 (page 10) suggests that large jurisdictions are particularly likely to have low concentrations of juvenile sex offenders among their juvenile violent offender population. It is also possible that these jurisdictions have higher rates of violent nonsexual juvenile offending, which lowers the relative percentage of juvenile sex offenders.

IMPLICATIONS

These findings suggest a number of implications for policy and practice. First, the statistics clearly highlight the fact that juveniles continue to constitute a substantial proportion—more than one-third—of those who commit sexual offenses against minors. This proportion is comparable to that found in reports from other samples and from earlier periods (Davis and Leitenberg, 1987; Snyder and Sickmund, 1999). Thus, any effort to prevent or intervene in sexual assault and child molestation must address the risk that juvenile sex offenders pose. Prevention and deterrence messages should be directed to youthful audiences in schools, youth organizations, on the Internet, on youth-oriented media, and even in families. Victimization prevention messages delivered to potential victims and their caregivers should be broadened to include information about the risk of sexual abuse not only from adults but also from juveniles.

In addition, perpetration prevention programs that have been targeted primarily toward at-risk adult populations need to begin earlier (Ryan, 1997), with youth younger than age 12, the age at which these findings suggest an escalation in offending occurs. Given the sharp increase in sex offense rates at this age, prevention messages delivered to boys prior to early adolescence may be essential to consider. The prevention messages for these preteens may need to focus on their risk for victimizing much younger children (ages 4–7). Families and institutions may need to stay vigilant about contexts that involve pairings of young teenage boys with much younger children. This is not to suggest that all young teenage boys pose a high risk for molesting children. Very few juveniles of any age commit sex offenses. Rather, it is simply that the risk of offending against children during this developmental period appears to be relatively higher than at other ages. Therefore, some increased vigilance may be appropriate. This might include taking additional care to check references when considering young teenage babysitters and exercising closer supervision or monitoring of interactions.

Different preventive priorities seem important for older teenagers. Given the older age profile for victims of older teenagers, prevention messages may need to shift as youth enter middle adolescence. Prevention messages for these older teenagers may be better focused on the dynamics of date and teenager-on-teenager rape. The Centers for Disease Control and Prevention (CDC) have developed a multilevel public health primary-perpetration prevention model that includes suggested prevention activities at the individual, relationship, community, and societal levels (Centers for Disease Control and Prevention, 2004), including a focus on juvenile perpetration prevention.

To ensure adequate intervention with the large proportion of juveniles among the sex offender population, police, prosecutors, and probation and parole officials need adequate training and resources to respond effectively and sensitively to juvenile sex offenders. They must conduct investigations and manage juvenile offenders in a way that best prevents reoffending. Fortunately, several intervention strategies have proven effective in reducing recidivism among teenage sex offenders, and communities should acquaint themselves with these approaches (Borduin and Schaeffer, 2001; Reitzel and Carbonell, 2007; Letourneau et al., 2009). Good results have also been reported across a number of short-term interventions with juvenile offenders younger than age 12 (Chaffin et al., 2008). Researchers found that one brief treatment for preteens reduced the risk of future sex offenses to levels comparable with those of children who had no history of inappropriate sexual behavior (Carpentier, Silovsky, and Chaffin, 2006).

Analysis of the study data also highlights certain features of juvenile sex offenders that policymakers should take into account. First, the findings emphasize the diversity among juveniles who commit sex offenses. This population clearly includes older and younger youth, males and females, those who offend against much younger children, those who offend against peers, those who offend alone, and those who offend in groups, among other diverse characteristics. This diversity indicates the need to avoid stereotypes about juvenile sex offenders and to develop prevention and response strategies that can accommodate many of these various types of youth and offenses. Similarly, public policies must reflect the diversity among juvenile sex offenders by adopting more nuanced and flexible procedures rather than broad mandates.

The analyses reiterate many findings from the clinical sample literature, notably, that individuals known to the victim, including family members, are those who most often commit sexual assaults; that around 90 percent of known teen offenders are male; and that preteens with sexual behavior problems include a higher percentage of girls. Given the natural reluctance to consider family members and other trusted persons among those who may pose a danger, these findings underscore the need for information about prevention to emphasize that risk can include family members or other well-known persons.

The findings show that young boys are highly vulnerable to offenses by other juveniles. Parents, schools, or prevention programs that have focused on limiting or supervising contact between female children and older male juveniles or adults must revise their messages to include examples involving young male victims, and perhaps even female perpetrators. Because boys younger than 12 are particularly at risk, it is important to give them prevention information that addresses the possibility of sexual misbehavior at the hands of older boys. Adults should be equally vigilant in protecting young boys as in protecting young girls.

Another significant finding is that juvenile offenders are more likely than adult offenders to commit illegal sexual behavior in groups. This finding mirrors recent work in other countries that also has shown that juveniles commit more sex crimes in groups (Kjellgren et al., 2006). Although some of these group-involved juveniles may have offended on their own, the findings suggest that peer influences play as much of a role in juvenile sexual delinquency as they do in nonsexual delinquency, underscoring the need for prevention efforts to look beyond individual pathology and consider male adolescent peer cultures. It may be possible to devise interventions that would help inoculate some malleable, but less delinquency prone, youth to resist such peer influence. Such efforts could be extensions of some of the work in the field to promote more prosocial actions by "bystanders" with regard to date rape (Banyard, Moynihan, and Plante, 2007).

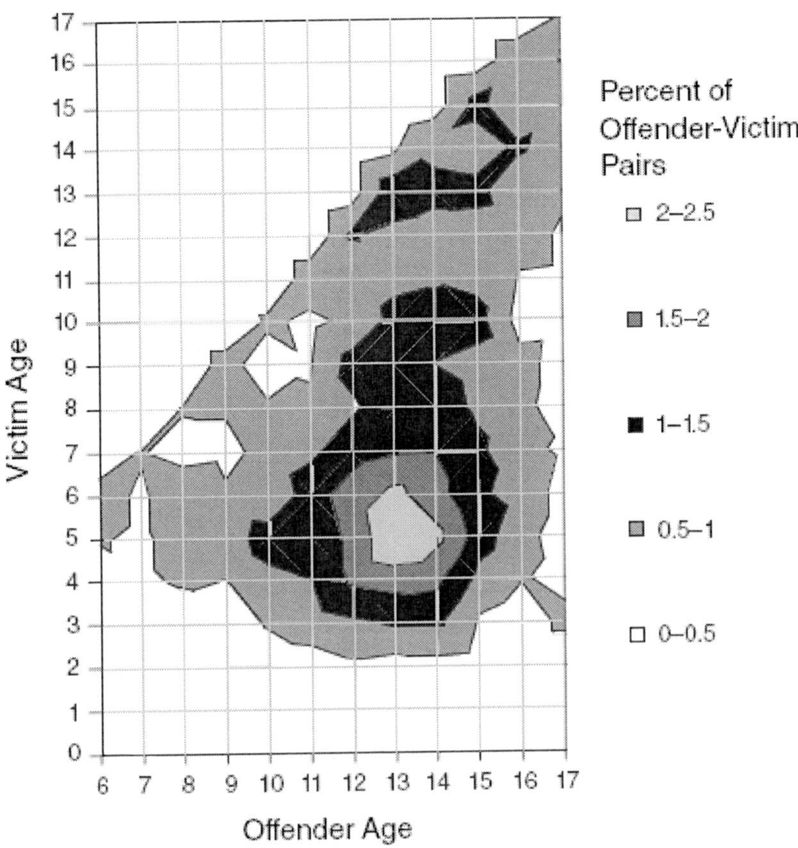

Source: U.S. Department of Justice, Federal Bureau of Investigation, National Incident-Based Reporting System, 2004.

Figure 4. Juvenile Sex Offenders Versus Male Juvenile Victims

Data from police reports also show that, overall, older offenders tend to choose older victims. Juveniles who commit sexual offenses tend to do so against their age mates or somewhat younger children. In fact, offenses against young children actually decline across offender age, as offenders move from early to middle adolescence. This contradicts an assumption behind some sex offender treatment that a fixed attraction to young children (i.e., pedophilia) is the sole or even predominant motivation for juvenile sex offenses. The relationships between victim and offender age found in this study may suggest developmental hypotheses for the clinical assessment of juveniles. To the extent that epidemiologically rarer events correspond to greater individual deviancy, cases of older teenagers victimizing much younger children might raise relatively more concern and pose higher future risk than cases where younger teenagers victimize young children. Because it is more common for younger teenagers than older teenagers to engage in illegal sexual behavior with younger children, this scenario may reflect comparatively lower levels of individual pathology.

Table 3. Characteristics of Juvenile Sex Offenders Who Victimize Minors, by Gender of Offender

Characteristic	Juvenile Sex Offenders (%)	
	Female ($N = 979$)	Male ($N = 12,450$)
Offender age (years)		
6–8	10.6	4.4
9–11	20.6	10.0
12–14	38.3	37.9
15–17	30.4	47.7
Multiple offenders in incident	36.1	22.9
Adult offender in incident	12.6	4.6
Multiple victims in incident	22.9	12.0
Victim identity (youngest victim)		
Family	26.4	24.9
Acquaintance	57.0	63.8
Stranger	0.6	2.6
Victim was also offender	6.3	0.4
Unknown	9.7	8.3
Incident location		
Residence/home	77.2	68.2
School/college	6.5	12.4
Store/building	4.8	3.8
Outside	4.3	7.3
Other/unknown	7.2	8.4
Victim gender (youngest victim)		
Male	36.6	21.4
Female	63.4	78.6
Age of youngest victim (years)		
0–6	39.8	25.6
7–10	20.2	17.8
11–14	26.0	39.2
15–17	13.9	17.4
Type of sex offense		
Forcible	91.0	90.4
Nonforcible	9.0	9.6
Injury in incident		
None	87.6	87.0
Minor	11.5	10.5
Major	0.9	2.5
Incident time of day		
Morning (6 a.m. to 12 p.m.)	27.4	26.6
Afternoon (12 p.m. to 6 p.m.)	41.5	43.1
Evening (6 p.m. to 12 a.m.)	27.0	25.1
Night (12 a.m. to 6 a.m.)	4.0	5.2
Arrest in incident	26.7	30.9

Source: U.S. Department of Justice, Federal Bureau of Investigation, National Incident-Based Reporting System, 2004.

Table 4. Juvenile Sex Offenders as a Percentage of All Juvenile Violent Offenders, by Agency Size

Agency population*	Percent	Quartile (%)	
		Lower	Upper
Less than 50,000	7.3	1.9	11.5
50,000–100,000	6.3	3.2	9.5
100,000–300,000	6.7	4.1	11.9
More than 300,000	4.7	3.4	12.1

*Table includes only agencies classified by NIBRS as cities (population more than 5,000) and which reported at least 10 juvenile violent offenders (N = 1,010 agencies).

Source: U.S. Department of Justice, Federal Bureau of Investigation, National Incident-Based Reporting System, 2004.

Juvenile sex offenders known to law enforcement appear to commit a greater number of group-involved cases and teenager-on-teenager cases than one might expect from studies of clinical populations in which a typical offender is a single teenager victimizing a younger child. Although the clinical literature on juvenile sex offenders has not emphasized teenager-on-teenager sexual assault, the NIBRS data suggest that this problem is very prevalent among middle- and late-adolescent males. It is possible that the juvenile justice system processes group-involved and teenager-on-teenager cases differently or that these offenders are less likely to receive services. How the system handles youth and how well current juvenile justice programming addresses their needs may need further examination. Peer assaults and date rapes have sometimes received less attention than the sexual abuse of young children by teenagers. However, peer assaults and date rape may be easier to prevent because the power differential or developmental difference between offender and victim in these cases is less than that between a teenager and a much younger victim. Because juvenile sexual assaults are more likely than adult assaults to occur at school or during afterschool hours, efforts to prevent juvenile assaults might benefit from actions focused on these settings.

This analysis found considerable variation across jurisdictions and communities in the proportion of juvenile offenses that were sexual in nature. There are a number of possibilities, including real differences in prevalence rates, different rates of overall crime or crime reporting, or differential willingness to report or investigate juvenile sex offenses in particular, that might explain this finding. Observation suggests real variation in community approaches to juvenile sex offending. In some communities, officials handle juvenile sex offense cases more within the child protection system than within the criminal justice system. Exclusive handling of a case within the child welfare system may occur more often when a young child commits the offense or when the offense occurs within the family, possibly causing these types of cases to be underrepresented in NIBRS data.

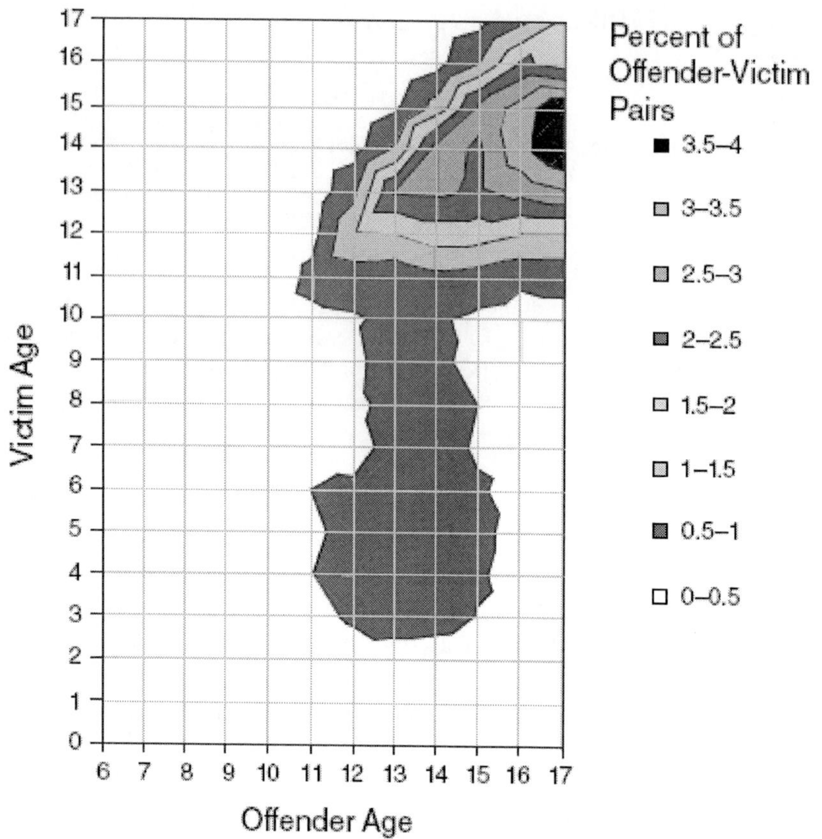

Source: U.S. Department of Justice, Federal Bureau of Investigation, National Incident-Based Reporting System, 2004.

Figure 5. Juvenile Sex Offenders Versus Female Juvenile Victims

If the variation is indeed due to differences in community practice, it may merit additional study, particularly to test whether more aggressive or more criminal-justice-oriented approaches to the problem have advantages over less aggressive approaches or ones that emphasize other institutions such as child protective services or mental health agencies. Some communities have clearly made this problem a law enforcement priority. Although there are many reasons to think that such a priority could have benefits for the community and victims and result in a reduction of sex offending, these are propositions that researchers must evaluate. On the other hand, questions have been raised about whether particularly harsh or stigmatizing community policies—for example placing juveniles on public sex offender registries or excluding these youth from normal social interactions—may have unintended negative consequences, such as deterring reporting, decreasing juvenile justice system involvement in cases, or hindering youths' prosocial developmental that may lead to increased crime risk (Letourneau and Armstrong, 2008).

CONCLUSION

The issue of juvenile sex offenses against minors, like most issues involving sex crimes and minors, will continue to attract considerable controversy and debate. Such debates can often continue unresolved or with questionable policy outcomes in the absence of good epidemiology and other research about the problem and its dynamics. The NIBRS dataset, which is growing to encompass an ever larger number of jurisdictions nationwide, is one resource that can help provide some empirical perspective and should continue to be analyzed for the insights it can offer.

FOR FURTHER INFORMATION

This Bulletin presents information taken from the *National Incident-Based Reporting System, 2004.*

REFERENCES

Alexander, M. A. (1999). Sexual offender treatment efficacy revisited. *Sex Abuse, 11(2),* 101–116.

Banyard, V. L., Moynihan, M. M. & Plante, E. G. (2007). Sexual violence prevention through bystander education: An experimental evaluation. *Journal of Community Psychology, 35*, 463–481.

Becker, J. V. (1998). What we know about the characteristics and treatment of adolescents who have committed sexual offenses. *Child Maltreatment, 3*, 317–329.

Borduin, C. M. & Schaeffer, C. M. (2001). Multisystemic treatment of juvenile sexual offenders: A progress report. *Journal of Psychology and Human Sexuality, 13*, 25–42.

Caldwell, M. F. (2002). What we do not know about juvenile sexual reoffense risk. *Child Maltreatment, 7(4)*, 291–302.

Carpentier, M., Silovsky, J. F. & Chaffin, M. (2006). Randomized trial of treatment for children with sexual behavior problems: Ten-year followup. *Journal of Consulting and Clinical Psychology, 74*, 482–488.

Center for Sex Offender Management. (1999). *Understanding Juvenile Sexual Offending Behavior: Emerging Research, Treatment Approaches and Management Practices*. Silver Spring, MD: Center for Effective Public Policy.

Centers for Disease Control & Prevention. (2004). *Sexual Violence Prevention: Beginning the Dialogue*. Atlanta, GA: Centers for Disease Control and Prevention. Retrieved March 25, 2009, from the Web: www.cdc.gov/NCIPC/dvp/SVPrevention.htm.

Chaffin, M. (2005). Can we develop evidencebased practice for adolescent sex offenders? In *Current Perspectives: Working With Sexually Aggressive Youth and Youth With Sexual Behavior Problems*, edited by R.E. Longo and D. *Prescott. Holyoke, MA:* NEARI Press, pp. 119–141.

Chaffin, M., Berliner, L., Block, R., Johnson, T. C., Friedrich, W. N., Louis, D. G., Lyon, T. D., Page, I. J., Prescott, D. S., Silovsky, J. F. (2008). Report of the ATSA Task Force on Children With Sexual Behavior Problems. *Child Maltreatment, 13(2)*, 199–218.

Chaffin, M., Letourneau, E. & Silovsky, J. F. (2002). Adults, adolescents, and children who sexually abuse children: A developmental perspective. In *The APSAC Handbook on Child Maltreatment,* 2nd ed., edited by J.E.B. Myers, L. Berliner, J. Briere, C.T. Hendrix, C. Jenny, and T.A. Reid. Thousand Oaks, CA: Sage Publications, pp. 205–232.

Davis, G. E. & Leitenberg, H. (1987). Adolescent sexual offenders. *Psychological Bulletin, 101*, 417–427.

Elliott, D. S., Huizinga, D. & Menard, S. (1989). *Multiple Problem Youth: Delinquency, Substance Use, and Mental Health Problems.* New York, NY: Springer-Verlag.

Hunter, J. A., Figueredo, A. J., Malamuth, N. M. & Becker, J. V. (2003). Juvenile sex offenders: Toward the development of a typology. *Sexual Abuse: A Journal of Research and Treatment, 15(1)*, 27–48.

Kjellgren, C., Wassbert, A., Carlberg, M., Langstrom, N. & Svedin, C. (2006). Adolescent sexual offenders: A total survey of referrals to social services in Sweden and subgroup characteristics. *Sexual Abuse: A Journal of Research and Treatment, 18*, 357–372.

Knopp, F. H., Freeman-Longo, R. & Stevenson, W. F. (1992). *Nationwide Survey of Juvenile and Adult Sex-Offender Treatment Programs and Models.* Orwell, VT: The Safer Society Press. Lambie, I., Seymour, F., Lee, A., and Adams, P. 2002. Resiliency in the victim-offender cycle in male sexual abuse. *Sexual Abuse: A Journal of Research and Treatment, 14(1)*, 31–48.

Letourneau, E. J. & Armstrong, K. S. (2008). Recidivism rates for registered and nonregistered juvenile sexual offenders. *Sexual Abuse: Journal of Research and Treatment, 20(4)*, 393–408.

Letourneau, E. J., Henggeler, S. W., Borduin, C. M., Schewe, P. A., McCart, M. R., Chapman, J. E. & Saldana, L. (2009). Multisystemic therapy for juvenile sexual offenders: 1- year results from a randomized effectiveness trial. *Journal of Family Psychology, 23(1)*, 89–102.

Letourneau, E. J. & Miner, M. H. (2005). Juvenile sex offenders: A case against the legal and clinical status quo. *Sexual Abuse: A Journal of Research and Treatment, 17(3)*, 293–312.

Parks, G. & Bard, D. (2006). Risk factors for adolescent sex offender recidivism: Evaluation of predictive factors and comparison of three groups based upon victim type. *Sexual Abuse: A Journal of Research and Treatment, 18(4)*, 319–342.

Reitzel, L. R. & Carbonell, J. L. (2007). The effectiveness of sexual offender treatment for juveniles as measured by recidivism: A metaanalysis. *Sexual Abuse: A Journal of Research and Treatment, 18*, 401–422.

Righthand, S., Prentky, R., Knight, R., Carpenter, E., Hecker, J. E. & Nangle, D. (2005). Factor structure and validation of the Juvenile Sex Offenders Assessment Protocol (J–SOAP). *Sexual Abuse: A Journal of Research and Treatment, 17(1)*, 13–30.

Ryan, G. D. (1997). Perpetration prevention: Primary and secondary. In *Juvenile Sexual Offending: Causes, Consequences and Correction,* edited by G.D. Ryan and S.L. Lane. San Francisco, CA: Jossey-Bass, pp. 433–454.

Silovsky, J. F. & Niec, L. (2002). Characteristics of young children with sexual behavior problems: A pilot study. *Child Maltreatment, 7*, 187–197.

Snyder, H. N. & Sickmund, M. (1999). *Juvenile Offenders and Victims: 1999 National Report.* Washington, DC: U.S. Department of Justice, Office of Justice Programs, Office of Juvenile Justice and Delinquency Prevention.

U.S. Department of Justice, Federal Bureau of Investigation. (2004). *National Incident-Based Reporting System, 2004.* Compiled by the U.S. Department of Justice, Federal Bureau of Investigation. ICPSR04468-v1. Ann Arbor, MI: Inter-university Consortium for Political and Social Research, 2006-09-20. doi:10.3886/ICPSR04468.

Widom, C. S. & Ames, M. A. (1994). Criminal consequences of childhood sexual victimization. *Child Abuse and Neglect, 18(4)*, 303–318.

Worling, J. R. (2004). The estimate of risk of adolescent sexual offense recidivism (ERASOR): Preliminary psychometric data. *Sexual Abuse: A Journal of Research and Treatment, 16(3)*, 235–254.

Acknowledgments

This Bulletin was prepared by David Finkelhor, Ph.D., professor of sociology and director, Crimes against Children Research Center, University of New Hampshire, Durham, NH; Richard Ormrod, Ph.D., research professor, Crimes against Children Research Center, University of New Hampshire, Durham, NH; and Mark Chaffin, Ph.D., professor of pediatrics, University of Oklahoma Health Sciences Center, Oklahoma City, OK.

Share With Your Colleagues

Juvenile Justice Clearinghouse
Publication Reprint/Feedback
P.O. Box 6000
Rockville, MD 20849–6000
800–851–3420
301–519–5600 (fax)
Web: tellncjrs.ncjrs.gov

This Bulletin was prepared under cooperative agreement number 2005-JL-FX-0048 from the Office of Juvenile Justice and Delinquency Prevention (OJJDP), U.S. Department of Justice.

The Office of Juvenile Justice and Delinquency Prevention is a component of the Office of Justice Programs, which also includes the Bureau of Justice Assistance; the Bureau of Justice Statistics; the Community Capacity Development Office; the National Institute of Justice; the Office for Victims of Crime; and the Office of Sex Offender Sentencing, Monitoring, Apprehending, Registering, and Tracking (SMART).

End Notes

[1] This Bulletin follows the common convention of referring to these youth as "offenders." However, very few of the youth described with this label in the National Incident-Based Reporting System data are convicted as adults would be. Many were only alleged to have engaged in illegal behavior, and, if subject to justice system action, were adjudicated delinquent rather than convicted of a crime. Thus, the term "juvenile offender" should not imply shared status with convicted adult offenders, legally or otherwise.

CHAPTER SOURCES

The following chapters have been previously published:

Chapter 1 – This is an edited, excerpted and augmented edition of a United States Department of Justice publication, dated August 2010.

Chapter 2 – This is an edited, excerpted and augmented edition of a United States Department of Justice publication, dated July 2010.

Chapter 3 – This is an edited, excerpted and augmented edition of a United States Department of Justice publication, dated December 2009.

INDEX

C

D

E

F

G

H

M

N

O

P

T